Comic Books and American Cultural History

Comic Books and American Cultural History

An Anthology

MATTHEW PUSTZ

continuum

Continuum International Publishing Group
80 Maiden Lane, Suite 704, New York, NY 10038
The Tower Building, 11 York Road, London SE1 7NX

www.continuumbooks.com

© Matthew Pustz and Contributors, 2012

ISBN: HB: 978-1-4411-6319-6
ISBN: PB: 978-1-4411-7262-4

Library of Congress Cataloging-in-Publication Data
A catalog record for this book is available from the Library of Congress.

Typeset by Newgen Imaging Systems Pvt Ltd, Chennai, India
Printed and bound in the United States of America

To my teachers, for making me a better student.
To my students, for making me a better teacher

CONTENTS

LIST OF FIGURES

NOTES ON CONTRIBUTORS

Ben Bolling is a graduate student and Jacob K. Javits Fellow in the Department of English and Comparative Literature at the University of North Carolina at Chapel Hill. His work focuses on post-1945 American literature and theories of history and form.

Matthew J. Costello is Professor of Political Science at Saint Xavier University in Chicago. His research focuses on American popular culture during the Cold War in film and comics. Recent works include "Spandex Agonistes: Superheroes Confront 9/11" in *Portraying 9/11*, edited by Veronique Bragard, Christophe Dony and Warren Rosenberg (2011), "The New Super-powered Conflict: Recent Portrayals of the Cold War in American Comics," in *Between Freedom and Fear*, edited by Kathleen Starck (2010), and *Secret Identity Crisis: Comic Books and the Unmasking of Cold War America*, Continuum (2009).

Yves Davo is Assistant Professor in English and American literature at Michel de Montaigne University of Bordeaux, France. He is a doctoral fellow whose Ph.D. research focuses on the impact of the 9/11 terrorist attacks on American culture through their representations in literature and cinema. He has presented some part of his work on the subject in numerous conferences in France and currently is a member of the ARTE program (Research Workshop on the Representation of Trauma) at the University of Paris-Sorbonne, France.

John Donovan is Assistant Professor of History at the United States Air Force Academy (USAFA) in Colorado Springs, Colorado. His research focuses on the Cold War and its impact on popular culture and American society. He is the author of "Atomic Age Monsters: Radioactivity and Horror during the Early Cold War" from *The Monster Imagined: Humanity's Re-Creation of Monsters and Monstrosity* (2010). A two-time winner of Instructor of the Year from Chapman University's Vandenberg Academic Center, he recently earned USAFA's 2011 Teaching Excellence in World History award. He is currently revising for publication his master's thesis on women and combat issues during the Cold War, "The Integration of Women onto Minuteman Missile Crews."

Jeanne Emerson Gardner lives in New York City, where she recently completed her M.A. in Decorative Arts, Design History, and Material Culture at the Bard Graduate Center.

Jeff Geers is a doctoral candidate in the American Cultural Studies program at Bowling Green State University. His dissertation focuses on the role of serial narrative structure and non-continuity narratives in superhero comics. He teaches film studies and communication at the University of Dayton.

William Grady is currently working on his M.A. (by research) in the Department of Film and Media at Manchester Metropolitan University, supervised by David Huxley and Joan Ormrod. His current research is looking at the Western genre's adaptation into comic books, considering classic and contemporary generic elements. For more information, visit williamgrady.wordpress.com.

Peter Lee is a graduate student in American cultural history at Drew University. He has published articles in *Americana: the Journal of American Culture* and has several other articles forthcoming.

A. David Lewis is the co-editor of *Graven Images: Religion in Comics Books and Graphic Novels* and an Editorial Board member for *The International Journal of Comic Art*. He is the founder of the Religion and Graphica Collection at Boston University's School of Theology Library. Lewis lectures nationally on Comics Studies and has authored a number of comics including the award-winning *Lone and Level Sands* graphic novel.

Martin Lund is currently working on his Ph.D. in Jewish Studies at the Centre for Theology and Religious Studies at Lund University, Sweden. His main research interest is in religion and popular culture, with a chief focus on Jews and Judaism in comics.

Alison Mandaville, M.F.A., Ph.D., University of Washington, is a Visiting Assistant Professor of English and Women and Gender Studies at Pacific Lutheran University. A specialist in multi-ethnic American and global literatures in English, she has taught more than a dozen college courses in comics literature. Her publications in comics scholarship include contributions to *Comics and the American South* (University Press of Mississippi, 2011), *ImageText: Interdisciplinary Comics Studies*, *Teaching the Graphic Novel* (MLA Press, 2009), *The International Journal of Comic Arts*, *Philology: Special Issue on Violence and Representation*, and *The Comics Journal*. Her current research interests include African American science fiction and women cartoonists.

Bridget M. Marshall is the author of *The Transatlantic Gothic Novel and the Law, 1790–1860* (Ashgate, 2010). She is an Assistant Professor at the University of Massachusetts, Lowell, where she teaches courses on the Gothic novel, the horror story, and American literature.

Todd S. Munson is an Associate Professor of Asian Studies at Randolph-Macon College in Ashland, Virginia. He earned a B.A. in English from the University of Massachusetts (1991), with an M.A. in East Asian Studies (2000), and Ph.D. in Japanese (2004) from Indiana University. His work on comics and Asian culture has appeared in the *International Journal of Comic Art, East Asian History, Early Modern Japan: An Interdisciplinary Journal,* and *Japan Studies Review,* among others. His essay entitled "Superman v. the 'Japs': The Man of Steel and Race Hatred in WWII" appears in *Understanding Superman: The Evolving Contexts of a Pop Culture Icon,* edited by Joseph Darowski (Continuum, 2012).

Jessamyn Neuhaus is an Associate Professor of U.S. history and popular culture at SUNY Plattsburgh. She is the author of two monographs—*Manly Meals and Mom's Home Cooking: Cookbooks and Gender in Modern America* (Johns Hopkins University Press) and *Housework and Housewives in Modern American Advertising: Married to the Mop* (Palgrave Macmillan)—as well as chapters in scholarly anthologies and articles in *Journal of Popular Culture, Journal of Women's History, Journal of the History of Sexuality, Journal of Social History,* and *American Periodicals.* Since beginning her teaching career in 1998, Neuhaus has given presentations on pedagogy at national, state, and specialized conferences, and recently published an article in *The History Teacher.*

Phillip G. Payne is a Professor of History at St. Bonaventure University, where he teaches a variety of courses on United States and Public History. Before joining the faculty at St. Bonaventure, he worked in public history. He holds degrees from Marshall University and the Ohio State University. He is the author of *Dead Last: The Public Memory of Warren G. Harding's Scandalous Legacy* (2009) and numerous essays and articles.

Matthew Pustz is the author of *Comic Book Culture: Fanboys and True Believers,* published in 2000 by the University Press of Mississippi. He has also contributed essays to *Inside the World of Comic Books* (Black Rose Books, 2007) and *Webslinger: Unauthorized Essays on Your Friendly Neighborhood Spider-Man* (BenBella Books, 2006). He currently lives in Massachusetts and teaches American Studies and history at Fitchburg State University and Endicott College.

Paul J. Spaeth is the Director of the Library and Special Collections Librarian at St. Bonaventure University. He regularly teaches courses in film, literature, history, and theology. Among his publications, he has been most active in writing about and editing the works of the poet Robert Lax.

INTRODUCTION

Comic Books as History Teachers

Matthew Pustz

As strange as it might sound, Spider-Man was one of my first history teachers. Oh, it wasn't that my parents didn't pay any attention to my education. My family frequently visited historical sites while on vacation and I had more than my share of "How-and-Why" books that talked about events like World War II and the American Revolution. And I'm sure that my elementary school teachers talked about history in a very rudimentary sort of way. But the first time I really remember thinking about the past, and how it was different from the present, happened when I was reading a Spider-Man comic book.

I was probably 10 or 12 years old when I bought a copy of *Marvel Team-Up* #42 featuring two of my favorite characters, Spider-Man and the android Avenger called the Vision. Although it was a typical super-hero comic of the 1970s, with brightly-costumed characters and battles between good and evil, it was also very different than any comic I had read before. This story took place, not in contemporary New York City or even somewhere fictitious like Metropolis or Gotham City, but rather in Salem, Massachusetts, in 1692, during the famous witch trials. The trials were, in fact, an important element of the story. Spider-Man and his co-star had gone back in time to search for the Vision's wife, the Scarlet Witch, who had been kidnapped from the present by a frenzied preacher named Cotton Mather.[1]

I didn't know at the time that Mather was a real person (albeit without the mystical powers he's depicted as having in the comic), but I did have some vague idea that the four-issue long story was based on reality, and I was fascinated by this. Looking back at the story as an adult, I can see why. The comics do a surprisingly good job of teaching readers about the events in and around Salem in 1692. Although *Marvel Team-Up* doesn't give us much of an interpretation as to why the witch hysteria happened, the comics spend a relatively large amount of time explaining the basic events. In issue #42, for example, three pages out of eighteen total pages of story in the comic are spent showing the initial accusations of witchcraft. There are two more pages of historical narrative in #43. Because of this, readers like myself came away from *Marvel Team-Up* knowing the basic outline of what happened in Salem in 1692. In fact, one fan responded to the story by claiming that writer Bill Mantlo did a better job of telling the story of the Salem witch trials than did his history professor.[2]

There are certainly some problems with the *Marvel Team-Up* version of the Salem witch trials, but it's probably too much to expect that a story in a superhero comic book would represent the events of the Salem witch trials with complete accuracy. In a way, though, *Marvel Team-Up* manages to capture one of the most powerful lessons to be learned from the witch hysteria. We can see this on the final page of the story arc (see Figure 0.1). Most of the characters have forgotten about the accused of Salem, but not Spider-Man. He returns to the village, but he's unable to stop the executions. This final image emphasizes the tragedy of the event: that innocent people died, that heroic efforts couldn't stop what by then had seemed to be the inevitable result of the hysteria.[3] It certainly was an image and lesson that could stick with a young reader (and certainly stuck with this particular young reader). Seeing Spider-Man's grief and anger, we understand that these were needless deaths. In this way, the presence of the superhero and readers' identification with him enhances the narrative impact of the historical information.

The *Marvel Team-Up* Salem witch trial story is a great example how comic books can contribute to what I call "casual learning." This concept is similar to "collateral learning," an idea developed by Steven Johnson in his book *Everything Bad Is Good for You* where he argues that disreputable entertainment like television shows and video games help to improve people's cognitive abilities.[4] According to Johnson, a video game, through its complicated system of quests, helps players think about multiple layers of problems and the steps that it would take to solve them. A complicated TV show like *Lost* makes regular viewers smarter by requiring them to hold multiple plot lines in their heads at the same time and demanding that they have a good memory of events from the series' first season so that they can make sense of the show's conclusion years later. Of course, this collateral learning is not the direct goal of video games and television shows. Depending on your level of cynicism, the purpose of a program like *Lost* is either entertainment or selling products through advertising. Johnson does not ignore this aspect of popular culture but argues that collateral learning takes place as an accidental by-product of certain aesthetic and

Figure 0.1 Learning about the outcome of the Salem witch trials. Bill Mantlo (w), Sal Buscema (a), and Mike Esposito (i). *Marvel Team-Up* #44 (April 1976), Marvel Comics, 31. Spider-Man, © and ™, Marvel. All Rights Reserved and used with permission.

economic trends that pushed the culture industries toward more complicated entertainment.

Casual learning is similar to Johnson's "collateral learning." It is certainly incidental to the main purpose of the cultural text, whether it is a television program, video game, or comic book. Casual learning, though, comes from the content of the text rather than its structure. It reflects knowledge or understanding more than a cognitive skill. In this sort of way, there are dangers involved with casual learning when the original text is flawed or inaccurate. For example, a story in DC's *World's Finest Comics* from 1969 features some elements similar to those in *Marvel Team-Up*.

The problem in this story, though, is that the creators have conflated almost a hundred years of American history into one vaguely "colonial" moment when both the Salem witch trials and the American Revolution took place simultaneously.[5]

Despite dangers like this, "casual learning" suggests that the medium of comics has a great deal of potential for the teaching of history. Stories like these can be useful for teaching historical facts (if they're accurate or if a teacher is able to help students identify the fiction and the mistakes) but they are probably more significant for their ability to help readers develop the skill of historical thinking. This concept involves a real, meaningful comprehension that life was different in the past, that *people* were different in the past, that those differences are determined by certain historical factors that are shaped by complex causes and effects that are driven by actual human beings actively working (but not always consciously working) to change society. There are, of course, many ways to learn this lesson, but if comic books can do this, we should be willing to use them. At the same time, I am not arguing that they should be used exclusively and every other tool for teaching about the past be thrown away. What the phenomenon of casual learning suggests, though, is that there is potential for the comics medium to teach serious topics in a way that might reach students differently and perhaps at times more effectively than more traditional texts. This potential also exists when comics are used as primary sources or as secondary texts that can be used to augment other pedagogical techniques.

It is the goal of the chapters in this book to illustrate some of the ways in which comic books can help teachers guide their students to a greater understanding of history. In their chapters, Jessamyn Neuhaus and Bridget M. Marshall explain how they used comic books in their classrooms. For Neuhaus, comic books were tools to teach her students about the methodologies of doing history. For Marshall, a particular graphic novel was the impetus for an analysis of primary sources in the study of American literary history. The chapters by William Grady and Alison Mandaville demonstrate how comic book creators themselves sometimes function as historians, perhaps by engaging in discourse with national historical myths or by using comics to create personal narratives that connect to key moments in American history.

The bulk of the chapters in this volume demonstrate how comic books can function as dynamic primary sources that can help scholars, teachers, and students to understand various periods of modern American history. For example, Martin Lund writes about the cultural, political, and economic forces shaping the creation of Superman during the 1930s. Jeanne Gardner examines the complex and often contradictory values of the era immediately following World War II by focusing on romance comics. John Donovan uses the Jack Kirby and Joe Simon comic *Fighting American* to help us think about the 1950s and its Cold War mentality. Chapters by

Peter Lee and Matthew Pustz analyze comic books that touch on different aspects of the 1970s. Finally, Matthew Costello examines how the series *American Flagg!* reflects certain aspects of Ronald Reagan's America.

Another section of *Comic Books and American Cultural History* demonstrates how comics and graphic novels derive their power from the use of historical identities. Todd Munson, for example, shows us how Gene Yang uses the racial stereotypes from the early twentieth century in his graphic novel *American Born Chinese*. Philip Payne and Paul Spaeth examine how creators have used Nick Fury as a symbol of the "Greatest Generation" to commemorate World War II. The queer identity of the superhero Northstar is the topic of Ben Bolling's chapter.

The final group of chapters examines contemporary history, in particular the events surrounding and produced by the terrorist attacks of September 11, 2001. Yves Davo shows how Alissa Torres tries to personalize and re-historicize 9/11 in her graphic autobiography *American Widow*. Jeff Geers shows us how the series *Ex Machina* reflects the cultural anxiety produced by 9/11. The impact of the wars in Afghanistan and Iraq on the role of superheroes is examined by A. David Lewis.

These chapters appear at a unique time for comic books. Suddenly, it seems, they have become respectable—or at least they have become respectable when they're called "graphic novels" and found in their own dedicated sections in Barnes & Nobles and independent bookstores all across the country. Librarians have come to realize that graphic novels are a great way to get adolescents to check out books from and spend time in the library. For adults, graphic novels have become an established—if still a little exotic—part of many Americans' regular diet of reading material. In early 2011, even my mother's reading group in Madison, Wisconsin, was talking about graphic novels.

One result of this increased respectability is that teachers are becoming more and more comfortable using graphic novels in the classroom. Most of this is happening in literature classes, but there is also the potential for comic books to be used to teach history. Some historically-themed graphic novels, like *A People's History of American Empire*, by Howard Zinn, Mike Konopacki, and Paul Buhle (2008), function as textbooks. The cover of *A People's History* announces that it is a "graphic adaptation" of the work of left-wing historian Howard Zinn who appears throughout the story as a narrator. One of the strengths of the book is that it integrates other kinds of visual material into the comics format. A section about labor activism at the end of the nineteenth century, for example, includes photographs, period drawings, and newspaper editorial cartoons, as well as more traditional comics.

Other historically-themed graphic novels feature cohesive narratives. Works like *Satchel Paige: Striking Out Jim Crow* (2007), by James Sturm and Rich Tommaso, and *Nat Turner* (2008), by Kyle Baker, are not especially analytical but instead tell compelling historical stories through comics. Sturm and Tommaso's book uses a simple style to emphasize the dignity of the African-Americans who were forced to deal with racism and inequality in the early decades of the twentieth century. Baker's work depicts the famous 1831 slave revolt in large, mostly silent panels that reflect the horror of the events depicted in the story with immediacy and darkness. His mastery of facial expressions adds to our understanding of the people involved, from the whites' desire for revenge to Turner's serenity with which he approached his death. Despite their focus on the visuals, neither work ignores the facts behind the stories they tell. *Satchel Paige* includes an afterword that features in-depth explanations of the historical context of particular panels that illustrate topics like the importance of the railroad in African-American culture and the ubiquitous presence of lynchings in the South. *Nat Turner* includes a bibliography and takes its text directly from historical documents.

The third category of comic books that could be used as secondary texts in the history classroom focuses on biography. The benefit of using comics for biography is that creators can emphasize the expressionistic experience of historical events. In *Maus*, for example, readers connect with the personal experiences of Vladek Spiegelman, and it is this connection that makes comics especially effective for historical biography. The immediacy of comics is what also helps it to be able to record events and emotions directly and personally. Comics as a medium is inherently expressionistic. As art, it is created, sometimes as a representation of reality and sometimes as an expression of emotion. When it is created by one artist, it reflects an individual point of view, and as such we almost instinctively know that it is personal. The expressionistic quality of comics allows us to experience a personal story more directly than we can in perhaps any other medium.

This is what happens in Josh Neufeld's *A. D.: New Orleans after the Deluge* (2009). Neufeld is able to take an event that we all remember, that we all think we know about, and make it new by focusing on the stories of a handful of people who survived the hurricane and the mistakes that happened afterward. Readers can feel the physical power of the storm, but more importantly they can feel the fear that people in New Orleans must have felt. Neufeld's art is simple and clear, and this helps the reader connect with the anger, sadness, and horror that the characters are feeling. As a work of history, Neufeld is able to capture the reality, the truth of the situation in a way that other kinds of texts might not be able to. One sequence, for example, focuses on a woman named Denise who, in the aftermath of the storm, finds herself waiting for help outside the convention center with thousands of other people. The people are frustrated and need food, water, and shelter. We learn about the sacrifice of strangers and how leadership sometimes came from people who might otherwise have been considered thugs. As the hours go by, tensions rise and the largely African-American crowd begins to feel like they've been abandoned. Rumors begin to spread that some of the levees were destroyed on purpose to flood the black community out. A double page spread, focusing a single panel on the faces in the crowd, crystallizes the fear: "There ain't gonna be no buses comin'! They gonna open the floodgates and drown us! They brought us here to die!" Amidst the crowd, seeing that people are dying, Denise slowly realizes that there might be some reality behind these fears.[6]

A. D. is among the best recent graphic novels, and among the comic books with the greatest potential to be used in a history classroom, because of its powerful use of the medium and its overall human significance. It provides us with a new way of looking at an event, and that is what is most important about using comic books as a way to discuss, study, and teach American history. However, I'm not recommending that we give up our textbooks, our primary written documents, or even our traditional classroom techniques. In her chapter in this volume, Jessamyn Neuhaus reminds us that comic books are as fraught with challenges as every other primary source that we might use. The same is true with comics as secondary sources. But what comic books and graphic novels do offer are new tools that could help make our teaching of American history more effective. Like a good documentary, fiction film, or, hypothetically, even historically-themed video game, comic books can be used by teachers to connect their students to difficult subject matter or simply to tell old stories in new, perhaps more effective ways. In particular, using comic books as primary documents in the classroom or in our own scholarship can open up new visions of American history, often by helping students develop the skills of doing history and thinking historically. In many ways, this is the most important job of any history professional, whether she is a high school teacher, college professor, or museum interpreter. While we cannot abandon the teaching of facts, what is more important is that the history profession helps people to develop and hone their history skills. It is the job of educators not so much to fill buckets as to light fires and give people the tools to learn—and to want to learn—for themselves.

Ultimately, I come back to my own experience as a comic book fan who was able to casually learn about the Salem witch trials from a Spider-Man comic book. What that story did was make me want to learn more. It taught me about causes and effects, about the consequences and emotions involved with historical events. The bottom line is that it made me want to study American history. And maybe that's the most important thing that we can do as history teachers: to convince our students that the past is worth knowing about and that doing history can be fun. Whether we're using them as primary sources during a classroom exercise or as a secondary source to help our students discuss Jim Crow, if comic books can help us to get people interested in learning about history, then they are a tool that we should embrace. *Comic Books and American Cultural History*, as an anthology, is not meant to be an exhaustive list of possible ways these tools can be used, but rather it is another step in the integration of comic books into the field of history.

Notes

1 Bill Mantlo (w), Sal Buscema (a), and Mike Esposito (i). "Visions of Hate!" *Marvel Team-Up* #42 (February 1976), Marvel Comics.
2 "Mail It to Team-Up" [Letters column]. *Marvel Team-Up* #46 (June 1976), Marvel Comics, 19.
3 Bill Mantlo (w), Sal Buscema (a), and Mike Esposito (i). "Death in the Year before Yesterday!" *Marvel Team-Up* #44 (April 1976), Marvel Comics.
4 Steven Johnson, *Everything Bad Is Good for You: How Today's Popular Culture Is Actually Making Us Smarter*. New York: Riverhead Books, 2005.
5 Bob Kanigher (w), Ross Andru (p), and Mike Esposito (i). "The Bat Witch!" and "The Demon Superman!" *World's Finest Comics* #86–87 (August–September 1969), DC Comics.
6 Josh Neufeld, *A. D.: New Orleans after the Deluge* (New York: Pantheon, 2010), 153.

PART ONE

Doing Cultural History through Comic Books

CHAPTER ONE

How Wonder Woman Helped My Students "Join the Conversation"

Comic Books as Teaching Tools in a History Methodology Course

Jessamyn Neuhaus

I'm not a comic book fan. I don't find comic books—from any era—especially entertaining or enjoyable to read. Maybe this seems like rank heresy in a volume such as this, however, I'm sure all of us contributors would agree that you do not need a closet full of mylar-encased comic books or a vast collection of superhero action figures to productively incorporate comic books into your academic work. I'm not a comic book fan but, as a scholar and teacher of popular culture and U.S. history, I *am* very interested in knowing how comic books function as significant cultural artifacts from the past, in understanding the enormous impact they continue to make on mainstream popular culture, and in exploring how comic books as a topic of study can facilitate successful student learning in my classes.

I currently use comic books as the content theme when I teach an undergraduate history methodology course called "Historical Practices," the first in a sequence of three required classes for all history majors and social studies adolescent education majors at my small state university.[1] The course introduces students to doing historical analysis, that is, primary source research rooted in an understanding of the pertinent historiography. In this chapter, I discuss how comic books help my students learn how to "do history" and to recognize history as an ongoing debate and "conversation" about the meaning of the past. Becoming familiar with a representative sampling of scholarship on comic books and discussing it in class effectively introduces students to the concept of learning the historiography of a particular topic. In addition, by examining actual comic books in class, students practice testing historical analysis against the primary source evidence itself—they "join the conversation."

However, history instructors hoping to beneficially utilize comic books need to address a persistent problem in student preparation for college-level work in the field of history. Taught throughout high school and reinforced by society at large that history simply uncovers "what happened," students usually do not realize that historians always contend with complex, often contradictory, primary sources that never completely reveal or explain the past.[2] Moreover, many students believe that the narrative of history should concern itself almost solely with the most dramatic events and prominent people of the past. Students thus truly struggle with the concept that, when examined by historians, comic books can help us understand the past and that, like all primary sources, comics are subject to scholarly debate about their historical significance. Instructors need to be prepared for the fact that students will regularly dismiss comic books as "bad" primary sources and scholarship on comic books as "not real history." This holds true for students who are ardent comic book fans, as well as those who've never read a comic book. Often deeply but unreflectively immersed in the media ocean of the twenty-first century, students view comic books as "entertainment" and entertainment as somehow irrelevant to historical practices. Instructors must therefore be careful to give students the analytical tools they need to identify the potential possibilities and limitations of *all* primary sources when introducing them to comic books as a site of historical inquiry.

Doing history with superheroes: Introducing key concepts with comic books

The growing interdisciplinary field of comics studies includes numerous historical analyses of comic books. For example, a number of scholars explore how Silver Age comic books of the 1950s and early 1960s reflect Cold War anxieties. Historians have also examined the comic book industry as a whole and have demonstrated how it offers insights into political, social, and cultural changes in the United States.[3] Others focus on superhero characters specifically, while some of the most interesting work advances our understanding of how race, gender, and sexuality play out in the pages of comic books.[4] As the field expands, it has become more nuanced, with work focusing specifically on different genres such as romance and war comics, and manga studies emerging as a whole separate category of investigation.[5]

Building on this growing body of knowledge, educators from a wide variety of fields have begun to advocate using comic books and graphic novels in the classroom, suggesting a broad range of roles that comic books and graphic novels can play in learning. Many literacy teachers argue that having students read (and create) different types of comic books can serve a valuable pedagogical function, and instructors at all levels in such diverse areas as English language arts (ELA), sociology, business, creative writing, and the sciences embrace using comic books in their classes.[6] I decided to use comic books as a content theme in my history methodology course for three reasons: First, in contrast to many possible topics, the scholarship analyzing comic books through a historical lens is diverse enough to give students a sense of historians debating the meaning of the past but small enough to satisfy my desire for students to understand the biggest issues in the relevant scholarship of a topic. Secondly, I could easily provide students access to a small sampling of relevant primary sources. Thirdly, I hoped that the novelty of comic books as a topic might grab students' attention in a new way.

My reading assignments offered a limited overview of the available historical scholarship on comic books.[7] The class began with Bradford Wright's chronological examination in *Comic Book Nation: The Transformation of Youth Culture in America*, continuing on to articles proposing specific historical analyses of different characters and storylines, and then examples of literary analysis focusing on issues of race, gender, and sexuality in comic books. Students also watched two documentaries: an overview of the major superhero characters and an examination of post-World War II crime comics and their cultural impact. We finished the semester by considering the use of comic books in secondary social studies classes (almost half of my students plan to become high school social studies teachers). Far more so than most classes I've taught, during class discussions many students referred back to earlier readings, comparing and contrasting that day's assignment with earlier assignments. While some students felt the readings were repetitive, class discussion and student written comments demonstrated that, by its end, a significant number of students left the course with an increased understanding that history is an ever-evolving "conversation" among scholars making arguments based on primary source evidence, with some arguments being much more convincing than others.[8]

In a good example of how student perceptions of their own learning don't always offer a complete picture of what they've actually accomplished, some of the students who most vocally objected to the repetitiveness of the reading showed in class and in their research papers that they completed the course with solid comprehension of a central methodological concept: in order to investigate any given topic in history, one needs to thoroughly delve into the secondary source literature. The narrow focus on comic books as opposed to a broader field of study helped students achieve this learning objective. A good number of students felt empowered by the sense that they possessed solid knowledge about the topic at hand during our class discussions, better enabling them to try to assess the strengths and weaknesses of the secondary source materials. Student perception that they were becoming well-read on the topic of comic books performed a critical function in helping students "join the conversation." I should acknowledge that this belief did not necessarily accurately reflect students' real understanding or knowledge of comic book history, but *feeling* confident that they had a solid grounding in the secondary source literature on comic books enabled students to better grasp that as history majors, they have to learn how to "do history." In sharp contrast to what most of them learned to do in their high school history classes, they knew they would now be required to pursue their own secondary and primary source research, make an argument, and then support it.

Student comments illustrated their comprehension of this key concept of actively engaging in historical analysis rather than passively receiving information. When asked to define "joining the conversation," one student wrote: "Know what others have already said. Then we can look for new evidence which we can interpret and then add to the ongoing 'conversation.'" For another, "joining the conversation" meant being able "to put or add your interpretation on a particular subject that has been discussed by historians by analyzing primary and secondary sources of that area." A third defined it as being able "to contribute to the secondary source conversation about history they must be able to evaluate primary and secondary sources and create thesises [sic] from the information." Another explained that "joining the conversation" meant "that history is a subject which has many interpretation[s] and arguments that are between scholars and we [as] history majors 'joining the conversation' have something to contribute to understanding the past through understanding and maybe arguing these different interpretations and arguments that scholars have made."[9]

For students to get to this point where they can truly "join the conversation," they needed to understand what it means to do primary source research. Here, the comic book theme effectively reinforced the key concepts of "doing history" and encouraged students to be creative in this kind of research. I chose to use comic books as a content theme because I could provide students the opportunity to examine in person the primary sources under consideration—comic books. With online archives proliferating, students rarely experience the unique pleasure of digging around and making actual discoveries in physical archives and library special collections, so they don't often get to see and touch preserved pieces of the past. Plus, as one student accurately pointed out, "Our library does not have a good collection of comics, this makes it hard to look at them." As previously mentioned, I don't own a comic book collection but in hopes of providing students with a semblance of the archival research experience so fundamental to historical practices, I turned to eBay.

The result was three different sets of comic books that I then brought to class. Students individually, in small groups, and as a class examined the comic books in light of the assigned course readings. For a class on post-World War II crime comic books, my budget did not extend to hard copies, but students examined a DVD-ROM with scanned issues of entire copies of crime comic titles such as *Authentic Police Cases, Crime Does Not Pay, Dick Tracy*, and *Justice Traps the Guilty*.[10] In another class, students examined a small random selection of mostly mainstream comic books published in the 1970s, 1980s, and early 1990s, including a disco-influenced *Dazzler; Black Lightning*, featuring an African American superhero; the introduction of Spider Woman; well-known titles like *The Hulk, Captain America, Silver Surfer, The Amazing Spider-Man, Superman, Iron Man, Green Arrow, X-Men*, and a juvenile comic book promoting environmentalism called *Conservation Corps*.[11] Finally, after reading Mitra C. Emad's *Journal of Popular Culture* article "Reading Wonder Woman's Body: Mythologies of Gender and Nation," students examined a small selection of Wonder Woman comic books published in the 1990s.[12] I gave each student a form to fill out with blanks for the title, creators, publication information of comic books, initial observations about the comic book, and ways that the source might support the assertion that "comic books can provide a window into the past by helping us better understand changing U.S. society and culture."

Examining comic books created the opportunity for students to try to apply what they'd learned from the secondary sources to the primary sources, including assessing the authors' interpretations of these sources. For example, based on the primary source evidence presented in class, they were quick to concur with Emad's assertions about the hypersexualization of Wonder Woman in the late 1900s and early 2000s.[13] In addition, students felt that they discovered some important aspects of comic books as primary sources that were not addressed in the scholarship we read. For instance, many of them expressed interest in the different kinds of advertising included in comic books, and what it might reveal about how publishers marketed the books and how the books functioned in conjunction with other pop culture sources and as consumer objects. With good cause, students felt that the comic book scholarship they read did not offer enough analysis of exactly who purchased and read comic books at different points in time, so fan letters printed in the comic books also attracted students' attention as a possible window into this vexing question of readership and reader response.

Based on an anonymous end-of-the-class survey, a good number of students found these exercises worthwhile, demonstrating that using comic books as the content area in "Historical Practices" helped them understand the wide diversity of primary sources historians may use. In their answers to the question "How did your study of the history of comic books this semester change your understanding of historical analysis in general?" many students affirmed that studying comic books helped them consider primary source research in a new light: "I'm now considering the historical implications of more things. At first I was skeptical about using comic books to understand historical analysis; now I am not." "It opened my eyes to using different things as primary and secondary sources. I had no idea that we could use them in such arguments." "Looking at history through comic books has helped me realize there is more to history than just what's in the textbooks." "That history can be found anywhere." "I did not realize that something written for America's youth could be so complex or hold so much history. Analyzing comic books showed me that I should be more open-minded and think out of the box when it comes to analyzing historical sources or choosing them." "That there are many more means of studying history than I had previously realized." "[T]here are many different mediums to look at to see history of the time." "Pop culture can be used to analyze history. I hadn't given that much thought before." As one student summarized, "For most everyone this is also their first time considering comics as historical artifacts. This allows us to expand our understanding of what can be used as primary sources which allows us to join the 'conversation' more easily."

These kinds of comments indicated that reading scholarly analyses of comic books, combined with examining comic books as primary sources, helped improve student learning of history methodology. In particular, many felt that the class focus on comic books effectively illustrated the depth and breadth of primary sources available to historians. However, as I discuss in the next section, this was not true for all students. During the primary source activities, for instance, some students found the comic books baffling on all levels. More troublingly, some students (including, interestingly, regular comic book readers) dismissed much of the content of the books as simply weird or silly. Despite being exposed to fairly thorough secondary source background information about using comic books to understand social history, youth culture, and national politics from different time periods, some of my students completely dismissed the idea that what they were holding in their hands might offer clues about the past.

"They are entertainment not history": Student resistance to comics as primary sources

When asked to list the most important advantages and disadvantages of using comic books as the content area for a methodology course, a good number of students expressed appreciation for the novelty of the topic, commenting that they did in fact enjoy the "change of pace" that comics provided. Or in the words of one student, "IT'S FUN!" Others pointed to the fact that a small overview sample of the still fairly new field of comic book scholarship offered them the opportunity to get a good sense of the field quite quickly. As one student commented, "The research done on this topic is limited [so] it is relatively easy to 'add to the conversation.'" And another asserted that h/she found it "interesting to see so many different interpretations of comics." A majority of students clearly grasped the concept that comic books can reflect the time period in which they were created. Listing advantages to using comic books, students wrote: "They give a broad understanding of the culture in the time they were written." "You can discover how comic books were influenced by the history of the time." "They represent popular ideas of their times."

But even if a student clearly stated that comic books could provide insights into the past, s/he was *also* quite likely to criticize comic books as being a problematically limited primary source. Students commonly described comic books as an incomplete record of the past when listing the disadvantages of using comic books. In other words, students criticized comic books for the exact same limitations inherent to every other imaginable type of primary source: "Biases." "Comic books are sometimes a false portrayal of history." "That they do not always tell or portray the whole historical event." "They only show certain aspects to [sic] that time period." "Not an exact account of history." "Very open to interpretation."

In part, such comments simply reflect students' very limited exposure to primary source research before college and widespread misconceptions about the use of sources—misconceptions that can persist even after they've successfully completed "Historical Practices" and can articulate that they understand key concepts in history methodology in other ways. Even if they can clearly state that history is made up of arguments and debates, they still often fail to fully grasp the significance of this, particularly when interpreting primary sources. History educators have extensively documented such misconceptions, as well as possible strategies for better facilitating student learning in this area.[14] In this way, there's nothing about comic books per se, as opposed to other types of primary sources, which hinders student learning.

However, I've found that many students have a kind of mental block to working with comic books because of how they perceive the nature of popular culture and the practice of history. Any educator who wishes to incorporate comic books into a history curriculum needs to address this problem. For instance, a significant number of my students characterized comic books as "entertainment," and "not history" when asked to list the disadvantages of using comic books as a content area: "They weren't written to be used as historical records but for entertainment." "Skeptical people, coming into the class people being skeptical on how we can use comics to study history. Some may seem them as only entertainment." "They are entertainment not history." A number of other students, when asked "Would you ever consider using a comic book as a primary source in your classroom if you were to pursue a teaching career?" gave similar answers: "Probably not, at the end of the day, comic books are for entertainment, not education." "No, because the entertainment aspect would undermine [the] historical value."

As one student put it, "It is a topic that not everyone feels deals with history in a serious manner." Many students become history majors because they love the dramatic sweeping epics of history as told on the History Channel, and while some students appreciate the change of pace of pop culture history (especially as they advance through their college program), many others strongly resist turning from what they've always consumed as "history"—dramatic military battles, major disasters, and presidential hagiography—and instead looking closely at primary sources to try to understand what the past was like for the majority of the people living at that time. For at least some students, comic books just plain trivialize what they see as the grand enterprise of history.

A history methods course therefore involves a great deal of unlearning for students, and even as we attempt to empower them to "do history," instructors need to be cognizant of student resistance to reframing the study of history in this way. Educators offer a variety of pedagogical techniques for using pop culture primary sources to both build students' critical thinking skills and help them better understand the nature of historical inquiry.[15] But as history teachers, we need to be more attuned to the fact that, in contrast to many of the other kinds of primary sources they might use during their college careers, most students arrive having already consumed literally thousands of hours of pop culture. Unlike other types of historical documents, students already "know" how to watch a movie, listen to music, or read an advertisement, and so they dismiss this activity as "entertainment" in contrast to the "history" they know from their high school textbooks. Their knowledge of pop culture does not usually encompass critical reflection, and for many students those activities appear to be entirely unrelated to the more "serious" undertaking of history. So historians who wish to use pop culture primary sources must not only address students' misconceptions about sources in general, but pop culture sources in particular as well. As history instructor Christopher Edwards writes about using Bob Dylan songs as primary sources in the undergraduate classroom, "The idea that a song is historical evidence demanding critical interrogation is not one that comes naturally or readily to students."[16] The same must be said of comic books.

In a vivid illustration of this challenge, some of the students who self-identified as enthusiastic comic book fans in "Historical Practices" stated unequivocally throughout the semester that comic book scholarship was not "real history."[17] At first, I was surprised by this, supposing that their love of the medium would make them eager to explore the historical significance of comic books. But students—and most Americans, for that matter—view consumption of and participation in popular media, even when it takes up a huge chunk of their daily lives, as somehow entirely separate from "history." Used to thinking about history as big wars and great men, they fail to see that those who try to understand the past must sometimes take a microscopic as well as macroscopic view. They resist the idea that a close study of a coherent group of primary sources such as comic books is one effective way of trying to understand the past. Instructors need to be mindful of this drawback: yes, comic books might appear to us more likely to engage students' attention than other kinds of primary sources, but the very fact that they are entertaining ironically makes them even more difficult for many students to use as a site for historical investigation. Students and instructors can definitely overcome this hurdle, as demonstrated by the student who answered the question "Would you ever consider using a comic book as a primary source in your classroom if you were to pursue a teaching career?" this way: "After taking this class I would because I understand how they can reflect a time period, prior to this class no because I did not view them as historically significant, just entertainment."

A good selection of secondary sources, focusing on using comic books as historical artifacts, is crucial to helping students develop their thinking regarding comic books in this way. Discussing at some length the pedagogical reasons for choosing to utilize comic books in a methodology course can increase student understanding, particularly for those students who may be pursuing teaching careers of the own.[18] This activity made an especially positive impact on my own students' learning. In the future, I also plan to include in-class comparison exercises with other types of primary sources from the relevant time period. Listing how historians might interpret different types of primary sources—side by side with comic books—could help students make the cognitive leap to seeing comic books as just another type of primary source, with both possibilities for advancing knowledge and limitations on what it can tell us about the past. Reading a number of contrasting and conflicting interpretations about more "traditional" primary sources such as diaries, photographs, speeches, or legal documents, and then introducing a similar debate around comic books as historical artifacts could help more students better understand comic book scholarship as "real history." Devoting at least a week to more rigorous and structured primary source exploration exercises when using comic books could also improve student understanding both of how to use primary sources and why comic books can be a useful primary source.[19] Finally, I suspect that more exposure to older comic books, even in electronic format, could build student appreciation for the historical significance of comic books as primary sources.

Conclusion: With great power . . .

Along with the great power we may gain when wielding comic books in the classroom, comes a great responsibility: ensuring that students understand that comic books, even with their limitations (like any other primary source), are significant cultural artifacts. By being aware of and assiduously addressing the potential pitfalls, history instructors can successfully incorporate comic books into a methodology course. My experience shows that doing so can help students comprehend some of the key concepts of both secondary source and primary source research more effectively.

Notes

1   I'm grateful to all the SUNY Plattsburgh students in my Spring 2010 and Spring 2011 "Historical Practices" classes for their thoughtful feedback and insights about using comic books as a content area for this course. I am also indebted to my colleague Dr. Richard Schafer for helping me apply the concept of "joining the conversation" to the methodology class.

2   See for example Caroline Hoefferle, "Teaching Historiography to High School and Undergraduate Students," *OAH Magazine of History* 21, no. 2 (2007), 44; David J. Voelker, "Assessing Student Understanding in Introductory Courses: A Sample Strategy," *The History Teacher* 41, no. 4 (2008), 505.

3   For historical studies, see for example Adam Capitanio, "'The Jekyll and Hyde of the Atomic Age:' The Incredible Hulk as the Ambiguous Embodiment of Nuclear Power," *Journal of Popular Culture* 43, no. 2 (2010): 249–270; Matthew J. Costello, *Secret Identity Crisis: Comic Books and the Unmasking of Cold War America* (New York: Continuum, 2009); Paul Gabilliet, trans. Bart Beaty and Nick Nguyen, *Of Comics and Men: A Cultural History of American Comic Books* (Jackson: University of Mississippi Press, 2009); David Hajdu, *The Ten-Cent Plague: The Great Comic-Book Scare and How It Changed America* (New York: Farrar, Straus, and Giroux, 2008); Gerard Jones, *Men of Tomorrow: Geeks, Gangsters, and the Birth of the Comic Book* (New York: Basic Books, 2004); Paul Lopes, *Demanding Respect: The Evolution of the American Comic Book* (Philadelphia: Temple University Press, 2009); Amy Kiste Nyberg, *Seal of Approval: The History of the Comics Code* (Jackson: University of Mississippi Press, 1998); Shirrel Rhoades, *A Complete History of American Comic Books* (New York: Peter Lang, 2008); Natalie Myra Rosinsky and Douglas Holgate, *Graphic Content! The Culture of Comic Books* (Mankato, MN: Compass Points Books, 2010); and William Savage, *Comic Books and America, 1945–1954* (Norman: University of

Oklahoma Press, 1990). Stephen Krensky's *Comic Book Century: The History of American Comic Books* (Minneapolis: Twenty First Century Books, 2007) is a historical overview for young adults. For a textbook introduction to the history of comic books, see Randy Duncan and Matthew J. Smith, *The Power of Comics: History, Form and Culture* (New York: Continuum, 2009).

4 On superheroes specifically, see for example Cary D. Adkinson, "The Amazing Spider-Man and the Evolution of the Comics Code: A Case Study in Cultural Criminology," *Criminal Justice and Popular Culture* 15, no. 3 (2008): 241–261; Danny Fingeroth, *Superman on the Couch: What Superheroes Really Tell Us About Ourselves and Our Society* (New York: Continuum, 2004); Geoff Klock, *How to Read Superhero Comics and Why* (New York: Continuum, 2002); Chris Knowles and Joseph Michael Linser, *Our Gods Wear Spandex: The Secret History of Comic Book Heroes* (Newburyport, MA: Wieser Books, 2007); Bradford Wright, "From Social Consciousness to Cosmic Awareness: Superhero Comic Books and the Culture of Self-Interrogation, 1968–1974," *English Language Notes* 46, no. 2 (2008): 155–174; Terrence R. Wandtke, *The Amazing Transforming Superhero! Essays on the Revision of Characters in Comic Books, Film and Television* (Jefferson, NC: McFarland, 2007). On race, see for example Jeffery Brown, *Black Superheroes, Milestone Comics, and Their Fans* (Jackson: University of Mississippi Press, 2000); Ana Pozzi-Harris, "Your Brain on Latino Comics: From Gus Ariola to Los Bros Hernandez," *International Social Science Review* 85, no. 3/4 (2010): 140–141; and Marc Singer, "'Black Skins' and White Masks: Comic Books and the Secret of Race," *African American Review* 36, no. 1 (2003): 107–120. On gender, see for example Aaron Taylor, "'He's Gotta Be Strong, and He's Gotta Be Fast, and He's Gotta Be Larger than Life: Investigating the Engendered Superhero Body," *Journal of Popular Culture* 40, no. 2 (2007): 344–360. On how Jewish identity has shaped comic book history, see for example Thomas Andres, et al., *Siegel and Shuster's Funnyman: The First Jewish Superhero, from the Creators of Superman* (Port Townsend, WA: Feral House, 2010); Danny Fingeroth, *Disguised as Clark Kent: Jews, Comics, and the Creation of the Superhero* (New York: Continuum, 2008); Aire Kaplan, *From Krakow to Krypton: Jews and Comic Books* (Philadelphia: Jewish Publication Society, 2008).

5 On specific comic book genres, see for example Michael Barson, *Agonizing Love: The Golden Era of Romance Comics* (New York: Harper Design, 2011); Alexander Clarkson, "Virtual Heroes: Boys, Masculinity, and Historical Memory in War Comics 1945–1995," *Journal of Boyhood Studies* 2, no. 2 (2008): 175–218; Jacque Nodell, "Love on the Racks: A History of American Romance Comics," *Journal of Popular Culture* 42, no. 3 (2009): 576–578. On manga, see for example Martha Cornag, "Eroticism for the Masses: Japanese Manga Comics and Their Assimilation into the U.S.," *Sexuality and Culture* 6, no. 1 (2002): 3–126; Hiromi Dollase, "Shôjo Spirits in Horror Manga," *U.S.-Japan Women's Journal: A Journal for the International Exchange of Gender Studies* 38 (2010): 59–80; John Ingulsrud and Kate Allen, *Reading Japan Cool: Patterns of Manga Literacy and Discourse* (Lanham, MD: Lexington Books, 2009); Toni Johnson-Woods, ed., *Manga: An Anthology of Global and Cultural Perspectives* (New York: Continuum, 2010); Mark McLelland, "The Love Between 'Beautiful Boys' in Japanese Women's Comics," *Journal*

of Gender Studies 9, no. 1 (2000): 13–35; Antonia Levi, Mark McHarry, and Dru Pagliassotti, eds, *Boys' Love Manga: Essays on the Sexual Ambiguity and Cross-Cultural Fandom of the Genre* (Jefferson, NC: McFarland, 2010); Eldad Nakar, "Memories of Pilots and Planes: World War II Japanese Manga, 1957–1967," *Social Science Japan Journal* 6, no. 1 (2003): 57–76; Jennifer Prough, "Marketing Japan: Manga as Japan's New Ambassador," *ASIANEtwork Exchange* 17, no. 2 (2010): 54–68; James Welker, "Beautiful, Borrowed, and Bent: Boys' Love and Girls' Love in Shôjo Manga," *Signs: Journal of Women in Culture and Society* 31, no. 3 (2006): 841–870.

6   See for example Michael Bitz, "The Comic Book Project: Forging Alternative Pathways to Literacy," *Journal of Adolescent and Adult Literacy* 47, no. 7 (2004): 574–586; Stephen Cary, *Going Graphic: Comics at Work in the Multilingual Classroom* (Portsmouth, NH: Heinemann, 2004); Kerry Cheesman, "Using Comics in the Science Classroom," *Journal of College Science Teaching* 35, no. 4 (2006): 48–51; Mark Crilley, "Getting Students to Write Using Comics," *Teacher Librarian* 37, no. 1 (2009): 28–31; Lila Christensen, "Graphic Global Conflict: Graphic Novels in the High School Studies Social Studies Classroom," *Social Studies* 97, no. 6 (2006): 227–230; Virginia Gerde and R. Spencer Foster, "X-Men Ethics: Using Comic Books to Teach Business Ethics," *Journal of Business Ethics* 77, no. 3 (2008): 245–258; Michael Gorman, *Getting Graphic! Using Graphic Novels to Promote Literacy with Preteens and Teens* (Santa Barbara: Linworth, 2003); Kelley Hall and Betsy Lucal, "Tapping Into Parallel Universes: Using Superhero Comic Books in Sociology Courses," *Teaching Sociology* 27, no. 1 (1999): 60–66; Katie Monnin, *Teaching Graphic Novels: Practical Strategies for the Secondary ELA Classroom* (Gainseville: Maupin House, 2009); Bonny Norton, "The Motivating Power of Comic Books: Insights from Archie Comic Readers," *Reading Teacher* 57, no. 2 (2003): 140–147; Adam Schwartz, "Understanding the Manga Hype: Uncovering the Multimodality of Comic-Book Literacies," *Journal of Adolescent and Adult Literacy* 50, no. 1 (2006): 40–49; Rich Shea, "Comics in the Classroom," *Teacher Magazine* 18, no. 2 (2006): 16–17; Willona Sloan, "No Laughing Matter: Comic Books Have Serious Educational Value," *Education Update* 51, no. 10 (2009): 1–7; Stephen Tabachnick, ed., *Teaching the Graphic Novel* (New York: Modern Language Association of America, 2009); Emma Weitkamp and Helen Featherstone, "Engaging Children Through the Use of Cartoons and Comics," *Primary Science* 113 (2010): 33–35; Bill Zimmerman, "Creating Comics Fosters Reading, Writing, and Creativity," *Education Digest* 74, no. 4 (2008): 55–57. See also The National Association of Comic Art Educators, "Teaching Comics," http:// www.teachingcomics.org (accessed June 1, 2011) and Gene Yang, "Comics in Education," http://www.humblecomics.com/comicsedu/index.html (accessed June 1, 2011).

7   I assigned students the following readings: Katherin G. Aiken, "Superhero History: Using Comic Books to Teach U.S. History," *OAH Magazine of History* 24, no. 2 (2010): 41–47; Linda Kelly Alkana, "Teaching World History with Graphic Novels," *World History Bulletin* 23, no. 2 (2007): 28–31; Lawrence Baron, "*X-Men* as J Men: The Jewish Subtext of a Comic Book Movie," *SHOFAR* 22, no. 1 (2003): 44–52; Michael Cromer and Penney Clark, "Getting

Graphic with the Past: Graphic Novels and the Teaching of History," *Theory and Research in Social Education* 35, no. 4 (2007): 574–591; Mitra C. Emad, "Reading Wonder Woman's Body: Mythologies of Gender and Nation," *The Journal of Popular Culture* 39, no. 6 (2006): 954–984; Mike Dubose, "Holding Out for a Hero: Reaganism, Comic Book Vigilantes, and Captain America," *The Journal of Popular Culture* 40, no. 6 (2007): 915–935; Robert Getner, "'With Great Power Comes Great Responsibility:' Cold War Culture and the Birth of Marvel Comics," *The Journal of Popular Culture* 40, no. 6 (2007): 953–978; Bernard Mergen, review of *Comic Book Nation: The Transformation of Youth Culture in America*, by Bradford Wright. *The Journal of American History* 89, no. 1 (2002): 295–296; Valerie Palmer-Mehta and Kellie Hay, "A Superhero for Gays? Gay Masculinity and *Green Lantern*," *The Journal of American Culture* 28, no. 4 (2005): 390–404; Cord Scott, "Written in Red, White, and Blue: A Comparison of Comic Book Propaganda from World War II and September 11," *The Journal of Popular Culture* 40, no. 2 (2007): 325–343; Nathan G. Tipton, "Gender Trouble: Frank Miller's Revision of Robin in the *Batman: Dark Knight* Series," *The Journal of Popular Culture* 41, no. 2 (2008): 321–336; Bradford Wright, *Comic Book Nation: The Transformation of Youth Culture in America* (Baltimore: Johns Hopkins University Press, 2001). We also watched two documentaries: *Comic Book Superheroes Unmasked* (2003), DVD, directed by Steve Kroopnick (New York: A&E Television Network, 2003) and *Tales from the Crypt: From Comic Books to Television* (2004), DVD, directed by Chip Selby (Reisterston, MD: CS Films, 2005).

8 I base my assertions on my observations during my classes, student course evaluations, student written work, and an anonymous survey I distributed to students in my Spring 2011 "Historical Practices" classes regarding the use of comic books in this course. A total of 33 students answered the survey. Survey questions included: "Explain what we mean when we say that every topic in historical study has a historiography." "In HIS 285, the history department requires history majors, minors, and social studies education majors to 'join the conversation.' What do we mean?" "In your opinion, what are the most significant disadvantages and advantages of using the history of comic books as a content area in HIS 285? [List at least three each.]" "How did your study of the history of comic books this semester change your understanding of historical analysis in general?" "Would you ever consider using a comic book as a primary source in your classroom if you were to pursue a teaching career? Why or why not?"

9 Of course "the conversation" encompasses more than historical scholarship, extending to public history, political rhetoric, debates about education, and so on. For purposes of "Historical Practices" and for teaching the research paper, we tend to focus on academic works of history.

10 "Crime on the Run," *Authentic Police Cases* v1 #2 (New York: St. John Publishing, May 1948); "The Payroll Bandits," *Justice Traps the Guilty* v10 #3 (New York: Headline Publications, June/July 1957); "The Savage Genna Brothers: Bootleggers," *Crime Does Not Pay* v1 #66 (New York: Gleason Publications, August 1948). No authors or artists available. See also for example Chester Gould, "Dick Tracy and the Case of Murder by Mistake," *Dick Tracy* v1 #73 (St. Louis: Harvey Publications, March 1954).

11 Tom DeFalco (w), John Romita Jr. (p), and Alfredo Alcala (i). "Where Demons
    Fear to Dwell." *Dazzler* #2 (April 1981), Marvel Comics; Tom DeFalco (w),
    Ron Frenz (p), and Brett Breeding (p, i). "The Sinister Syndicate." *The Amazing
    Spider-Man* #280 (September 1986), Marvel Comics; Tom DeFalco (w),
    Keith Pollard (p), Joseph Rubinstein (i). "Day of Judgement." *X-Men Vs. The
    Avengers* #4 (July 1987), Marvel Comics; Mike Grell (w), Dan Jurgens (p),
    Dick Giordano (i), and Frank McLaughlin (i). "Moving Target." *Green Arrow*
    v1 #14 (January 1989), DC Comics; Tony Isabella (w), Trevor Von Eeden
    (p), and Frank Springer (i). "Merlyn Means Murder." *Black Lightning* v1 #2
    (May 1977), DC Comics; Stan Lee (w), Marie Severin (p), and Frank Giacoia
    (i). "He Who Strikes the Silver Surfer." *Marvel Superheroes* #48 (January
    1975), Marvel Comics; Stan Lee (w), Jack Kirby (p), Joe Sinnott(i), and Syd
    Shores (i). "The Claws of the Panther." *Marvel Double Feature* #21 (March
    1977), Marvel Comics; Stan Lee (w), John Buscema (p), and Sal Buscema (i).
    "Worlds Without End." *Fantasy Masterpieces* v2 # 6 (May 1980), Marvel
    Comics; Paul Castiglia (w) and Dan Nakrosis (a). "A Fish Out of Water."
    Conversation Corps #2 (September 1993), Archie Comics; Len Kaminski
    (w), Kevin Hopgood (p), and Steve Mitchell (i). "Into the Void." *Iron Man* v1
    #295 (August 1983), Marvel Comics; Marv Wolfman (w) and Jerry Ordway
    (a). "From the Dregs." *The Adventures of Superman* #426 (March 1987), DC
    Comics.
12 John Byrne (w, a). "Claws." *Wonder Woman* v2 #118 (February 1997), DC
    Comics; John Byrne (w, a). "The Men Who Moved the World." *Wonder
    Woman* v2 #117 (January 1997), DC Comics; George Perez (w), Jill
    Thompson (p), and Romeo Tanghal (i). "Embrace the Coming Dawn." *Wonder
    Woman* v2 #50 (January 1991), DC Comics; George Perez (a), Brian Bolland
    (a), Marie Severin (a), Cynthia Martin (a), Linda Medley (a), Kevin Nowlan
    (a), Adam Hughes (a), Chris Bachalo (a), Matt Wagner (a), P. Craig Russell
    (a), and Sergio Aragones (a). "Wonder Woman Gallery." *Wonder Woman* v2
    #50 (January 1991), DC Comics; George Perez (w), Mindy Newell (w), Chris
    Marrinan (p), and Romeo Tanghal (i). "The Ties that Bind." *Wonder Woman*
    v2 #41 (April 1990), DC Comics.
13 Emad, "Reading Wonder Woman's Body," 969, 976.
14 See for example Keith Barton, "Primary Sources in History: Breaking Through
    the Myth," *Phi Beta Kappan* June 2005: 745–753; Michael Coventry, et al.,
    "Ways of Seeing: Evidence and Learning in the History Classroom," *The
    Journal of American History* 92, no. 4 (2006): 1371–1402; Heather Owen,
    "Beyond the Flapper: The Problem of 'Snapshot' History," *OAH Magazine
    of History* 21, no. 3 (2007): 35–40; Roy Rozenzweig Center for History and
    New Media, "Historical Thinking Matters," http://historicalthinkingmatters.
    org/index.php (accessed June 2, 2011); Joel M. Sipress, "Why Students Don't
    Get Evidence and What We Can Do About It," *The History Teacher* 37, no. 3
    (2004): 351–363; Susan Veccia, *Uncovering Our History: Teaching with
    Primary Sources* (Chicago: American Library Association, 2003); Wilson
    Warren, "Closing the Distance Between Authentic History Pedagogy and
    Classroom Practice," *The History Teacher* 40, no. 2 (2007): 249–255; Laura
    Westhoff, "Lost in Translation: The Use of Primary Sources in Teaching
    History," in Rachel Ragland and Kelly Woestman, eds, *The Teaching American*

History Project: Lessons for History Educators and Historians (New York: Routledge, 2009), 62–78.

15 See for example Scott Allsop, "'We Didn't Start the Fire:' Using 1980s Popular Music to Explore Historical Significance by Stealth," *Teaching History: A Journal of Methods* 137 (2009): 52–59; LeRoy Ashby, "Not Necessarily Swill Time: Popular Culture and American History," *OAH Magazine of History* 24, no. 2 (2010): 7–9; Ron Briley, "A Teaching Note: Incorporating Popular Culture Into a History Classroom," *Teaching History: A Journal of Methods* 36, no. 1 (2011): 28–30; Harvey Cohen, "Music in the History Classroom," *Perspectives* 43, no. 9 (2005): 18–21; Christopher Edwards, "Down the Foggy Ruins of Time: Bob Dylan and the Concept of Evidence," *Teaching History: A Journal of Methods* 140 (2010): 56–63; Richard Hughes, "Race, Music, and Meaningful Approach to Teaching Historical Methods," *Teaching History: A Journal of Methods* 25, no. 2 (2010): 59–67; Jessamyn Neuhaus, "'Shake This Square World and Blast Off for Kicksville:' Teaching History with WWII Prescriptive Classroom Films," *The History Teacher* 44, no. 1 (2010): 35–50; Rowland Weston, "Introducing Theoretical Issues Through Popular Historical Films," *Teaching History: A Journal of Methods* 35, no. 2 (2010): 92–102.

16 Edwards, "Down the Foggy Ruins of Time," 57.

17 Even more troublingly perhaps, the three students who chose to do research papers on comic-book related topics, and who clearly recognized that comic books could be historically significant primary sources, struggled to actually apply this knowledge to their own work.

18 John Shedd, "Glimpsing at Pedagogy while Teaching History: A Mixture of Metacognition, Bird-Walking, and Quick Tips for Future Teachers," *The History Teacher* 43, no. 3 (2010), 450.

19 For an example of a structured primary source exploration activity, see Hughes, "Race, Music, and Meaningful Approach to Teaching Historical Methods," 63.

CHAPTER TWO

Comics as Primary Sources

The Case of *Journey into Mohawk Country*

Bridget M. Marshall

Many contemporary comic books (or graphic novels) "do" history, in a wide variety of ways: Art Spiegelman's classic *Maus* (1986) details the history-biography of his father's life during the Holocaust; Marjane Satrapi's *Persepolis* (2004) depicts her experiences as a young girl during the Iranian Revolution; Joe Sacco's *Safe Area Gorazde: The War In Eastern Bosnia 1992–1995* (2002) recounts life in a late twentieth-century war zone.[1] The stories of numerous historical events have been told through the medium of comics: C. C. Colbert and Tanitoc's *Booth* (2010) offers a version of Lincoln's assassination, and two books by Sid Jacobson and Ernie Colón—*The 9/11 Report: A Graphic Adaptation* (2006) and *Anne Frank: The Anne Frank House Authorized Graphic Biography* (2010)—present official findings, reprint and refer to historical documents, and include bibliographies documenting sources. Even long before the arrival of such upscale graphic novels, history comics—in the form of educational comics, real-life adventure stories or true-crime tales—held popular appeal, as demonstrated in part by the numerous history-based mid-twentieth-century series like *True Comics*, *Classics Comics*, and *Classics Illustrated*.[2]

But the graphic narrative *Journey into Mohawk Country* (2006), the subject of this essay, is unique among the historical comic crowd: it represents a collaboration between a twenty-first-century comic artist, George O'Connor, and a seventeenth-century Dutch explorer, Harmen Meyndertsz van den Bogaert. O'Connor's design and artwork (with coloring by Hilary Sycamore) illustrate the words of the original 1634 journal kept by Van den Bogaert as he explored what is now New York. I have been teaching O'Connor's comic version of Van den Bogaert's journal for four semesters in my History of American Literature course. My students and I have found it to be a fascinating primary source, an engaging story, and perhaps most importantly, a great lesson in critical reading.

Comics—history-based and otherwise—are increasingly being used in the classroom, in particular in history and literature classes.[3] In many cases, teachers see these texts as the "hook" that will get students interested in a historical moment or a work of literature. In *Comic Books as History: The Narrative Art of Jack Jackson, Art Spiegelman, and Harvey Pekar,* Joseph Witek suggests that the goal of such history-based comics as *Classics Illustrated* was "to encourage young readers to grow beyond their infatuation with comic books to a love of 'real' literature," and that "their essential endeavor is to make themselves obsolete."[4] Following this positioning of comics as the "spoonful of sugar" that helps the "medicine" of actual academic content more palatable for students, many teachers would argue that comic books help reach students (of whatever age) and get their attention, so that they can then read the "real" literature that is the required (and purportedly more appropriate) assignment. However, many recent graphic novels actually do present remarkable historical detail, evidence, and research, and are appropriate and useful as literary and historical texts in themselves. In a review of O'Connor's book for *Library Media Connection,* Donna Reed writes, "This book represents a happy marriage between a primary document and a graphic novel."[5] As such, *Journey into Mohawk Country* presents a unique opportunity, as it is both original source and contemporary interpretation working in tandem.

As a primary document, Van den Bogaert's original journal—filled with very specific, rather dry detail—is the stuff historians love, and (many) student readers hate. Van den Bogaert's handwritten journal was first published in an English translation in 1896; the 22-page journal was kept over a 2-month period when Van den Bogaert traveled through Mohawk and Oneida Indian territory in an attempt to secure trade relations with the natives. Van den Bogaert encountered members of several tribes, including Mohawks, Oneidas (whom he calls "Senecas"), and Onondagas;[6] in fact, Van den Bogaert's journal is the earliest known written account of these tribes. Although brief, the journal is full of impressive detail about Native culture that Van den Bogaert observed in his travels; anthropologist Thomas S. Abler explains, "The ethnographic data in the journal are profuse."[7] The journal has been praised by scholars for its clear detail and the surprising open-mindedness of the author; according to historian E. A. Schwartz, "it describes what the author saw in ethnographically useful detail, with little ethnocentricity and objectification."[8] In 1988, a new translation of the journal was published in a scholarly edition by Charles T. Gehring and William A. Starna, scholars at the New Netherland Project at the New York State Library.[9] It was this heavily footnoted and annotated edition that O'Connor used to create his comic.[10] As O'Connor explains in his introduction to the volume, "None of [Van den Bogaert's] entries have been altered or abridged; all is as Van den Bogaert recorded it."[11] While the first part of O'Connor's statement is indeed quite true—every word of Gehring and Starna's translated text of Van den Bogaert appears, and no text has been added—it is not entirely truthful to say that O'Connor's version is "all as Van den Bogaert recorded it," since the framing and the images make the text a different one, no matter how faithfully O'Connor attempts to render his images.

And, in fact, this is not exactly a faithful interpretation of the text— O'Connor has added numerous elements that appear nowhere explicitly in Van den Bogaert's text. As Witek explains, "sequential art narratives establish a visual text parallel to the verbal one, a narration both immediate and subliminal, one which can reinforce, contrast, or even contradict the verbal level of the story."[12] While O'Connor's visual images often reinforce the verbal narrative, they also repeatedly contrast with and contradict that narrative in ways both obvious and subtle. A *Booklist* review of O'Connor's rendition explains, "More than simply illustrating the account, O'Connor fills it with a new life, expanding on ideas only touched upon, creating action and conflict, casting some welcome humor into the Dutchman's somewhat dry original commentary."[13] O'Connor's humorous tone—which slightly undermines the solemnity of Van den Bogaert's text—is apparent in the very first pages of the book, when Van den Bogaert is explaining his journey and introducing the members of his exploratory party. On an eight-panel page, text boxes in the top two panels explain, "Because trade was going very badly" and "So for these reasons I went with Jeromus LaCroex and Willem Tomassen," while the final text box of the page, appearing in the lower right panel reads, "May the Lord Bless our Journey."[14] This rather plainspoken prose is undercut by the images appearing in the panels, in which we see Jeromus and Willem in a sort of slapstick, bumbling attempt to cross a river; they are unsteady, they push one another, they fall, they yell, and they end up wrestling one another in the middle of the river.

Later, in another example, the text of the original journal is reproduced faithfully, but O'Connor's images inflect Van den Bogaert's "May the Lord bless our journey" with a very different tone. While Van den Bogaert's narration doesn't necessarily imply exasperation with his travel companions, that is certainly one possible interpretation of his words. In fact, it's an interpretation that seems completely appropriate given O'Connor's images, but one that students probably wouldn't have considered if they were only reading the text without the images to suggest this possibility. Certainly no evidence exists to demonstrate that these men were particularly inept, or argumentative, or for that matter, that one was short and squat and the other tall and thin. But we also don't know what these men did look like. I see this text as an opportunity for students to more fully imagine these historical figures as real people, something that is typically very difficult for students to do when they are studying such dry older texts. As historian and blogger J. L. Bell wrote of *Journey into Mohawk Country*, "By focusing his book on Van den Bogaert's report, O'Connor replicates what historical researchers do most of the time: interpreting documents in an attempt to understand the past."[15] Like Bell, I see the strength of *Journey into Mohawk Country* in O'Connor's unique method of historical interpretation—presenting a primary document in its original (translated) form along with a visual interpretation that unfolds in the panel images.

As Witek writes "much of the action of a comic-book story takes place between the panels, in the gutters, so to speak, which separate the panels."[16] It is the separation of panels and the presence (or absence) of the gutter that is one element of comics that helps improve students' reading skills more generally—not just of comic texts, but of non-comic ones as well. While students can usually read what is on the page, they are often unable to—at least on their own—read what is not on the page. So when a historical journal skips a day, or a person in a narrative disappears, students rarely stop to imagine that things happened in that missing day, or that the missing person went off to have a life (or possibly not). The panel format presses students to imagine the things that are happening that are not on the page, and that are not included in the original text—the accidental as well as the willful choices of the first-person narrator. As one online review of the book explained, "O'Connor's work here illustrates the first-person narrative's slippery claims on truth and the limited viability of a 'true' historical account."[17] While students are likely to take such an account at face value as a "true" telling of what happened, it is essential for students to consider the problematic nature of such first-person narratives, whether they are from the seventeenth century or from our own times. O'Connor's book forces them to see that there are things happening between the journal entries, and between the words. While what O'Connor specifically portrays may not be what was happening, the fact that anything is happening at all that isn't appearing in the written word is an important lesson.

Potential problems: Depicting native culture

While I see great value in teaching *Journey into Mohawk Country*, it is not without its problems; however, I see some of these problems as openings for further discussion and exploration that can enlighten students not only about the original text, but also about cultural ideas about Native Americans that have been around since Van den Bogaert's times. As Michael A. Sheyahshe explains in *Native Americans in Comic Books: A Critical Study*, Native Americans have appeared in comic books since the start of the publishing format. However, "for the most part, Indigenous people became plot devices to move the story along and make the central character (most always a white man) more heroic"; they are most typically "flat, two-dimensional characters who were mere caricatures of real Native people."[18] On this point, O'Connor's comic differs from these stereotypical portrayals of Native Americans in comics. Van den Bogaert's text is not fiction, and indeed, the Native figures are not mere plot devices; the Natives—their trade practices, beliefs, and behaviors—are, in fact, the main reason for his exploration of their country. It is true that the white men (Van den Bogaert and his companions) are more fully fleshed out than the Native figures, but a wide array of Natives is portrayed, with individual personalities and variations; they are certainly not relegated to caricatures or side-kick status.

Sheyahshe describes a recurrent theme in comic books (indeed, in American literature more generally) that he terms the "Mohican Syndrome," in which "the hero is a white male pretending to be Indian," as seen in comic books he cites such as *White Indian* (1949), *Tomahawk* (1950), and Scalphunter, the main feature in *Weird Western Tales* beginning with issue #39 (April 1977).[19] Over the course of O'Connor's version of Van den Bogaert's story, the men do at times pretend to be Natives, but only to a degree. On page 124, after text boxes explain that "It was very cold and I was not able to start a fire. Therefore, I had to walk around the whole night to keep warm," in a series of wordless panels, Van den Bogaert takes the quill he has been using to write his journal, and sticks it behind his ear in the fashion of a Native headdress; for the next six nearly wordless pages, the feather-wearing Van den Bogaert stalks through the winter night, appearing to be on a sort of "spirit walk" in which he encounters (perhaps imagines) both beavers and a wordless Native American man who eventually lead him to safety. Van den Bogaert wears this feather in his hair through the end of his narrative, when he finally returns to Fort Orange. Over the course of the story, the three Dutchmen begin to look more and more like their Native hosts. The appearance of all three men from the beginning of the book to the end changes, as O'Connor explains in a blog sketchbook with a "before" and "after" sketch of the main characters[20] (see Figures 2.1 and 2.2).

O'Connor describes the differences between these two images: "They've lost some things, and gained some others. These shots are the alpha and omega. Artwise, I gradually brought them from the clean cut image in the

Figure 2.1 The "before" sketch of the main characters. George O'Connor (a). From *The First Second Blog*, http://www.firstsecondbooks.com/authors/oconnorBlogMain.html. Based on characters from *Journey into Mohawk Country*, art by George O'Connor, words by Harmen Meyndertsz van den Bogaert, translation by Charles Gehring and William Staarna (NY: First Second Books, 2006). Copyright George O'Connor, 2005.

before shot to the ragged, but wiser, final image."[21] The men learn over the course of their journey that Dutch ways are not ideal (their clothing, in particular their shoes, is quite inadequate for the environment); coupled with this acknowledgment of their own culture's limitations is their adoption of native dress and practice. In general, the three Dutchmen are mostly ill-suited to the challenges of life in the wilderness, whether due to their inadequate clothing, their physical limitations, or their lack of basic knowledge. If anything, O'Connor undermines the idea of "the Mohican Syndrome" by showing that the Natives are clearly stronger, smarter, and more capable than the Dutch explorers. Throughout their travels, the Dutchmen rely upon the Natives they meet to serve as guides, as well as to help them find shelter and food. When the Dutchmen take on Native habits and behaviors, it is clearly because these ways of living are more effective and appropriate to their environment.

Figure 2.2 The "after" sketch of the main characters. George O'Connor (a). From *The First Second Blog*, http://www.firstsecondbooks.com/authors/oconnorBlogMain.html. Based on characters from *Journey into Mohawk Country*, art by George O'Connor, words by Harmen Meyndertsz van den Bogert, translation by Charles Gehring and William Staarna (NY: First Second Books, 2006). Copyright George O'Connor, 2005.

Potential problems: Depictions of gender and sexuality

While most critics approve of the comic's (and the original journal's) depiction of Native culture,—Karp's *Booklist* review claims "The diary is absent of racism"[22]—its depiction of gender and sexuality has raised concerns for some readers. In "Our Minds in the Gutters: Sexuality, History, and Reader Responsibility in George O'Connor's Graphic Novel *Journey into Mohawk Country*," Melissa L. Mellon specifies her serious concerns with bringing this text into the classroom, where she fears the audience will not be sufficiently knowledgeable about Native American culture to adequately situate the story. Mellon writes: "In O'Connor's hands, *Journey into Mohawk Country* exists less as a document relating to the Dutch/Mohawk fur-trading business of the seventeenth century and more as a generalized narrative of Anglo-Indian contact both actual and mythologized."[23] Mellon's concern in particular is with O'Connor's portrayals of the women who appear in Van den Bogaert's narrative. As she explains, there are very few women actually mentioned in the original text, and none of them are named; yet O'Connor has chosen, at nearly every mention of a female Native, to sexualize these figures. She claims that O'Connor turns Van den Bogaert's narrative into a "comfortable 'boy meets girl' story"[24] that undermines the credibility of the portrayal and also makes troubling assumptions about gender and sexuality across time and culture. In O'Connor's images, Van den Bogaert is repeatedly depicted "checking out" Native ladies. In the first instance, the text reads, "no one was there but women,"[25] which O'Connor signifies in a panel depicting a group of half-undressed Native women. Following this panel, Van den Bogaert and his friends are shown in a huddle, after which they announce (as per the original text): "we would have then continued on, but I could not move my feet because of the rough going."[26] While the men's interest in Native women may well have motivated their decision to stay, that is not explicitly indicated by the text; however, O'Connor's images make the female nudity (and presumably hoped-for intimacy) the reason for a longer stay in this particular village. Later images depict Van den Bogaert flirting with an Indian woman,[27] despite text boxes that are entirely focused on issues of trading salmon and tobacco. While Van den Bogaert appears to have no luck with the women he admires,[28] his companion Willem apparently develops a more serious relationship with a Native woman, with whom he is shown later in a joyous reunion.[29] For several pages of panels, Willem runs off with his Native woman friend[30] while the text focuses on the details of a trade deal with no mention whatsoever of Willem's antics or the Native woman. In the final pages, it appears that the Native woman has returned to Fort Orange along with Willem, another element that goes unmentioned by the text and appears nowhere in the historical record. While it's entirely possible that a relationship between a Dutchman of the exploration party and a Native woman occurred, there is no evidence to support it; moreover, the particular and rather modern romantic vision of the relationship hardly seems likely given contemporary culture on both the Dutch and Native side.

O'Connor's visual interpretation, with its tale of romantic interactions, is not entirely defensible, but also is not outside the bounds of the possible, given some of the historical evidence. O'Connor includes a brief "glossary" at the end of the narrative, but it is much shorter than the word list created by Van den Bogaert himself and included at the end of his original journal, which Gunther Michelson (a collaborator with Gehring and Starna) has called "the earliest known philological treatment of the Mohawk language in existence."[31] Buried within the expected terms for a variety of foods, animals, numbers, and directions, are translations for somewhat more surprising words, such as "prostitute" and "(to have) intercourse."[32] Noting these words, Mellon reasonably questions, "are Van den Bogaert and/or his companions 'given' the sexual favors of the women they encounter?"[33] The question of the willingness of the Native women to participate in courtship or sexual relations with white explorers is not clear, either in this specific (imagined) case or in such situations generally. Further, as Mellon points out, historical records tell us that Van den Bogaert, though a husband and father of several children, was forced to flee the New Netherland colony in 1647 to avoid prosecution for homosexual acts—a capital crime under Dutch colonial rule at the time—after he was caught having intercourse with his black servant Tobias.[34] Although this incident happened 10 years after Van den Bogaert completed his journal, the information is included in Gehring and Starna's introduction to the journal; however, O'Connor makes no mention of this detail of Van den Bogaert's life. Throughout the images, O'Connor portrays all romantic or sexual interest as heterosexual, despite the fact that homosexual affection and intercourse were no doubt an element of life at this time, too. Ultimately, Mellon concludes that O'Connor's version of the journal "remakes history in a myopic way."[35] Her point is well-taken, particularly considering the evidence regarding Van den Bogaert's sexuality; upon fleeing from the Dutch colony, he returned to the Mohawk tribes he had encountered 10 years prior, where he was welcomed. While O'Connor's interpretation encourages readers to consider possibilities they might not otherwise have imagined—that the Dutch men had relationships with Native women—his interpretation limits some other possibilities that readers might also want to consider, and sidesteps the fact that ideas about sexuality and criminality vary over time and culture.

Despite these concerns, O'Connor's illustrations draw attention to the fact that they are interpretations, and students are well aware of the distinctions between what appears in the text (and was written by Van den Bogaert) and what appears in the images (and may be imagined by O'Connor). Some students in my courses were bothered by the gulf between what they sometimes called "the real story" and O'Connor's version, particularly the depiction of the relationship between Willem Tomassen and the Native woman. Numerous student papers proclaimed "he shouldn't do that" or "he can't do that," and that as student readers, they felt they were "led astray" by the sideline stories that were invented by O'Connor. His liberties with the text certainly caused some anxiety among alert readers, but they also prodded less engaged readers to question their own assumptions about texts and what they can and can't infer from primary sources. As Witek explains, "The synthesis of words and pictures in comic books finally becomes a narrative gestalt combining verbal movement and sequence with pictorial stasis and simultaneity, and vice versa."[36] It is this "narrative gestalt" that students questioned far more readily than they questioned our other more traditional, text-based reading assignments. The images, it seems, gives them a way into the interpretation that the purely text-based version does not. O'Connor's interpretive leaps, while they may frustrate some historians and readers, provide possibilities that can expand a student's view of history, or at the very least, engage the student in serious consideration of how interpretation works.

Benefits of the comic format:
Slow down, read closely

After teaching *Journey into Mohawk Country* over multiple courses, I found that students actually read this text more closely than other texts in the course, and were able to recall more details from this journal than from other journals and narratives of early America that we read, such as the 1682 *Narrative of the Captivity and the Restoration of Mary Rowlandson*. One student explained, "It helped me slow down while reading." To me, this was a huge win, as I'm always trying to get them to read carefully and slow down while they are reading their assignments. That the comic form would have this effect came as a surprise to me, as I had imagined that students would read a comic more quickly than plain text. Indeed, many student comments ran counter to the slowing-down effect, with several students specifically calling it "a quick read" (which they saw as a compliment). With these students, I found myself wondering about their reading practice, and whether they had stopped to "read" the images in addition to the text. Every semester, a couple of non-comic reading students admit that they skimmed or skipped the pictures entirely, assuming that all they needed to do was read the text boxes. One student, who had never read comics, said the text was "difficult to follow," because "rather than reading text in normal form, you are reading text in 'bubble' form." This made it clear to me that students needed help to prepare for the reading of comics, as many of them were not familiar with the form. Just as I wouldn't assign a poem without some discussion of the formal elements of poetry, I've realized that students need some guidance on how to read and discuss a comic.

I asked students if they thought the book was appropriate for a college-level course; many of them enjoyed it and thought I should teach it again, but voiced some concern that it was "childish." At least one student suggested that while it was an appropriate text for a survey (200-level) course such as ours, it wouldn't be appropriate for a more advanced course. Several reviews of O'Connor seemed to suggest that the book was for a younger crowd; *Kirkus Reviews* said that it would "engage younger teens and spark interest in a potentially dull and little-known segment of American history."[37] The review harkens back to the idea that comics are a trick, and that teachers can use them to get students to read something they otherwise wouldn't. The review goes on to explain, "Several facial expressions are presented with exaggerated juvenile quirkiness, marking the work's interest level as definitely middle school."[38] This purported correlation between "juvenile" artwork and a juvenile readership continues to dog reactions to comics and graphic novels; I found it interesting that both critics and students had concerns about whether the text was appropriate for adult readers in the college classroom. One student suggested that the book would actually be more problematic for younger readers, who might not understand that the images are not "real" and thus would think that O'Connor's love story and other additions were part of the actual history. This student felt that such interpretations were more appropriate for older readers, who understood the layering of primary document and interpretation, and could read the book more critically.

One thing I particularly like about O'Connor's version of the journal is that it reproduces the original text unabridged; all the words within the comic are those of Van den Bogaert (translated), so my student readers aren't missing anything. What they're getting instead, we might think of as visual footnotes. While the reader of the scholarly edition might page back to the 100-plus (excellent) footnotes explaining a particular ritual or food or animal or plant, the reader of O'Connor's version just sees it played out on the page. While this involves a certain amount of interpretation on O'Connor's part, so, too, do the footnotes in Gehring and Starna's edition. Overall, *Journey into Mohawk Country* continues to excite my students and me; they have suggested to me that it offers "a nice change of pace," and, "it may not be the most factual [reading assignment], but it is the most refreshing." In a midterm paper, one student wrote, "Reading comics for class kind of makes students feel like they're getting away with something, but they're learning a lot at the same time." I suppose some of my unease with teaching the comic is the idea of "getting away with something"; this urge that students (and perhaps all of us) have is not necessarily something I want to encourage. But ultimately, I believe the text helped us to achieve a key goal that I have for the course, which is to help students understand the history of early America—its exploration and founding—as not just history, but as the lived experiences of real people. If we have some fun on the way, perhaps I'm really the one who's getting away with something—sneaking historical lessons into their otherwise entertaining comic book.

Another reason that I find this particular text important is that it fills a profound gap in the texts available for student readers. The literature of early America—used both in literature and history classrooms—is heavily weighted toward several well-anthologized texts—Bradford's *History of Plymouth Plantation* and John Smith's *Virginia* are typical of such anthologies, and are well-known to students and scholars alike. Narratives of the Dutch colonization in early America have not received nearly as much critical (or student) attention, for a number of reasons.[39] One key factor is the fact that narratives of Dutch settlement must be translated; many of these texts have yet to appear in English translations, and those that have been translated (particularly in the eighteenth and nineteenth centuries) are often lacking in both readability and accuracy. While many more of these Dutch narratives are available for scholars now,[40] they are rarely included in the standard American literature anthologies that typically appear on university syllabi for American Literature courses.[41] While this is slowly beginning to change, it has meant a long gap in standard texts taught in the course that will no doubt continue even long after new texts are made available. As Cathy Davidson explains in *Revolution and the Word: The Rise of the Novel in America*, "literary history is a history of the most available texts."[42] As scholars and publishers continue to discover, recover, and explore long lost, forgotten, and overlooked texts, more texts become available to a wider audience. O'Connor's version of Van den Bogaert's journal expands access to this incredible document. Although it raises concerns, so should any and all literary or historical documents; as Davidson warns, "no documents . . . can simply be 'read' as if they were objective, scientific data produced or preserved as some pure product of a people and the abiding record of their times. The record always suppresses more than it tells."[43] While students often like to think that there is some "objective" source out there for historical information, Davidson reminds us that this is not the case, and that all historical documents require active interpretation. The journal of Harmen Meyndertsz van den Bogaert is no exception, and George O'Connor has done an excellent job of providing an accessible, not to mention entertaining, interpretation of this document. O'Connor has opened up the text with new possibilities that engage a wider readership, and perhaps more importantly, his collaboration with van den Bogaert encourages readers to contemplate the complicated ways in which we make history.

Notes

1 For more discussion of different ways in which comics have presented history, see Joseph Witek, *Comic Books as History: The Narrative Art of Jack Jackson, Art Spiegelman, and Harvey Pekar* (Jackson, Mississippi: University Press of Mississippi, 1989). He suggests some of the various ways in which comics interpret history, explaining that the three authors of his title "embody a spectrum of historical narrative which ranges from Jackson's overtly politicized rendering of the history of social groups, through world history focused by means of biography and autobiography in Spiegelman's work, to Pekar's history of an individual life" (4).
2 Witek provides background regarding these precursors to the rise of history comics in the chapter "Comic Books as History: The First Shot at Fort Sumter," 11–47.

3   See Katherine G. Aiken, "Superhero History: Using Comic Books to Teach U.S. History," *OAH Magazine of History* (April 2010), 41–47. The 2009 publication of *Teaching the Graphic Novel*, edited by Stephen E. Tabachnick, published in the MLA's Options for Teaching series, also signals the more general acceptance of these texts on college campuses.

4   Witek, *Comic Books as History*, 36.

5   Donna Reed, "Van den Bogaert, H. M. *Journey into Mohawk Country*," *Library Media Connection* (January 2007): 64.

6   All three tribes are part of the Iroquois Nation; at the time when Van den Bogaert was writing, the Mohawks were the most numerous of the five (today six) tribes considered the Iroquois.

7   Thomas S. Abler, "*A Journey into Mohawk and Oneida Country, 1634–1635: The Journal of Harmen Meyndertsz van den Bogaert*. Translated and Edited by Charles T. Gehring and William A. Starna," Book Review. *Ethnohistory* 38, no. 3 (Summer 1991): 342.

8   E. A. Schwartz, "*A Journey into Mohawk and Oneida Country, 1634–1635: The Journal of Harmen Meyndertsz van den Bogaert*," *The American Indian Quarterly* 18 (1994): 119. Academic OneFile. Gale. (A15295301).

9   Charles T. Gehring and William A. Starna, trans., *A Journey into Mohawk and Oneida Country, 1634–1635: The Journal of Harmen Meyndertsz van den Bogaert* (Syracuse: Syracuse University Press, 1988).

10 O'Connor's publisher, First Second, has a blog that includes many guest posts from O'Connor where he describes his design and research process in developing the comic, http://firstsecondbooks.typepad.com/mainblog/george_oconnor_guest_blogger/ (accessed November 21, 2011).

11 George O'Connor, introduction to *Journey into Mohawk Country* (New York: First Second, 2006), 4.

12 Witek, *Comic Books as History*, 20.

13 Jesse Karp, "O'Connor, George. *Journey into Mohawk Country*," *Booklist* 104, no. 4 (October 15, 2006): 38. Infotrac (A153707046).

14 O'Connor, *Journey*, 10.

15 J. L. Bell, "Getting into Mohawk Country," *Boston 1775* (December 4, 2007), http://boston1775.blogspot.com/2007/12/getting-into-mohawk-country.html (accessed November 21, 2011).

16 Witek, *Comic Books as History*, 22.

17 "*Journey into Mohawk Country*—Van den Bogaert and O'Connor," *Biblioklept* (August 3, 2007), http://biblioklept.org/2007/08/03/journey-into-mohawk-country/ (accessed November 21, 2011).

18 Michael A. Sheyahshe, *Native Americans in Comic Books: A Critical Study* (Jefferson, NC: McFarland, 2008), 9.

19 Ibid., 14.

20 Images from O'Connor's sketchbook, http://www.firstsecondbooks.com/authors/oconnorBlogMain.html (accessed November 21, 2011).

21 George O'Connor, *First Second Blog*, http://www.firstsecondbooks.com/authors/oconnorBlogMain.html (accessed November 21, 2011).

22 Karp, "O'Connor, George. *Journey into Mohawk Country*," 38.

23 Melissa Mellon, "Our Minds in the Gutters: Sexuality, History, and Reader Responsibility in George O'Connor's Graphic Novel *Journey into Mohawk Country*," *ImageTexT: Interdisciplinary Comics Studies* 4, no. 3 (2009): par. 34.

24 Ibid., par. 16.

25 O'Connor, *Journey*, 16.

26 Ibid.

27 Ibid., 32.

28 Ibid., 86–87.

29 Ibid., 79.

30 Ibid., 114–117.

31 Gunther Michelson, "Wordlist," *A Journey into Mohawk and Oneida Country, 1634–1635: The Journal of Harmen Meyndertsz van den Bogaert* (Syracuse: Syracuse University Press, 1988), 51.

32 Ibid., 54, 59.

33 Mellon, "Our Minds in the Gutters," par. 24.

34 This incident is discussed in greater detail in Russell Shorto, *The Island at the Center of the World: The Epic Story of Dutch Manhattan, the Forgotten Colony That Shaped America* (New York: Doubleday, 2004), 187–189.

35 Mellon, "Our Minds in the Gutters," par. 32.

36 Witek, *Comic Books as History*, 34.

37 "O'Connor, George: *Journey into Mohawk Country*," *Kirkus Reviews* 74, 17 (September 1, 2006), 910.

38 Ibid., 910.

39 For discussion of the literary canon and anthologies, see Raymond F. Dolle, "The New Canaan, the Old Canon, and the New World in American Literature Anthologies," *College Literature* 17, 2/3 (June/October 1990), 196–208.

40 For examples, see *Narratives of New Netherlands 1609–1664*, edited by J. Franklin Jameson.

41 *The Norton Anthology of American Literature Seventh Edition* (2007) and *The Bedford Anthology of American Literature* (2008) include no works of Dutch origin. *The Heath Anthology of American Literature Sixth Edition* (2008) added one Dutch colonist, but previous editions had no representations of Dutch settlement. Across anthologies and syllabi, despite new and expanded selections in geographic areas such as "Chesapeake," "New France," "New Spain," and Native American texts, there have been only limited advances in the representation of Dutch colonization or "New Netherland."

42 Cathy Davidson, *Revolution and the Word: The Rise of the Novel in America* (New York: Oxford University Press, 2004), 359.

43 Ibid., 360.

CHAPTER THREE

Transcending the Frontier Myth

Dime Novel Narration and (Jesse) Custer's Last Stand in *Preacher*

William Grady

Filmmakers working in the Western genre, such as John Ford, have often created sophisticated mythic narratives that reflect key moments in American history. In doing so, they created, out of myth, a vision of America that came to be accepted as reality. Ford himself revealed his own artifice in *The Man Who Shot Liberty Valence* (1962). James Stewart stars as Ransom Stoddard, a lawyer long feted as the man who vanquished famed outlaw Liberty Valence. In reality, this is not true, and in a flashback the film tells the real story. Stoddard is interviewed by the newspaper reporter and tells him the truth about the killing of Valence. The reporter burns his notes, stating, "This is the West, sir. When the legend becomes fact, print the legend."[1]

Fiction, whether on film or in print, can draw on myths and legends as an abstraction of reality and construct a history—a series of linked events over time—which is neither reliable nor accurate but seen as true nonetheless. This appears to be a paradoxical statement, but one that can be explored by analyzing the comic book series *Preacher*.

The *Preacher* series, written by Garth Ennis and illustrated by Steve Dillon, ran from 1995 to 2000, with a total of 75 issues (66 monthly issues, and 9 special issues). The plot focuses on a flawed Texas preacher, Jesse Custer, whose body plays host to Genesis, an all-powerful being who has escaped from Heaven. With Genesis' entry into Jesse's body, Custer learns

of God's flight from heaven. From this discovery, he sets off on a journey across America in his search for God, who he holds accountable for
his life's mishaps. Following him on his adventure are his girlfriend Tulip
O'Hare and Prionsias Cassidy, Jesse's Irish vampire friend. Throughout
their journey, they encounter, saints, serial killers, and a secret organization (the Grail) that has sustained the bloodline of Jesus in the hope of
reinstating Christ as king of men upon the apocalypse (prophesized for the
year 2000).

The series' timeline extends across a number of historic scenarios from
the Vietnam War to the Irish War of Independence, and heavily encapsulates multiple aspects of popular culture. However, the most self-aware
aspect of the series is the Western—or rather the Frontier myth that birthed
it. This essay will examine the impact of the Frontier myth on the *Preacher*
series, considering a number of actual myths from the American frontier
and assessing their uses. This will inform the study's consideration of a
number of uses of myth in Ennis' tales, including the creation of his own
myths of the frontier in the form of the *Saint of Killers* story arc collected
in *Preacher: Ancient History*.[2] The series also examines the impact of historical scenarios and their myths upon its characters. This is exemplified
by Custer's Last Stand, which Ennis mimics in the series' final battle, as
featured in *Preacher: Alamo*.[3] Here, Jesse Custer must face his own "last
stand." This transforms the original "Custer's Last Stand" from a historical battle, inflated through myth into a mystical battle between a Preacher
and a Vampire.

History repeated and the Frontier myth

I learned everything from this first spectacle: I saw how the white
(French), superior, plutocratic, civilized world founded its powers on
the repression of populations who had become "invisible" . . . I saw
the great, noble, "advanced" countries establishing themselves by
expelling what was "strange"; excluding but not dismissing it; enslaving
it. A commonplace gesture in History: there have to be two races—the
masters and the slaves.[4]

Here, Helene Cixous, an Algerian French Jew, speaking of her experience
during the Algerian War of Independence, explains a basic lesson of history: that difference often results in oppression. As Robert Young suggests,
"History . . . cannot tolerate otherness or leave it outside its economy of
inclusion."[5] As such, the evolutionary narrative of Eurocentrism demands
that the Other become absorbed into this binary: the master and slave,
the oppressor and the oppressed, the civilized and the barbarian. This has

happened in India, where (for Europeans) the history of that nation was defined by having been taken over by Britain, and in North America where the Native Peoples were made to fit into the imagination and mythology of the "civilized" Whites settling their land. This, in fact, came to be how their oppression would be justified through the Frontier myth and ideas like Manifest Destiny.

According to historian Richard Slotkin, "The myth of the Frontier is [the United States'] oldest and most characteristic myth, expressed in a body of literature, folklore, ritual, historiography, and polemics produced over a period of three centuries."[6] With its roots in the taming of the wilderness and extermination of the Native Americans, the myth was a vital tool for the justification of the peopling of the American colonies, which was in fact an act of mass extermination of the natives of America's land. But as the colonies expanded, the economy grew, and the nation developed as a powerful state, so too has the myth expanded to explain the development of the United States. The history of America is one based on violence, from the Indian wars to the slave trade—events predicated on brutality. Again, Slotkin explains, "What is distinctively 'American' is not necessarily the amount or kind of violence that characterizes our history but the mythic significance we have assigned to the kinds of violence we have actually experienced, the forms of symbolic violence we imagine or invent."[7]

The myth lies in the boundaries of cultural history, with Slotkin asserting that the concepts of ideology, genre, and myth are three related aspects of the culture making process.[8] Ideology equates to the basic beliefs and values of society. Genre is a form of classification and a way of articulating ideology. Finally, myth is a form of expression, or, as Roland Barthes asserts, "a type of speech."[9] Claude Lévi-Strauss takes this further by showing that before there were archives to trace history and myth, "there is only a verbal tradition."[10] Thus, in the most primitive of terms, myth originates from word of mouth. Barthes too draws his theory from this idea of myth as word of mouth. Myth always starts as a system of communication. While this is a basic premise for the tradition of myth, what can develop from this is the communicative form of myth, and more importantly, the storytelling aspect of myth. These stories are "drawn from a society's history that has acquired through persistent usage the power of symbolizing that society's ideology and of dramatizing its moral consciousness."[11] Over time, persistent retellings of these stories see them whittled down to the resonant symbols that these tales signify. Slotkin uses events such as "Pearl Harbor," "The Alamo," and "Custer's Last Stand" as examples, suggesting the very names "evoke an implicit understanding of the entire historical scenario that belongs to the event."[12]

As Garth Ennis remarks in his foreword to *Ancient History*, "The American myth originally intended to disguise this rather feisty past [i.e. the conquering and destruction of Native Peoples] is, of course, the Western."[13] He lists examples like General Custer, stating his "reputation as an Indian fighter—prior to the spectacular piece of military incompetence that was the Little Bighorn—was based on a massacre of women and children."[14] While Ennis is speaking in the present day, back in the nineteenth century, Custer was a revered Indian fighter (even more so after his death). Likewise Jesse James never "robbed from the rich to give to the poor."[15] However, he was depicted as doing so in the dime novels of his escapades back in his time. While the historical figures Ennis describes were, in reality, no heroes, the tales written about them would secure their legendary status. As Slotkin asserts, "The 'Frontier' was . . . a complexly resonant symbol, a vivid and memorable set of hero-tales—each a model of successful and morally justifying action on the stage of historical conflict."[16] The telling of these "hero-tales" that fit into the Frontier myth will be the focus of this study.

The dime novel

Before these mid-to-late nineteenth century heroes (such as Custer and James), the Frontier hero-tales were dominated by the likes of Hawkeye from James Fenimore Cooper's "Leatherstocking Tales," and historical figures such as Benjamin Church and Davy Crockett. However, it was in the dime novels of the mid-late nineteenth century America that these already codified hero-tales were combined with new heroes to make a specific frontier mythology. Brothers Irwin and Erastus Beadle founded their company Beadles Publications, and produced the first dime novel in 1860. Charles Harvey, writing in 1907, states that the initial purpose of the dime novel was to offer "a picture of American wild life," adding, "A real frontier in 1860 along the line of the Missouri and the Arkansas, with thousands of fighting Indians beyond that line, and some of them east of it, gave the reader an ardent concern in the adventures."[17]

Jean Paul Gabilliet's *Of Comics and Men* argues that the dime novel and later pulp magazines laid the foundation for the mainstream comic book narratives of the 1930s and 1940s.[18] Also significant is the fact that the dime novel industry collapsed in 1903, the year the first Western film (*The Great Train Robbery*) was released.[19] This demonstrates how these mythic hero-tales quickly made their transition to film. The association between *Preacher* and the Western film genre is very clear, but the connection between the series and the dime novel has been less noted. But it is important, as writer Garth Ennis tells a tale similar to the narratives of the dime novels in the *Saint of Killers* story arc to create his own myths.

Preacher: Ancient History

Ennis admits in the foreword to *Ancient History*, "I can honestly say, with my hand on my heart, that Westerns are my favorite."[20] The indelible influence of the Western on the series is already affirmed in the prior three volumes (collecting issues #1–26) with the inclusion of such tropes as the gunslinger, the desert locales, John Wayne (both as apparition to Jesse and in physical form handing Jesse's father a Zippo lighter in Vietnam), and also revisionist western genre tropes in the form of the strong female lead—Tulip O'Hare. However, while these genre conventions, old and new, are present, Ennis states in his foreword that "the Western remains a form of legend. The stories happen long ago and far away, in a land so wild and brutal we cannot imagine it. The characters who ride its streets and canyons are giants, the words they speak echo forever . . ."[21] For this legendary tale, Ennis needed a character who had these virtues, explaining he wanted someone who "would directly represent the Old West, who had walked straight out of history, and who brought with him the horror and terror of those times."[22] *Preacher: Ancient History* collects together the story arcs *The Story of You Know Who* (the story of how Arseface became disfigured) and *The Good Old Boys* (a tale about Jody and T. C.), which especially offer more of a back-story to the series, but it is the *Saint of Killers* story arc that adds depth.

We are introduced to the Saint early on in the series as he is ordered to retrieve Genesis from Jesse. The *Saint of Killers* story arc introduces us to the character before he became the Saint, and illuminates his quest for vengeance against God later in the series. We never learn his true name, but we know he served in the Confederate Army during the American Civil War. Upon his journey across the Old West in search of medicine for his sick wife and child, the Saint is delayed from returning with the medicine by a group of outlaws resulting in his and subsequently his family's death. In Hell, the Devil allows him to become the "Saint of Killers," thus granting him access to Earth to take vengeance for his family's death. Before being put to rest, he is called upon to apprehend Jesse.

Ennis changes the use of narrative voice in this story, arguably making it just like a classic dime novel. This raises two questions, though. What is dime novel narration? And how does Ennis transcend generic narrative voice in his series to become more akin to dime novels in this story arc?

Narrative voice

In *Narrative Discourse*, Gerard Genette coins two terms: heterodiegetic ("the narrator [is] absent from the story he tells") and homodiegetic ("the

narrator [is] present as a character in the story he tells," be it as hero—
autodiegetic—or secondary character—homodiegetic).[23] As Genette further states, "Absence is absolute, but presence has degrees. So we will have
to differentiate within the homodiegetic type at least two varieties: one
where the narrator is the hero of his narrative and one where he plays only
a secondary role, which almost always turns out to be a role as observer
and witness."[24] This terminology describes traditional ways of describing
narratives in the first, second, and third-person forms, and Julia Round has
proved that these terms can be applicable to comic books as well.[25]

Before analyzing the narration that is similar to that of dime novels
in *Preacher*'s *Saint of Killers* story arc, it is worth describing the narrative voice in the rest of the series. Throughout the 66 issues of the main
story arc of the *Preacher* series (excluding the *Ancient History* volume),
Ennis barely uses any third-person heterodiegetic narration. Exceptions do
include the context of time as the series drifts back and forth in time and
space, examples of which include captions reading "six months earlier."[26]
Homodiegetic first-person narration (from the point of view of one of the
characters) does occur occasionally. One example can be found in *Preacher:
Proud Americans*[27] (see Figure 3.1). Jesse meets Billy Baker, one of his
father's friends from the Vietnam War, who begins to tell Jesse the history
of the Zippo lighter his father received during the war. Thus, the narration

Figure 3.1 Jumping from homodiegetic first-person narration and dialogue.
Garth Ennis (w) and Steve Dillon (a). *Preacher: Proud Americans*. (NY: DC
Comics, 1997), 14. © DC Comics. Used with Permission of DC Comics.

by Billy switches between the past and present, as he is first narrating the panels that depict the past when telling the story of John Wayne handing Jesse's father the lighter (homodiegetic first-person narration) and then reverts back to the present (in the airport) as the narration returns to dialogue with Jesse gazing in awe at the lighter that was originally in the hands of John Wayne. However, these instances of homodiegetic first-person narration are limited and are only used in cases of characters telling a tale that requires them to refer to the past. Round describes these minimal instances of homodiegetic first-person narration and third-person heterodiegetic narration in the *Preacher* series but concludes that "Ennis chooses to tell his story predominantly in dialogue."[28] However, Round's study only looks at the 66 issues of the main story arc, and she does not apply this taxonomy to the *Saint of Killers* story arc.

The dime novel also takes a number of narrative stances. However, most employ the third-person heterodiegetic narrator; while the narrator is not present at the events he narrates, he is all-knowing in regard to those events.[29] Typically, these dime novels would open with the narrator's address to the reader. For example, Edward L. Wheeler's *Deadwood Dick's Doom; or, Calamity Jane's Last Adventure* opens with "DEATH NOTCH! Did you ever hear of a more uninviting name for a place dear reader?"[30] Col. Prentiss Ingraham's *California Joe, the Mysterious Plainsman* opens with "'Who was California Joe?' Kind reader, that question I cannot answer . . ."[31] This allows for the narrator to assume a conversational voice. As quoted previously, "myth is a type of speech," thus the narrator becomes a storyteller of these myths.

Ennis is working on the norms of dime novel narrative structure when creating his own tale. However, while he does not have a narrator addressing the reader, he begins *Saint of Killers* with a conversation between a pizzeria owner and a murderer. This returns Ennis' work to the basic premise of narrative as the object point of communication; as Barthes reminds us, "There can be no narrative without a narrator and a listener (or reader)."[32] The metafictive nature of this arrangement sees an omniscient and detached narrator telling the story of how a pizzeria owner is telling a murderer the story of the Saint of Killers in third-person heterodiegetic narration: "And he told the kid the version he'd been told, of the story that's about to begin."[33]

It is fair to note that the story is again scripted in dialogue. However, the third-person heterodiegetic narration is more present here and aids each scene. The combination of both dialogue (that aids the action depicted in the panels) and the narration (that is similar to the narration of a dime novel) arguably adds to the mystique of the narrative.[34] For example, before the Saint is killed in Ratwater, McCready (leader of a group of bandits) hides behind an innocent woman, stating, "You shoot [me] and you kill her."[35] The following panel shows the Saint shoot his gun regardless of the

Figure 3.2 Combining third-person heterodiegetic narration and dialogue. Garth Ennis (w) and Carlos Ezquerra (a). *Preacher: Ancient History.* (NY: DC Comics, 1998), 53. © DC Comics. Used with Permission of DC Comics.

woman, at which point the narrator notes, "And he damned himself"[36] (see Figure 3.2).

While the presence of a narrator is apparent, there is no obvious reason for the use of this dime novel/mythic form of narration in Ennis' work. A case study of William "Buffalo Bill" Cody, a character inflated by myth and elevated to mono-mythic status through dime novel tales, will offer an understanding of the mythic space of the dime novel, and why Ennis may use this form of narration in his tale. This will allow for an examination of how the mythic space of Ennis' dime novel tinged tale can impact on the Saint of Killers character in the rest of the *Preacher* series.

Buffalo Bill Cody

One of the most striking sidelights of the creation of our Western mythology is that it was being fabricated, recast, and enlarged upon almost immediately after the events upon which it was based were taking place. . . . The heroes . . . joined in the process by portraying themselves and re-enacting their supposed deeds.[37]

The mono-mythic hero William Cody, famed for his stage name Buffalo Bill, had some 1,700 stories written about his "heroic" adventures in the American frontier. This would make him the most written-about frontier character with the exception of Jesse James, placing Bill in the "traditional pantheon of frontier heroes derived from Boone, Hawkeye, Carson, and Crockett."[38] Even in dime novels written about him, the authors would place him in the same sentence as such heroes. For example, Colonel Prentiss Ingraham writes, "Glancing back over the past, we recall a few names that have stood out in the boldest relief in frontier history, and they are Daniel Boone, Davy Crockett, Kit Carson and W. F. Cody, the last named being Buffalo Bill, the King of Bordermen."[39]

William Cody was born in Iowa in 1846. A scout for the U.S. Army, popularized in Ned Buntline's *Buffalo Bill: The King of the Border Men*, and the star of his Wild West traveling show, he is a prime example of the transformation of reality into myth. A notable example of this can be seen in his duel with a Native American, Yellow Hand, in 1876. Working with the 5th Cavalry to stop a group of Cheyenne from joining with Sitting Bull in the run up to the Battle of the Little Bighorn, Cody was challenged by Yellow Hand. The fight was over instantaneously. Yellow Hand, without a firearm, was shot twice by Cody who was grazed during the skirmish. This differs from later newspaper accounts that would describe "137 bullet, arrow and tomahawk scars in the defense of civilization."[40] The mystique of the scenario derived from bits of everything: Cody scalping his fallen foe, the efficiency of Cody's victory, and even this clothing. Cody was aware that the day would see conflict, and selected an outfit from his theatrical trunk. "It consisted of a Mexican suit of black velvet . . . These costumes, fictional and actual, illustrate the blending of Cody with his theatrical role to the point where no one—least of all the man himself—could say where the actual left off and where dime novel fiction began," explains Smith.[41] The retelling of the event was recounted in a number of fictitious ways. One example is from Ingraham's *Adventures of Buffalo Bill from Boyhood to Manhood*:

> Together both fired, the chief with his rifle, and Buffalo Bill with his revolver, and down dropped both horses. Buffalo Bill nimbly caught on his feet, while the Indian was pinned by one leg under his and with his war-cry the scout rushed upon him. As he advanced the chief succeeded in releasing his leg from beneath his horse and again fired, as did Buffalo Bill, and both of them with revolvers. The Indian's bullet cut a slight gash in Bill's arm, while he struck the red-skin in the leg, and the next instant sprung upon him with his knife, which both had drawn. The hand-to-hand fight was hardly five seconds in duration, and Buffalo Bill had driven his knife to the broad red breast, and then tore from his head the scalp and feather war-bonnet, and waving it over his head, shouted in ringing tones: "Bravo! The first scalp to avenge Custer!"[42]

It was such events, and their subsequent dramatizing and mythologizing, that would win Cody a Medal of Honor. While considered unwarranted in hindsight, it is undeniable the indelible impact Cody had on the portrayal of the Frontier, informed by the countless cultural products that succeeded him in death.[43] These tales would elevate people like Cody to mythic status. This is what Ennis attempts to do when writing about the Saint of Killers. The Saint cannot write his own tales, so, like Ingraham, Ennis in the *Saint of Killers* story arc takes on the role of mythic narrator telling the tale. Since the Saint has a story narrated like legend, this lore elevates the character to the mono-mythic hero type in the rest of the series.

The Saint of Killers as mono-mythic hero?

As noted, it is the storyteller that adds to the myth and mystique of the character about which he or she is writing. Ingraham illustrates this as he placed Cody in the same pantheon as other frontier heroes such as Crockett in the introduction to one of his tales. In similar fashion, the narrator to the opening of the *Saint of Killers* sets the scene:

> There was Bowie and Crockett and Travis and a hundred and eighty men, who took the Alamo with them into history. . . . There was Ethan Edwards, who rode a trail of hate for five long years. . . . And Jesse James, who died at the hands of a traitor and a coward. . . . And William Munny, who one black night in 1880 was to scorn a hail of bullets and kill six men, and ride out unscathed from a town too terrified to face him.[44]

The narrator concludes, "It's been so long since then that I no longer know just which of [these stories] are truth . . . and which are only legends."[45] As Ingraham sets up one of his tales by first addressing the heroes before Cody, so Ennis too uses this to great effect, placing the Saint in the same league as these mono-mythic characters. Furthermore, by listing film characters (Ethan Edwards from *The Searchers* and William Munny from *Unforgiven*) along with historical figures (Crockett and Jesse James, et al.), he blurs the line between fiction and non-fiction. Where the acts of Jesse James and Crockett were real, the fiction and legends that succeeded them would inflate fact to fiction. This illustrates the point that whether the people listed are part of history or are characters in a film, their legends make them one and the same.

Ennis admits that the Western *Unforgiven*[46] and the main character William Munny (played by Clint Eastwood) were a large inspiration for this tale. In the film, Munny's legend as a child killer, bank robber, and murderer precede him. While we do not see these past acts, his reputation means that other characters fear him or seek his services. In a sense, throughout the *Preacher* series (set in present day), the Saint is like Munny, living off the power of his legend. But while we do not see Munny's past in *Unforgiven*, the *Saint of Killers* arc offers this legendary story where we can see the Saint's origins. When the character with no name takes on the title of the Saint of Killers in Hell, he then returns to the town of Ratwater to take his vengeance on McCready and the bandits who killed him. Rather than extracting revenge on just the group of thugs, the Saint takes revenge on the whole town, even killing a child in true William Munny fashion. This makes for a more poignant polarity in character. We do not see Munny killing the supposed children he murdered earlier in his life, and just see him killing the sheriff, Bill Daggett (Gene Hackman), for his wicked deeds. This allows for more likeable qualities in Munny's character. There are not meant to be any likeable qualities in the Saint. The depiction of him killing innocent people makes him more of an abhorred character. This detracts from the typical use of the dime novel narration, which would feature characters in a tasteful light, making their actions sound heroic. Even the dime novels featuring Jesse James, a bank robber, would imbue James with likeable qualities, in a sense depicting banditry favorably. However, this is not the point of Ennis' use of dime novel styles. He uses the dime novel narrative voice purely to create a legendary tale that resonates throughout the series.

As the story of *Saint of Killers* concludes, we return back to present day with the pizzeria owner and the murderer. "So the old man finished the version he knew, of the story that's just been told. He watched the young killer grow pale in the streetlight, and he realized . . . Holy God, the kid had aged five years."[47] Stating that the pizzeria owner finished "the version he knew" suggests that it may have differed from the story the narrator tells the reader. But this is illustrative of the Frontier myth in general, the exaggeration and changing of facts from the story. As noted previously, Cody would receive a slight wound from his fray with Yellow Hand, but it was later reported as "137 bullet, arrow and tomahawk scars." This in turn inflates fact from fiction. But it also leaves us wondering whether the narrator's story of the Saint is true or inflated by myth. As the narrator remarks, "so much blood has flowed since then that I no longer know how much of it is truth . . . and how much only nightmare."[48]

The Saint's legend haunts his presence throughout the series. The murderer (from the present day) at the end of the tale remains speechless after hearing about the Saint's legend. In the first volume of the series, the Adephi (the spirits that look after Heaven in the absence of God) gather to discuss their plan for retrieving Genesis. They decide to wake up the Saint to find Custer (who holds Genesis), to which Fiore responds, "You can't . . ."[49] in fear. The reader, at this point, has not come across the Saint, but already we know this character must be threatening. This illustrates the point of the

Saint's legend preceding him. The Adephi are reluctant to wake the Saint knowing his past full well, but we the readers also already fear him as we see how the other Adephi react at the prospect of waking up the Saint.

Ennis states that the legend behind the Saint is one "whispered from killer to killer down the years."[50] To that effect, it works. Due to this legend that precedes the Saint, the rest of the *Preacher* characters fear him. Even in the last volume, *Preacher: Alamo*, Jesse, who has on many occasions clashed with the Saint throughout the saga, reflects how "this part I never can get used to, not even a little bit"[51] as the Saint appears from the dark of the night to meet one more time with Jesse before the climactic ending. However, the Saint does not just have an impact on the characters in these scenes, but also on the reader. While the Saint's legend allows for the characters to fear him, Ennis, creating a legend/dime novel-type story, allows the reader to understand the character as a myth.

We have classified the mythic space of the dime novel, and how Ennis creates his own myth that impacts his work. To demonstrate how those Frontier myths resonate in culture and have worked their way into Ennis' work, it is instructive to study General Custer and his "Last Stand." This is a typical frontier paradigm of Cowboys versus Indians, and mirrors the conclusion of *Preacher: Alamo*, which sees Jesse Custer face off against his vampire nemesis Cassidy, thereby transforming the original scenario.

General Custer and The Last Stand

As noted previously, the thousands of restive Indians in the 1860s and 70s would be the topic of these dime novels and "gave the reader an ardent concern in the adventure." Just as, as Cixous observes, there would be no Nazis without the Jews,[52] without the Native Americans, there would be no resonant hero-tales in the dime novels and frontier mythology. The case of "Custer's Last Stand" is a prime example. Mythologized through the press at the time, and subsequently transcending to the level of myth through a number of cultural media, this event came to fit a number of scenarios.

The Battle of the Little Bighorn took place between the 25th and 26th of June, 1876. Famed later as "Custer's Last Stand," the battle saw George Armstrong Custer killed and his Battalion suffer a major defeat in one of the more famous battles in the Great Sioux War of 1876–77. There were various factors to the defeat: Custer's frosty relations with fellow officers, each of whom wanted their own battalion's personal victories in the battle; the map of the terrain that was based on "estimated guesses";[53] and the difficulty in getting a good estimate on the number of Indian fighters they were up against, among other factors.

An article in the *Brooklyn Daily Eagle* noted how General Custer was becoming quite the celebrity in the run up to the campaigns against the Indians.[54] As a result, the reportage on Custer's defeat was sensationalistic. Initially, when reports were just coming in from the battle, it was described as the "Montana Slaughter"[55] by the *Brooklyn Daily Eagle*. A follow up report by the same newspaper renamed it "The Custer Massacre"[56] when it appeared that he was the most famous fatality. The *Jacksonville Republican* reported how Custer and his men "fought like tigers"[57] and the *Brooklyn Daily Eagle* reported how Custer's killer (Rain-in-the-Face) cut out Custer's heart, retreated, but "occasionally halted and had a dance around the bloody trophy."[58] Of course, this ceremony was completely fabricated. But this was how the press would paint this picture of the brave and courageous Custer fallen at the hands of the "savage native." This created a typical good versus evil paradigm, and illustrates how mythologizing of an event could start so early on.

Nathaniel Philbrick argues that the battle was ultimately "the story of how America, the land of liberty and justice for all, became in its centennial year the nation of the Last Stand."[59] However, in this time of celebration, there was shock that the country's famed Indian fighter had been defeated. Thus, like coping with the settling of the wilderness of America through the Frontier myth, the only way for the country to comprehend this defeat was to transform this battle into myth. As Slotkin argues, "The process of transforming history into myth requires a series of creative acts of transmutation and associative linkage."[60] This translation of the Battle of Little Big Horn into the myth known as Custer's Last Stand started with journalists immediately after the event. As noted above, initially the event was termed a "massacre" before finally being transformed into "Custer's Last Stand." Journalists had already created the paradigm of good versus evil. But this allowed them to conjure links with the battle to other historic events like the Alamo, another "Last Stand" scenario, which also pitted a good (the mostly Anglo Texans) versus an evil (the Mexican army). This association gave some mythic credence to the "Last Stand," as historic scenarios such as the Alamo were already metaphors for America "winning the West."

Slotkin refers to the work of journalists and myth makers (such as Cody) as the progenitors of "establishing Custer and the Last Stand as an important ideological object—a myth whose terms, however variously interpreted, would seem to contain and refer to the conflicts of value that most concerned America."[61] The "Last Stand" as ideological object is malleable enough to be adapted as a metaphor to conflicts of universal interest, not just American. Nathaniel Philbrick, for example, looks at the "Last Stand" as an ideological object at the end of his book *The Last Stand: Custer, Sitting Bull, and the Battle of the Little Big Horn* (2010). However, he attempts to use the scenario to predict the future; he suggests,

"Instead of several hundred dead and a guarantee of eternal fame, a Last Stand in the future might mean the devastation of a continent."[62] Or, in the case of Ennis' *Preacher*, it might involve the collapse of a secret organization (the Grail), the death of God, and a fight between a clergyman and a vampire.

Jesse Custer and The Last Stand

The generic set up of the last stand is a scenario that has been repeated throughout history and within a variety of cultural texts.[63] It is this particular scenario that Garth Ennis picks up on when creating his own last stand with his own Custer. Ennis understands that the reputation of General Custer as a famed hero is based on the murder of innocent Natives. However, he is not using the negative underpinnings of Custer's character, but adapting scenarios and names to offer mythic credence to his tale, as seen in *Preacher: Alamo*.

Alamo is the climatic end to the *Preacher* series. Once good friends, Jesse Custer and Prionsias Cassidy became enemies midway through the series as Jesse learns of Cassidy's true self. Cassidy agrees to meet with Jesse outside the walls of the Alamo for one last fight. Meanwhile, the secret organization called the Grail has failed to restore order to the post-apocalypse world and their leader, Herr Starr, instead sets a trap to kill Custer at the Alamo, as Starr holds Custer responsible for the Grail's failings. In a sense, we see Custer in a last stand against a number of foes.

At face value, this scenario seems to be a stretch from the initial Battle of the Little Bighorn, but they are connected through the Alamo. As noted earlier, the battle reportage by the press in the following months would create an association between the "Last Stand" and the Alamo to give the major defeat positive mythic associations. However, in Ennis' scenario, he literally binds the two as Custer (Jesse) has his own "last stand" outside the Alamo. As noted earlier, such historic terms as "Alamo," through persistent usage, allow for implicit understanding of the scenario. Setting is one thing, but names, like Jesse (associating to Jesse James) and Custer, also create mythic reinforcement.[64]

In essence, Ennis has in effect already established Jesse as a mythic hero by using Custer as his surname. The resonant image conjured by the name only takes full effect in the final battle between him and Cassidy, though. As the battle ensues, Ennis quotes Evan S. Connell's book *Son of the Morning Star*, a piece of non-fiction about the life of George Armstrong Custer. The quote, "Custer! His name reverberates like the clang of a sword,"[65] is juxtaposed with the image of Jesse punching Cassidy in the face. Clearly, Ennis understands the resonant weight of the name. But he exploits it to great effect as the image shows Custer, all-powerful, defeating Cassidy in a bare-knuckle fight. Arguably, this allows Jesse himself to be elevated into a mythic pantheon like the other heroes before him.

Another factor Ennis hones is narrative voice. The *Preacher* series (when set in the present day) features a very limited mix of homodiegetic first-person narration and dialogue. The only time then, in essence, that third-person heterodiegetic narration is used is when Ennis adopts the mythic form of storyteller narrating in the *Saint of Killers* dime novel-infused story. However, there is one instance of it featured in *Preacher: Alamo*. As Cassidy burns in the rising sun, Jesse is shot in the head by one of the Grail's soldiers. The omniscient narrator returns, commenting, "And that was how they killed him, covered in the ashes of his dearest friend."[66] As has been established, this form of narration is reserved for legendary storytelling in Ennis' series. Ennis readopts this mode of narration to finally add some mythic credence to the main character Jesse Custer. With this final act, outside the Alamo and with a Custer, Ennis attempts to transcend his own mythic Last Stand by adding the mythic storyteller narrator. By this point in the story, we have come a long way with Jesse on his quest, making his final transformation into the realm of mythic hero very fitting.

Conclusion

As Slotkin asserts, "The Myth of the Frontier is arguably the longest-lived of American myths, with . . . a powerful continuing presence in contemporary culture."[67] This presence is felt most prominently in the Hollywood Western, of course. In recent years, though, Hollywood has seen a trend of Weird Westerns,[68] suggesting that something quintessential in the genre seems to be lost. Furthermore, with some Hollywood elite hailing the Western genre as "dead,"[69] some might consider the Frontier myth as a mythos in decline.

In *Preacher*, Ennis exemplifies that there is a continuing presence of the Frontier myth in contemporary westerns. As he concludes in his foreword to *Ancient History*, the Saint's "story is a myth. All westerns are. Writing my own was the joy I always knew it would be."[70] While this quote is from the foreword of *Ancient History*, we can extend Ennis' proclamation of his affection for myth-making to be extended to the rest of the series. Ennis uses myth when creating this multi-layered narrative in two distinct ways. First, through the use of storytelling through word of mouth, he returns myth to its early communicative form.[71] Secondly, his readaptation of actual Frontier myths (here, Custer's Last Stand) and dime novel narration, mimics more nineteenth century forms. This relies on binding allegory, fact, and fiction together to allow his characters to be elevated into a similar mythic pantheon. Set in the present, the series can be associated with other contemporary Weird Westerns, but clear narrative functions link the series directly to the Frontier myth. In a period where the Western seems unsure of its classic underpinnings, *Preacher* is a useful text for reminding us of the stories that continue to inform popular culture and identity. It draws out the subtleties, complexities, and ironies of life and encapsulates them in legendary form. To repeat the dialogue that concludes *The Man Who Shot Liberty Valance*, "When legend becomes fact, print the legend!"

Notes

1 *The Man Who Shot Liberty Valance*. Directed by John Ford (1962; Paramount Home Entertainment, 2005), DVD.
2 Garth Ennis (w) and Steve Pugh, Carlos Ezquerra, and Richard Case (a). *Preacher: Ancient History* (London: Titan Books, 1998).
3 Garth Ennis (w) and Steve Dillon (a). *Preacher: Alamo* (London: Titan Books, 2001).
4 Helene Cixous and Catherine Clement, *The Newly Born Woman*, trans. Betsy Wing (Manchester: Manchester University Press, 1986), 70.
5 Robert Young, *White Mythologies, Writing History and the West* (London and New York: Routledge, 1990), 4.
6 Richard Slotkin, *The Fatal Environment: The Myth of the Frontier in the Age of Industrialization, 1800–1890* (Connecticut: Wesleyan University Press, 1986), 10.
7 Richard Slotkin, *Gunfighter Nation: The Myth of the Frontier in Twentieth-Century America* (New York: Atheneum, 1992), 13.
8 Ibid., 5.
9 Roland Barthes, "Mythologies," in Anthony Easthope and Kate McGowan, eds, *A Critical and Cultural Theory Reader* (Buckingham: Open University Press, 1994), 14.
10 Claude Lévi-Strauss, *Myth and Meaning* (London: Routledge, 2003), 32.
11 Slotkin, *Gunfighter Nation*, 5.
12 Ibid., 6.
13 Ennis, et al., *Preacher: Ancient History*, 3.
14 Ibid.
15 Ibid.
16 Slotkin, *Gunfighter Nation*, 3.
17 Charles M. Harvey, "The Dime Novel in American Life," *The Atlantic Monthly*, 1907, 42.
18 Jean Paul Gabilliet, *Of Comics and Men: A Cultural History of American Comic Books*, trans. Bart Beaty and Nick Nguyen (Jackson: University Press of Mississippi, 2010), 13.

19 Michael Denning, *Mechanic Accents: Dime Novels and Working-Class Culture in America* (London: Verso, 1987), 159–160.

20 Ennis, et al., *Preacher: Ancient History*, 3.

21 Ibid., 3.

22 Ibid., 4.

23 Gerard Genette, *Narrative Discourse*, trans. Jane E. Lewin (Ithaca, NY: Cornell University Press, 1980), 244.

24 Ibid., 244–245.

25 Julia Round, "Visual Perspective and Narrative Voice in Comics: Redefining Literary Terminology," *International Journal of Comic Art* 9, no. 2 (2007): 316–329.

26 Garth Ennis (w) and Steve Dillon (a). *Preacher: Salvation* (London: Titan Books, 1999), 5.

27 Garth Ennis (w) and Steve Dillon (a). *Preacher: Proud Americans* (London: Titan Books, 1997), 14.

28 Round, "Visual Perspective and Narrative Voice in Comics," 326.

29 There are exceptions to this rule. For instance, William Cody, when writing his own dime novels about his alter ego's escapades, would employ first-person homodiegetic narration as he is talking about himself.

30 Edward L. Wheeler, "Deadwood Dick's Doom; or, Calamity Jane's Last Adventure," in *Deadwood Dick Library*, vol. 3, no. 39 (New York: Beadle and Adams, 1899).

31 Col. Prentiss Ingraham, "California Joe, the Mysterious Plainsman" in *Beadle's Boy's Library of Sport, Story and Adventure*, vol. 3, no. 54 (New York: Beadle and Adams), http://www-sul.stanford.edu/depts/dp/pennies/texts/ingraham2_toc.html (accessed February 14, 2011).

32 Roland Barthes, *Image Music Text*, trans. Stephen Heath (London: Fontana Press, 1977), 109.

33 Ennis, et al., *Preacher: Ancient History*, 7.

34 It is fair to note that Ennis is not the first to use third-person heterodiegetic narration in a comic book; for example, fellow Vertigo writer Neil Gaiman uses third-person heterodiegetic narration in his *Sandman* series. However, arguably the purpose of this narration is somewhat different.

35 Ennis, et al., *Preacher: Ancient History*, 53.

36 Ibid.

37 John Burke, *Buffalo Bill: The Noblest Whiteskin* (New York: G. P. Sons, Capricorn Books, 1973), 95.

38 Slotkin, *Gunfighter Nation*, 74.

39 Colonel Prentiss Ingraham, "Adventures of Buffalo Bill from Boyhood to Manhood. Deeds of Daring, Scenes of Thrilling, Peril, and Romantic Incidents in the Early Life of W. F. Cody, the Monarch of Bordermen," in *Beadle's Boy's Library of Sport, Story and Adventure*, vol. 1, no. 1 (New York: Beadle and Adams, 1882), http://www-sul.stanford.edu/depts/dp/pennies/texts/ingraham1_toc.html (accessed February 28, 2011).

40 Cf. Don Russell, *The Lives and Legends of Buffalo Bill* (Norman: University of Oklahoma Press, 1960), 188.

41 Henry Nash Smith, *Virgin Land: The American West as Symbol and Myth* (Cambridge: Harvard University Press, 1950), 108.

42 Ingraham, "Adventures of Buffalo Bill."
43 This can be a number of things, including the 700 stories written about him, *Buffalo Bill Weekly* (a pulp magazine) that ran up until 1919, and countless films featuring or referencing to his character.
44 Ennis, et al., *Preacher: Ancient History*, 9.
45 Ibid.
46 *Unforgiven*. Directed by Clint Eastwood (1992; Warner Home Video, 1998), DVD.
47 Ennis, et al., *Preacher: Ancient History*, 106.
48 Ibid., 105.
49 Ennis, *Preacher: Gone to Texas*, 21.
50 Ennis, et al., *Preacher: Ancient History*, 4.
51 Ennis, *Preacher: Alamo*, 34.
52 Cixous, *The Newly Born Woman*, 71.
53 Nathaniel Philbrick, *The Last Stand: Custer, Sitting Bull and the Battle of the Little Big Horn* (London: Random House, 2010), 97.
54 Uncredited journalist, *Brooklyn Daily Eagle*, May 6, 1876, 4, http://gethelp. library.upenn.edu/guides/hist/onlinenewspapers.html (accessed February 22, 2011).
55 Uncredited journalist, "The Battle," *Brooklyn Daily Eagle*, July 13, 1876, 3, http://gethelp.library.upenn.edu/guides/hist/onlinenewspapers.html (accessed February 22, 2011).
56 Uncredited journalist, "The Story of the Custer Massacre," *Brooklyn Daily Eagle*, September 9, 1876, 2, http://gethelp.library.upenn.edu/guides/hist/ onlinenewspapers.html (accessed February 22, 2011).
57 Uncredited journalist, *Jacksonville Republican*, July 15, 1876, 1, http://gethelp. library.upenn.edu/guides/hist/onlinenewspapers.html (accessed February 22, 2011).
58 Uncredited journalist, "The Battle," 3.
59 Philbrick, *The Last Stand*, xxii.
60 Slotkin, *The Fatal Environment*, 435.
61 Ibid., 436.
62 Philbrick, *The Last Stand*, 312.
63 See a number of scenarios, from the Battle of Thermopylae (popularized by Frank Miller's *300*), in which a small number of Greeks stood against the might of the Persian army, to the Battle of the Alamo itself seeing a last stand of Texans against an overwhelming number of Mexicans.
64 Slotkin, *The Fatal Environment*, 15.
65 Ennis, *Preacher: Alamo*, 155.
66 Ibid., 191.
67 Slotkin, *The Fatal Environment*, 15.
68 Weird Western is a subgenre that combines tropes of Westerns and genres such as horror and fantasy. Examples include *Jonah Hex* (2010), *Priest* (2011), *Rango* (2011), and *Cowboys & Aliens* (2011). This is not to disregard a number of classic Westerns released in recent years, such as the TV series *Deadwood* (2004–2006) and the remake of *True Grit* (2010), however, this current trend for the weird is apparent.

69 One such assertion has been made by Ridley Scott, see Dalya Alberge, "Sci-fi Films Are As Dead As Westerns, Says Ridley Scott," *The Times*, August 30, 2007, http://entertainment.timesonline.co.uk/tol/arts_and_entertainment/film/article2351086.ece (accessed March 20, 2011).

70 Ennis, et al., *Preacher: Ancient History*, 4.

71 Similarly, Carlyle notes that Norse God, Odin, was elevated to myth not through books but word of mouth. See Thomas Carlyle, *On Heroes, Hero-Worship, and the Heroic in History* (Cirencester: The Echo Library, 2007), 35.

CHAPTER FOUR

"Duel. I'll Give You a DUEL"

Intimacy and History in Megan Kelso's *Alexander Hamilton Trilogy*

Alison Mandaville

What is history? In the preface to her collection of stories *One Hundred Demons*, cartoonist Lynda Barry asks, "Is it autobiography if parts of it are not true? Is it fiction if parts of it are?"[1] The same questions might be asked of historical narratives. In her trilogy of short stories about Alexander Hamilton, cartoonist Megan Kelso uses the close dance between words and images in the comics form to reimagine a more intimate and dynamic relationship between individuals and key events in the past than one might receive in either traditional works of history or primary literature.[2] In these stories, Kelso depicts ordinary scenes in the lives of extraordinary figures in American history, humanizing and connecting them to the lives of ordinary, more contemporary Americans. She depicts moments in which contemporary Americans, particularly girls and women, interact with these events of the past to stubbornly ground history in its highly localized, personal effects.

As part of a new generation of female creators who are influenced by and draw significant inspiration from other women cartoonists rather than male predecessors, Kelso represents an important shift in the field of comics. Though aware of an alternative comics scene as a student at Evergreen State College (Matt Groening, Lynda Barry, and Charles Burns all attended college there), it was not until she read work by Julie Doucet that Kelso was able to see herself making comics.[3] She went on to teach herself the form,

authoring a 1990s self-produced indie zine "GirlHero," which offered serialized stories over the course of six issues.[4] Her first short story collection *Queen of the Black Black* brought together a selection of stories from
"Girlhero."[5] Her second comics short story collection *Squirrel Mother* was
well reviewed in many national publications including *People* and *Time*
magazines[6] and was followed by an invitation to produce a serial comic for
the *New York Times Magazine*. The result was "Watergate Sue," a story in
24 installments about an American family impacted by social and political
changes during the Watergate era.[7] Most recently, she published the graphic
novel *Artichoke Tales*, a fictional story set in an imaginary land populated by people with artichoke-like caps for hair.[8] The novel draws together
elements of recent and historical civil conflicts to explore the after-effects
of war on individuals, families, communities, and their environments.

Many of Kelso's stories take up questions of history: how we make it,
what we choose to make it from, and what the effects of our historical
tales are. In "Pickle Fork," from her collection *Squirrel Mother*, the story
of one woman's collection of silverware and dishes, accumulated over a
lifetime together with her loving industrialist husband, is told largely from
the perspective of the maid who cleans the silver and looks on as the older
woman is wooed by an ambitious and calculating museum acquisitions director.[9] The story offers a visual critique of the odd distance museums create
between people and their intimate, even if historical, domestic objects. In
the move from home to museum, from experience to history book, our life
stories, our close relationships with history itself, are often lost, even appropriated for others' personal gain. In *Artichoke Tales*, Kelso focuses on the
stories individuals tell each other about both family and national history in
the aftermath of war. The novel explores the ways that the histories we tell
and retell can have profound and long-lasting effects on lives in the present
and future, shaping our personal as well as political relationships.

Kelso's fascination with history, she says, goes back to Laura Ingalls
Wilder's *Little House* series which was read to her as a child.[10] This multi-
volume story about a pioneer family told through the eyes of a young girl
"made [her] love and appreciate 'old-fashioned' things."[11] This attachment
eventually turned into a full-blown adult passion for history. Kelso studied
history and political science at Evergreen State College, which is where she
said she was "made" to read the "Federalist Papers," a set of documents
that would become a central topic in her Alexander Hamilton trilogy (here-
after referred to as AHT).[12]

In her comics, Kelso sticks to accessible, cartoony line art, friendly pastel
colors, and spare use of prose. The reader can see and move through the
literal events of the stories rather easily and quickly—there is little sense of
immediate difficulty. Yet, not unlike the ostensibly child-like works by Barry
that were, for a long time, largely ignored by scholars, Kelso's seemingly
simple narratives work hard at the tension endemic to the comics form, the

friction between words and pictures, gutter and frame. Her stories advance right at the edge of reader understanding. The often surprising endings of her stories encourage multiple readings, encouraging readers to revisit and study the narrative for clues. The need to intensively reread Kelso's stories is also produced by the particularities of the comics form itself—elements that also make the medium especially appropriate for historical narratives. In her recent study exploring autobiographical women's comics, *Graphic Women: Life Narrative and Contemporary Comics* (2010), Hillary Chute writes that "[t]he medium of comics can perform the political and aesthetic work of bearing witness powerfully because of its rich narrative texture."[13] Later she writes more specifically about writing history that the form of "graphic narrative" is "a representational mode capable of taking up complex political and historical issues with an explicit, formal degree of self-awareness, which explains why historical graphic narratives are the strongest emerging genre in the field."[14] Indeed, Kelso uses the form's "rich narrative texture" to "bear witness" to a world she herself imagines and constructs, tethered by historical facts to our "non-fiction" world, but not bound to mirror it.

With friendly colors and cartoon images, Kelso's comics invite the reader in as a co-witness, even co-creator of her historical landscapes. Scott McCloud emphasizes the intimacy created by "closure"—the work a comics reader must do: creating narrative content in the gutters between frames and investing what might be cartoony and simple images with depth and detail. He writes, "Closure fosters an intimacy surpassed only by the written word."[15] I and many others have further developed this idea, arguing that comics is especially powerful for the intimacy it offers as a recursive and dialogic form that invites continual "play" between words/pictures, frame/contents, events (known)/gutter (unknown), and, in independent comics especially, high culture/low culture. Building on McCloud's above claim, I wrote in an article exploring the role of comics in prose fiction that "as a dialogic, explicitly sensual and recursive form, comics is closer to oral narrative than prose and so is, potentially *more* intimate [than prose]."[16] Chute argues that autobiographical narratives such as Marjane Satrapi's *Persepolis* and Alison Bechdel's *Fun Home* have been especially powerful precisely because they make use of this intimacy that the comics form can evoke. She emphasizes the "graphic" nature even of the words within a comic, noting how the handwritten text used in many of these works "creates an intriguing aesthetics of intimacy."[17] Certainly comics may offer an intimacy that intensifies personal narrative—but this is an intimacy that can be brought to the writing of public history and fiction as well.

It is important to note that, particularly when it comes to historically based narrative, McCloud has been criticized for his emphasis on "closure" and proscribed "types" of frame-to-frame transitions by some who argue this view of the comics-reading experience privileges the "wholeness" of story at the expense of the important ways comics narrative also comes to the reader in fragments. Teresa Tensuan, for example, suggests that, more significantly than the closure it requires, the comics form effectively mirrors how memory, or any story for that matter, consists of filtered bits of events and experiences, and that the form therefore offers a particularly powerful medium for materializing those histories that have never been told, or not told whole, for reasons of trauma and exclusion or oppression.[18] While acknowledging the helpful way McCloud addresses how comics "keeps readers' minds in the gutter" and invites them to "transform separate frames into a coherent narrative framework," Tensuan makes the perceptive observation that he nevertheless "retreats from the radical possibilities he opens up in his analysis" when he focuses on reader "closure" in the service of conventional narrative transitions (for example, moment-to-moment or action-to-action). She underscores the many possibilities the episodic form offers to "[create] narrative trajectories and tensions that move beyond the parameters of conventional narratives . . . in which a plot is mapped out along a one-directional arc of conflict and resolution."[19] That is, as a fragmented and episodic form, comics offers a particularly fruitful medium for mobilizing past events to retell stories from new perspectives.

Kelso not only makes use of this fragmentation of the comics form to create stories that are historically "incomplete" or even feel unfinished (we get only slices of her characters' lives in narratives that often end abruptly), but she also explicitly labels her work as fiction, resisting the idea that she is writing any kind of "accurate" history. She says of her work in fictional history,

> I can't imagine trying to do a kind of "objective/educational" historical narrative with comics. Part of the fun for me is that I make the world through how I draw it, and I get to emphasize and slant things and mess with things for my own purposes. It would kill the fun of it for me if I had to be fair and accurate all the time. I recently met Larry Gonick, the guy who does the *Cartoon History of the Universe* books. He has a very pointed left wing slant to his comics—and they are funny, but in his way, he is still attempting a certain accuracy and fairness. I have always done fictional stories precisely because I do not want to be bound by reality or what actually happened, so I think my history comics are always going to be a bit warped, and not particularly reliable sources in the educational sense. I guess in a way I would hope that those stories might pique the interest of readers to know more, but that is not really the intent of that work. For me, taking on historical periods is an arena that I am fascinated by to play around in and tell stories.[20]

Not only does Kelso take advantage of the way that comics offers a potentially more visceral experience of both story and history, but her texts also positively revel in the "play" the fragmented form offers—a word she also used several times during a 1998 roundtable with other cartoonists to describe her work and interest in comics: "it's this odd, mushy language of symbols that *is* really playful."[21] Discussing her sense of the formal play of comics in terms often used to describe human relationships, she says,

> I think that a really huge part of comics is chemistry. The images that you put together from panel to panel, or the words that you include within this panel, compared to the words that you include in that one. All of these combinations, where things are always bumping up against each other. The trick is learning how to understand how that chemistry works, what kind of effect you're going to get by putting particular things together—one panel that's silent or one that has lots of words or one that's all words—and I think that's one of the most difficult things. I think people often get too bounded up with things like "I do silent comics" and don't just break out and do anything and everything to figure out how things work together, and how the chemistry works.[22]

Kelso's view of comics emphasizes the "trans" nature of the form, saying that "in comics, there's a place where words get to dress up as pictures and pictures get to dress up as words. And you do get to force the idea that there isn't such a boundary between the two as you might think."[23] In fact, she likes the idea that words and pictures are involved in a kind of battle in the comics form.[24] In other words, for Kelso, comics does not set up the boundary between words and pictures, but rather plays with a socially constructed boundary that is not unlike the boundaries between nations that we collectively "imagine," as Benedict Anderson explores in his book *Imagined Communities*.[25]

Indeed, Kelso's approach to history is closely informed by this parallel between imagined narrative boundaries and national boundaries. She says,

> I have always felt very self-consciously American as a citizen and an artist. I remember first developing my own sense of what "American" was as a teenager. Of course it has evolved a lot since then, going through various stages of loving and loathing and on and on, but I definitely think that part of my history comics are me trying to get at that question of what it is to be American. In college I was so awestruck by the idea that what has always held us together has not been ethnicity or heritage, or even land, but a willingness to agree on the idea of this country. It still gives me chills that no matter how abused and tattered and torn those ideas, they are still what hold us together as a nation.[26]

The comics form mirrors Kelso's understanding of nation, and specifically the United States itself: both comics and nation are constructed through a process of communal agreement on ideas. A dialogic form, comics requires close exchange not only between words and pictures, frame and gutter, but also between reader and text to agree upon and construct the narrative. Moreover, comics is experienced as an explicitly visceral form in its making and reading, evoking the closeness of oral storytelling. Most "alternative" comics authors hand draw and letter their work, so that not only does comics, as Chute says, "put the body on the page" in concrete visual form, but it keeps foremost in the reader's experience of that page the writer's body *at work*, echoed in the embodied work of reading.[27] Chute writes, "There is an intimacy to reading handwritten marks on the printed page, an intimacy that works in tandem with the sometimes visceral effects of presenting private images."[28] I would add to this that comics images are visceral not only by way of private content, that is, when illustrating apparently private scenes, but also because, like the words of comics, the scenes—and, in Kelso's case, even their panel boundaries—are hand-drawn. This sets the literal craft of the narrative front and center as the reader's eyes trace the lines and curves, often imperfect and uneven, of what hands have so obviously made. In this sensual exchange, comics is a form that mimics conversation, even "battle" or argument, invoking both the writer and the reader's bodies in the material play of the narrative. In turn, this process evokes Kelso's very sense of America as formed through "a willingness to agree on the idea of this country." Kelso's use of the comics form makes very explicit the dynamic work and interchange between people's bodies that narratives, and also histories and nations, require.

Because comics relies on icons and, like language, on the commonly held and agreed upon cultural concepts and definitions triggered by those icons to construct narrative, her fictional comics offer insights, not only into possibilities for what our history was and might have been, but also into our contemporary cultural assumptions about that history. About the particular challenges of selecting and using such stereotypes to construct her "period" pieces, Kelso writes,

> Well, it's important to get the period feel, but not be overpowered by feeling like you have to be historically accurate at all times. I mainly concentrate on architecture, furniture and dress to evoke a period, but of course quite simplified and cartoony. I usually wind up picking out a few key details and repeating them—in the Hamilton stories, beards, the wigs, waistcoats, federalist architecture . . . It's stereotyping to be sure, but comics are not illustration—you make use of icons, so hopefully the icons of a certain historical period, combined with the specificity of character and story add up to a fully realized world in the mind of the reader.[29]

Indeed, the use of icons explicitly taps into and connects with contemporary culture in a way that realistic illustration and photography cannot.

Photos may have more detail, but those details do not serve as placehold-ers for cultural concepts and ideas right out in the open as icons do. In a recent interview about his editing choices in drawing details and transcrib-ing interviews while writing "history" through comics, journalist Joe Sacco says of the inevitable slant this gives to any historical "truth,"

> The arc of a story can be true, but you cannot say that everyone has the same memory of the arc of that story. There's always an objective truth, but then there are many tellings. And what history is is a telling. It's not necessarily the objective truth. If there are many tellings of that point, many tellings can point to an objective truth, and I think that's what I'm also trying to get across.[30]

There is, therefore, always a gap between a "telling"—history—and "object-ive truth." Kelso makes use of this gap, or, to use comics terminology, the "gutter" between "objective truth" and "history" to create "tellings" that "point to an objective truth"—marked and anchored by the accuracy of dates and names for the public historical events in her stories—drawn and imagined from new, more intimate feminist and democratic perspectives. Dealing with events more than two centuries past, the Alexander Hamilton Trilogy offers an example of the ways in which comics can create a per-sonal and immediate narrative of key moments in American history.

The political is personal: The Alexander Hamilton stories

This trio of stories focuses on a modern-day female character[31] who, as an adolescent, "falls in love" with the historical figure Alexander Hamilton while doing a report for school. Although Hamilton is the ostensible sub-ject of the trilogy, it is the relationship the modern-day female characters forge with the historical figure through narrative that is the center of these pieces. In every story, the act of writing itself is depicted. Human hands, both in the past and in the present, put ink down on tangible paper that often curls up to meet it. Paper, pens, and/or the act of writing appear in fully 13 of the 17 pages that make up this trilogy.[32] In one remarkable scene, Hamilton holds a feathered "pen" during a scene of physical intim-acy with Madison.[33] History and its very concrete process of creation are made literally sensible—and sensual (see Figure 4.1).

Through the eyes of the modern-day female characters, Kelso play-fully reimagines key moments in Alexander Hamilton's life: his role in the Federalist Papers, his (sometimes intimate!) relationships with the other Founding Fathers, and his eventual demise in a duel. As the modern-day

Figure 4.1 Alexander Hamilton, James Madison, and the process of making history. Megan Kelso (w, a). *Squirrel Mother* (Seattle, WA: Fantagraphics Books, 2006), 108. © Megan Kelso. Used with Permission.

character ages, we learn of the different periods of Hamilton's daily life in detailed artwork, with occasional explanatory narration and snippets of dialog as she imagines them. As a result of this intimate connection with the commonplace events of the past depicted in the stories, Hamilton's character, and the momentous history with which he is associated, is thoroughly and concretely humanized. Further, in AHT, by basing the stories on the connections that modern-day female characters make with Hamilton and his era, Kelso makes a place for girls and women in a historical narrative that has almost categorically excluded them.

In "Publius," the first Hamilton story, the intensity of an adolescent's simultaneous awakening of her sexual and political interests is expressed through a romantic vision of Hamilton and Madison "getting physical" together.[34] The story begins and ends as the modern day character chooses her topic, embarks on her research, stays up late writing, and finally turns in her passionate and completed essay to her bemused teacher. Sandwiched between this contemporary frame, the characters Hamilton and Madison, who worked together on the Federalist Papers, are depicted becoming increasingly close as they argue political theory. The comic shows their literal physical closeness as they meet and talk ideas: walking together, arms around each other; going home together and facing each other, seated over a glass of wine; leaning close in an increasingly passionate engagement that is eventually depicted through images alone.

As words dry up and images take hold, the central, modern-day character, dozing off as she does her research, becomes fully, bodily, identified with her subject. Through this imagery, American politics becomes embodied as an all-encompassing, visceral passion—not just words passed down on paper. And it becomes a passion in which the reader too partakes, gazing at the sensuous way the eighteenth-century men's pants hug—and fall away from—their figures as the two men embrace and kiss. Hamilton and Madison not only *think* and *talk* about politics; Kelso depicts them as having some serious "skin" in the game—like the artist whose hands traced these sensual lines. Kelso says, "I remember first developing my own sense of what 'American' was as a teenager." And she uses emotionally charged words to describe that sense of being American, of developing an identity as a citizen both "loving" and "loathing" America.[35] This is an identity that circulates through intimate passion, depicted visually: when the young girl awakens from her fantasy about the two men, her cheeks are burning with a blush that echoes the rosy cheeks Hamilton is depicted as having as well—and that the girl's teacher shares when he sees the hearts drawn on the cover of her report and realizes how personally she has taken her research.

When I taught this text, it was this story that provoked the most productive discussion and questioning in my class: What was going on? What did it mean to be so free with the personal lives of such iconic Founding Fathers? Where did fact and fiction begin and end? How could we be sure? This free hand with history provoked a real and increased curiosity in these characters and helped students think of history as something lived and made by individuals deeply invested in their world and the lives of others.

In "The Duel," the second story, the central present-day character continues her intense relationship with history as a young college-age woman who explores the mutual enmity of Hamilton and Thomas Jefferson.[36] Hamilton represents the interests of the Federalists—urban merchant/industrialists who are anti-slavery and keen on a strong federal government and taxation to provide for the common interest and to create a common stake in the nation. Jefferson stands for the interests of the republicans—landed gentry who are agrarian, pro-slavery, and favoring strong states' rights with little federal power, responsibility, or taxation. The story presents how these competing points of view inform two very different approaches to governance, both still reflected in political tensions in the U.S. today.

After learning of Hamilton's end in a college seminar, the young woman laments his death in a duel with a man she feels was an unworthy opponent, Vice-President Aaron Burr, "a failure . . . a lame duck . . . trying to jumpstart his own career."[37] That "Hamilton's career was basically over" meant, the narrator says to her companions in the story, with a dejected and grumpy look on her face, "[t]hey dueled from positions of weakness over petty insults."[38] In this piece, the narrator imagines and reenacts a different duel for Hamilton, through which she celebrates her much-loved historical figure's stature as a key political thinker, as well as her own engagement with American history, creating a tale that reminds us that history is a series of very local and specific "what-if"s.

Reversing the staging of the first story, in which contemporary time frames historical events, this story is framed by the historical events, between which are sandwiched two sets of frames from the contemporary period. The story begins with three panels depicting the "actual" historical events—the two men rowing across the river from New York, where dueling "was illegal," to New Jersey, where the Burr gives Hamilton a "hand up" to the bank from the boat—a visual that underscores, without a word, both the physicality of this event and the stupidity of the violence about to ensue between the men willing to give and take each other's hands. Hearing of this event in a classroom from a professor who simply "sighs" as she says that "the greatest political thinker in American history dies in a duel with the sitting Vice-President," the central character at first looks sad, then, increasingly angry. As she emerges from class into the city and heads through the subway turnstiles, a red spot appears on her cheek, echoing the rosy blush with which Hamilton is always depicted in close-ups in the story. She blurts out, with spark lines emanating from her forehead, "Duel, I'll give you a DUEL." In a subsequent frame, now seated in the subway car, no longer frowning but smiling with an almost devilish look, arms around knees drawn up, feet resting on the edge of the seat, she goes on to say, "Hamilton versus Jefferson. Now *that's* a fucking Affair of Honor."[39] Her companions, on either side of her, are rapt. One exclaims, "Whoa."

The change in the expression on the character's face from sadness, to anger, to a kind of fierce and joyful engagement encapsulates her movement from a sense of helplessness to empowerment. Simultaneously, images of the physical shifts in the character as she orients to the history she has learned mirror a political awakening: She transforms from sitting student, to striding thinker, to seated storyteller getting comfortably into the intimate physical space of storytelling in the very public space of the subway, and finally to lively actor, reenacting the historical event in (presumably) Central Park—also a very public space.

The story that ensues is thereby framed by a sense of "public history," that is, history that is personally relevant, that engages the personal within the public, communal sphere. It is a reimagined history, one that traces the origins of the very real discord between Jefferson and Hamilton and brings them, in the end, to an alternate duel in which Jefferson, on the verge of becoming America's second president, dies instead of Hamilton, thereby possibly altering the future power balance of American politics. What is particularly important here, though, is not the history that is reimagined, so much as it is the way in which it is done: on a subway, emerging from a subway, reenacted in a park, with others getting involved in the play with history. When she gets to the "new version" of the duel, one of her friends (also a woman) is drawn into the new "story" and begins, with the central character, to perform the alternate duel of Jefferson versus Hamilton. She ends the story with a penultimate and satisfactory image of the historical Jefferson shot and killed by Hamilton "for those of us who chafe at the unfairness of historical reputation."[40] The final panel shows an image of the Hudson River, the cliffs and bushes of New Jersey on one side and the heavily built up Manhattan on the other, no bridge in sight. Across the water between the two shores the comic narrates, "But that duel never happened. Instead they remain forever opposed, pistols cocked, aiming for each other's heads and we the people suspended between them."

The image—of a New Jersey in which duels are legal, facing of against a New York, in which they are not; of ideals facing off against each other in such visual, carefully drawn form reinforces the visceral sense Kelso gives to her dramatization of and connection to history and to the ways we tell it. As she says of her own viscerally felt sense of the United States, "It still gives me chills . . . those ideas . . . are what holds us together as a nation."

In the third installment of the trilogy, "Aide de Camp," the central, now much older character's passion for her historical subject gives a lecture to an assembly of the "Daughters of Federalists" on Hamilton's "backstory" and how he first came to the attention of Washington as his Aide de Camp during the Revolutionary War.[41] The name of the imaginary organization she speaks to is at once a play on the Daughters of the American Revolution, at one time a very exclusive, conservative, and racist organization and also a gender turn-about, as the "daughters" engage and carry on the history of the "fathers." The story she tells in her lecture imagines the initial relationship between Washington and Hamilton, one a young, smart man, the other an older, demanding character. Their exchanges, as depicted by Kelso through an older woman, reinforce how patriarchy operates to privilege not only men, but *older* men. Hamilton's choice to eventually leave Washington's service because of this ill treatment illustrates a resistance to that arbitrary and punitive authority. That the relationship between the two men nevertheless continued for their lifetimes, suggests that Hamilton's demands for respect may have borne fruit—or, he just grew older, joining the privileged ranks.

In this final story, the central female character's presence not only frames the historical portion of the tale, but indeed, through the visual slides she uses to accompany her talk, creates a portal through which that history is literally and visually "projected" into the present. As she talks, images of Hamilton and Washington appear on the wall beside her, drawn in the same style as the rest of the story. More than being reported on, or being reenacted, the two time periods are here visually merging in the same frames, foreshadowing the final scene (see Figure 4.2).

After polite clapping and a reception, the woman leaves the event alone—but a figure waving to her from a window of a waiting limousine turns out to be the ghost of Hamilton appearing to share her journey. Her projection of the past into her present seems to have materialized. Now not only does the past appear in images within the present, the present-day character now literally interacts with the historical character. Their tête á tête in the car's back seat sensually ties together events of the story's "present" to the past,

Figure 4.2 Alexander Hamilton celebrates with the main character. Megan Kelso (w, a). *Squirrel Mother* (Seattle, WA: Fantagraphics Books, 2006), 121. © Megan Kelso. Used with Permission.

a connection reinforced when Hamilton makes a dual-purpose champagne toast to the retirement of his companion, the woman lecturer, and to the resignation of President Richard Nixon. He quips, "Here's to your retirement and here's to that poltroon finally resigning from the oval office. 'Tis a night for jubilation!"[42] The physical intimacy depicted here—note the ghost of Hamilton's hand on the woman's knee—echoes the passionate daydream of the young, report-writing girl in "Publius." Though alone in the end, this woman's happy demeanor as she converses with her imaginary friend underscores a satisfying lifetime of passionate engagement with the creative work of politics and history.

It's a warm ending, and as such it comes down firmly on the side of the benefits of having an intimate relationship with history—not only for an informed awareness of one's country's politics that are clearly and succinctly detailed throughout the three parts of the story but also for the personal satisfaction that it seems to offer. It is as if, for Kelso, history *is* literally a *relationship* between teller and tale, a relationship that, for U.S. History anyway, may involve "loving" and "loathing" but must be intimate if it is to be productive.

Getting intimate with time

Given her explicit and graphic illumination of connections between the personal and the public political/historical spheres, it is no coincidence that many of Kelso's stories, such as AHT, foreground women's perspectives.

The feminist (and very American feminist, at that) mantra "The personal is political" finds accessible, concrete visual form in Kelso's comics short stories and novel.[43] At times she explores the particular intersections of gender within a class context— in "Pickle Fork," we see the story through the eyes of a maid, a wealthy wife, and an intellectual museum curator. Her war protest piece "Fuck the Troops" exposes the many ways in which the enlisted, mostly young male, frontline troops are "fucked" both at home and abroad in all wars across history, by those in power, usually older men and the upper classes. And in her work on personal relationships, under pressure from challenging and gendered circumstances of abortion, mental illness, or the effects of institutionalized as well as individual violence (sexual abuse, murder, capital punishment, war), Kelso almost relentlessly ties together the public and the private, exposing those ties in ways that allow few places, if any, to hide from the hardest aspects of human life that haunt our stories of the past.

Thus, in some ways, Kelso's work with fiction and history echoes what many of her female cohorts are currently doing in autobiography and memoir. Chute, interested in women's use of personal non-fiction, or "life narrative" comics to approach history, indeed to "(re)imagin[e] history in different ways,"[44] writes that these authors' works are "unquestionably attuned to the political," and "provoke us to think about how women, as both looking and looked at subjects, are situated in particular times, spaces and histories."[45] Having previously discussed how comics are a form offering strategies for constructing potentially more ethical historical narratives, Chute writes of the five cartoonists in her study that, "even as they deliberately place stress on official histories and traditional modes of transmitting history, they are deeply interested in their own accuracy and historicity."[46]

Included in her introductory list of women comics' authors,[47] but not a part of Chute's study, Kelso departs from the autobiographical formulation of women's graphic narrative by choosing to write stories that, while they certainly "place stress on official histories and traditional modes of transmitting history," also show her as less interested in "accurate" "self-representational storylines" than in the play of public history as it intersects with the (imaginary) individual—and, in turn, the individual's own play with that history. Though careful about the accuracy of many historical details she uses in her stories—note the repeated attention to historical names and dates in AHT as well as the "bibliography" of sources that appears at its end—she nevertheless deliberately chooses to write these details into fictional stories where she can play with the context for these "known" facts and, further, invent other sets of imaginary "facts" to create parallel "history." Kelso mixes fact and fiction to explore the plastic potential "story" has for showing us how to see the play that exists, therefore, in "history" as well. The stories in AHT, while they depend on accurate knowledge of the past, are not about simply recreating that past. Indeed, her female characters, knowing the facts, seek to consider how it might have been different—and so practice an understanding not only of civic history, but of the possibilities of civic change.

After W. J. T. Mitchell's work in *Iconology*, Chute calls comics itself a "feminized" form "not only because of its 'low' and 'mass' status, but also because of its traffic in space," where the feminine has often been assigned to (the less privileged) category of materiality in the Cartesian mind/body split.[48] She argues that the form "lends itself to the autobiographical genre in which we see so many authors—and so many women authors in particular—materializing their lives and histories."[49] Kelso certainly makes use of the forms' potential to powerfully figure the female body within history, saying that "I think it is still a radical act simply for female artists to draw the female figure! To draw themselves and other women as they see themselves. Subjectively! This is still so new and comparatively rare."[50] But, rather than writing autobiography, she uses the materiality and intimacy the comics form offers to create an integrated view of the public and the private in historical fiction. Her choice to stick to fiction resists the implicit stereotype of autobiographical, inward focus for women writers without rejecting the power of a "personal" approach that the intimacy of the comics form offers. That is, while the personal does matter very much in Kelso's stories, her "personal" has an explicitly large and public field of "play."

Kelso's stories set up explicitly constructed "histories" that suggest that while the past might not be alterable, "perspectives" on the past—the stories we *make* of the past, our *histories*, personal and public—are infinitely malleable. And what she herself chooses to make of the past is one in which the personal and the political are integrated in a continual and dynamic narrative that invites the reader to take an active part. This seems to me to be a deeply democratic approach to creating historical narrative in a very American sense of *participatory* democracy. If, in the level of interaction it explicitly requires of the reader, comics is a highly "participatory" form of story, and the United States is a nation held together through story, then perhaps the comics form can offer more than just a reflection and reimagining of American history, but indeed a practicum in participatory democracy, in "being American."

At its core, the phrase "The personal is political" ignites friction and suggests connections between the divided (and heavily theorized) categories of the public and the private. Kelso's comics enact a graphic collapse of these spheres through an intimate telling of history that, while personal, resists the label of "personal narrative." Through the medium of comics, Kelso offers a complex, strongly feminist, and thoroughly democratic view of American political history and of the average citizen's potentially intimate relationship with her nation's past and the evolving present. At a time when women in comics are being lauded for their powerful autobiographical narratives, Kelso's stories, particularly those that directly address specific moments in U.S. history, always push outward, using the particularities of the comics form to creatively explore and articulate the place and power of the person in community, in politics, and in the (thankfully) imaginary and pliable space of nation.

Notes

1 Lynda Barry, *One Hundred Demons* (Seattle, WA: Sasquatch Books, 2005), 7.
2 The first and second installments of Kelso's Hamilton trilogy, "Publius" and "The Duel," appeared in *The Comics Journal Winter Specials of* 2001 and 2004, respectively. The final section, "Aide de Camp" was published in 2006 together with the previously published pieces in Kelso's second collection of graphic short stories, *Squirrel Mother* (Seattle, WA: Fantagraphics, 2006), 105–121. The latter is the edition of all three stories used for this article.
3 Megan Kelso (Presentation at Pacific Lutheran University, October 19, 2010).
4 Megan Kelso (w, a). *GirlHero* #1–6 (1991–1996), self-published.
5 Megan Kelso (w, a). *Queen of the Black Black* (Cambridge, MA: Hightower Books, 1998).
6 S. C., review of *Squirrel Mother, People* 66, no. 9 (August 28, 2006): 48; Andrew D. Arnold, "5 Gripping Graphic Novels for Grownups," *Time* 168, no. 15 (October 9, 2006): 70.
7 Megan Kelso (w, a). "Watergate Sue," *New York Times Magazine* 25–31 (April 1–September 9, 2007), 25 (same page all issues).
8 Megan Kelso (w, a). *Artichoke Tales* (Seattle, WA: Fantagraphics, 2010).
9 Kelso, *Squirrel Mother*, 65–74.
10 Megan Kelso, Email interview with the author, June 16, 2011.
11 Kelso, Email Interview.
12 Kelso, Email Interview; Alexander Hamilton et al., *The Federalist Papers*, Library of Congress, http://thomas.loc.gov/home/histdox/fedpapers.html (accessed November 21, 2011).
13 Hillary Chute, *Graphic Women: Life Narrative and Contemporary Comics* (New York: Columbia UP, 2010), 4.
14 Ibid., 9.
15 Scott McCloud, *Understanding Comics* (New York: Harper, 1994), 69.
16 Alison Mandaville, "A Visitation of Narratives: Dialogue and Comics in Randall Kenan's *A Visitation of Spirits*," in Brannon Costello and Qiana Whitted, eds, Forthcoming in *Comics and the American South* (Jackson, MS: UP of Mississippi, December 2011).
17 Chute, *Graphic Women*, 6.
18 Teresa Tensuan, "Comics Visions and Revisions in the Work of Lynda Barry and Marjane Satrapi," *Modern Fiction Studies* 52, no. 4 (2006): 947–964.
19 Ibid., 950.
20 Kelso, Email interview.

21 Mark Nevins (moderator), Megan Kelso, James Kochalka, Gilbert James, Scott Gilbert, Dylan Horrocks, and Tom Hart, "New Voices in Comics 1998: A Roundtable," transcribed by Rich Pettus, *International Journal of Comic Arts* 1, no. 2 (1999): 233.
22 Ibid., 229.
23 Ibid., 236.
24 Ibid.
25 Bendict Anderson, *Imagined Communities* (New York: Versa, 1991).
26 Kelso, Email interview.
27 Chute, *Graphic Women*, 10.
28 Ibid., 11–12.
29 Kelso, Email interview.
30 Sam Adams, "Joe Sacco: Interview," *The American Voices Club*, June 10, 2011, http://www.avclub.com/articles/joe-sacco,57360/1/ (accessed November 21, 2011).
31 Initially, the central twentieth-century character in each story seems to be the same individual who carries a fascination with Hamilton throughout her life. Kelso herself admits that she thinks of the central character as the same person (Email interview with the author). Closer examination reveals that the fashions of the characters make this presumption a bit shaky, for the timelines don't quite match up. As Kelso explained, because she wrote the third installment much later, and then "timed" its contemporary setting to match the date of the resignation of President Nixon—an event her version of Hamilton celebrates— they can't "logically" be the same character. However, this is, after all, fiction, and, for the purposes of analysis in this piece, I read the character as the same, despite the "logical" problems. In the way the stories depict a young girl, a young woman, and then a middle-aged woman, the trilogy implies the progression of political engagement throughout a lifetime.
32 Kelso, *Squirrel Mother*. See images of paper, pen and/or the act of writing on pages 105, 106, 108, 109, 110, 111, 113, 114, 116, 117, 118, 119, 120.
33 Ibid., 108.
34 Ibid., 105–108.
35 Kelso, Email interview.
36 Kelso, *Squirrel Mother*, 109–115.
37 Ibid., 109.
38 Ibid.
39 Ibid., 110.
40 Ibid., 115.
41 Ibid., 116–121.
42 Ibid., 121.
43 Carol Hanisch, "The Personal is Political." Personal Website, http://www.carolhanisch.org/CHwritings/PIP.html (Originally published in *Notes from the Second Year*, Shulie Firestone and Anne Koedt, eds, New York: Self-published, 1970). This saying "The Personal is Political" seems to first appear in the title of Carol Hanisch's article written in 1969 and published in 1970 as part of the self-published anthology *Notes from the Second Year* edited by Shulie Firestone and Anne Koedt (New York). According to Hanisch, the title was

chosen by the editors; the sentence does not appear in the body of her article—though women's negotiation of the public and the personal is the piece's subject matter.

44 Chute, *Graphic Women*, 27.
45 Ibid., 3.
46 Ibid.
47 Ibid., 1.
48 Ibid., 10.
49 Ibid.
50 Kelso, Email interview.

PART TWO

Comic Books as Cultural Artifacts

CHAPTER FIVE

American Golem

Reading America through Super-New Dealers and the "Melting Pot"

Martin Lund

Superman first appeared in *Action Comics* #1, cover dated June 1938. In a mere 13 pages, his creators, Jerry Siegel and Joe Shuster, are credited with inaugurating, arguably in a frantic and somewhat haphazard way, what has become known as the "Golden Age" of comics.

Much of what is "known" about Superman today does not stem from that original version of the character. Superman was introduced as an alien from a destroyed planet whose much more evolved physique gave him his powers. This was a Superman who could not fly, who inhabited a world without the deadly threat of Kryptonite, where petty crime and corruption—not cosmic beings or supervillains—were the big threats.

The world's first encounter with Superman occurred in a story already halfway to its conclusion, with the hero carrying a murderess to the governor's mansion. His mission is to free a woman about to be executed for a crime she did not commit. Having ensured that justice in the legal sense of the word has been served, the newcomer proceeds to thwart an incident of domestic violence after being tipped off to a wife-beating in progress through the offices of the newspaper where he works in disguise.

Having convinced his fellow reporter Lois Lane to go out with him, Superman—in the guise of his alter ego, journalist Clark Kent—encounters Butch Matson, a brute with a short fuse and low impulse control. Matson cuts in on their dance, pushes Clark aside, and tells the unwilling Lois that she will dance with him, "and like it!" Having been rebuked and slapped in the face by his recalcitrant dance partner, Matson promptly kidnaps her, complaining that he had let the "yellow" Clark off too easy. Again, justice moves swiftly as Superman, shaking the kidnappers out of their get-away car and smashing it to bits on a rock, overtakes Butch and leaves him suspended from a telephone pole, humiliated and terrified.

In the story's final episode, Superman turns his attention to the capital, where he observes Alex Greer, "the slickest lobbyist in Washington," pushing the passing of a bill. The senator he is talking to assures Greer that it "will be passed before its full implications are realized. Before any remedial steps can be taken, our country will be embroiled with Europe." The story ends in a cliffhanger with Superman, running along telephone wires with a mortified Greer in his arms, trying to figure out who the lobbyist's backers are.[1]

Looking back at it, the creation of Superman was not necessarily revolutionary. In fact, the argument has often been made that he contained a mix of elements and tropes lifted from Biblical stories and various mythological characters. Further, the popular culture of the time is widely recognized as having played an important role in Superman's conception, from pulps and science fiction, to the daily comic strips and Hollywood icons like Douglas Fairbanks; even the self-styled pinnacle of human physical potential, Charles Atlas, can be found in the patchwork that made up the original character.

More importantly, from a broader cultural history perspective, this paper argues that the Superman which debuted in *Action* #1 is not rooted, as is often assumed, in the religio-cultural heritage of his creators. Rather, I will argue—not in spite of the fact that Siegel and Shuster were "two Jewish kids from Cleveland," but in large part because they were—that in contradiction to the contemporary lived reality of many Jews in America, Superman expressed the beliefs, values, and norms offered up by the Roosevelt White House and the long-held theory of assimilation that painted the country as a great cultural "Melting Pot."[2]

On Golems and Supermen

Among the sources often cited as important inspirations contributing to Superman's genesis is the myth of the Golem of Prague, as related by Yudl Rosenberg in the 1909 book *Niflo'es Maharal im ha-Golem*, or *The Wondrous Deeds of the Maharal of Prague with the Golem*.[3]

Rosenberg's story, in short, reads as follows: Rabbi Judah Loew, a learned man and mystic, created a humanoid servant known as a Golem from clay taken from the bottom of the Moldau River. The creature, named Yossele, was tasked to protect Prague's Jewry from a resurgence of anti-Semitism and Blood Libels—an old staple of anti-Semitism wherein Jews are accused of murdering Christian children to use their blood in rituals, or in the baking of matzo bread. Yossele's primary purpose was to patrol the streets at night, on the look-out for people carrying bundles large enough to conceal children murdered by accusers to provide "proof" of such allegations.

The Golem succeeds in his task, legislation against Blood Libels is enacted, and a year passes without hint of new accusations. With the crisis over, Yossele is laid to rest in Prague's Altneuschule, where he is said to still rest in case his protection should again be needed.

Over the course of the past century, the Golem story has proliferated in popular culture, through movies, science-fiction, comic books, and television.[4] It is not surprising, then, that a "Golem theory of Superman" should appear as attention turned to Siegel and Shuster's Jewish backgrounds. Reading the *Niflo'es Maharal*, one sees the lure of drawing conclusions based on structural similarities: both characters are, in essence, created superhuman beings whose overriding purpose is to protect the weak and oppressed. But most such readings of the early Superman seem too literal and are difficult to support historically.

In 1998, a series of 60-year anniversary issues of *Superman: The Man of Steel* had the character inexplicably transported back in time to relive the plot of his first appearance and then battle Nazis in occupied Poland and the Warsaw ghetto.[5] Meanwhile, two young boys dream up an angelic protector in their time of need. Upon hearing their descriptions, and seeing a drawing of the character (who bears an uncanny resemblance to the as-yet unencountered Superman), their grandfather tells them that what they have created sounds more like a Golem than an angel. When Superman arrives to protect the ghetto inhabitants and fight back against the Nazis, the connection the authors wanted to make becomes apparent: Superman is a Golem, created by two young Jews as protection against the Nazis.

There are many other examples of this interpretation. Discussing Superman, Simcha Weinstein invokes images of Kristallnacht (the Night of Broken Glass), November 9–10, 1938, when German Jews were attacked, their stores and synagogues destroyed. "The planet needed a hero—fast," he writes. While he leaves the explicit Golem connection to Captain America, Weinstein's descriptions of the 1998 *Man of Steel* issue and Michael Chabon's *The Amazing Adventures of Kavalier and Clay* leave little doubt that he supports the Superman as Golem argument.[6] Comics creator Frank Miller claimed in a 2006 interview that Superman, who like "[a]ll of the major superheroes through the 1940s [was] created by the Jews" during a "time of persecution," is a Golem.[7] Also worth noting is that Curt Leviant, translator of the *Niflo'es Maharal*, points out that Rosenberg "fused the anti-Semitism that pervaded Europe during his own time" and makes the connection to Siegel and Shuster, writing that this was "not unlike Superman, the comic strip hero created in the late 1930s by two American Jews to protect the innocent and battle evil."[8]

The Golem claims cited above are all based on the assumption that Superman's creation is rooted in the time immediately prior to America's entry into the Second World War, and that they are connected to Nazism's increasing power and brutality in Germany.

The rise of Nazism

The rise of Nazism in Germany did not immediately "elicit exceptional responses" from world leaders because its fascism and persecution of Jews were not uniformly viewed as "exceptional circumstances."[9] Stories about Nazi anti-Semitism were initially underreported in the American press—including in Jewish-owned newspapers like *The New York Times*—and some reports from Europe were viewed as exaggerated and accounts of Nazi atrocities were dismissed as "beyond belief."[10] Hitler was simply not yet taken seriously by some. Others saw Nazism as an anomaly in enlightened Germany, as a phase that would soon pass.[11] To this effect, Gerard Jones quotes movie mogul Irving Thalberg's report from a 1934 trip to Germany: "A lot of Jews will lose their lives . . . [but] Hitler and Hitlerism will pass, and the Jews will still be there." He continues, adding that "[t]here was even something faintly ridiculous about crazy Adolf. Jewish teenagers hooted at him in the newsreels. . . . The Nazis would probably come crashing gloriously down before they did any real harm."[12]

The responses of Jewish leaders in the United States (including those from the political, religious, and lay communities) to the rise of Nazism in Germany were varied and equivocal, and rarely explicit.[13] Fearing accusations of un-patriotic or un-American behavior, many chose not to raise the struggle for European Jewry as a Jewish issue. Instead, they sought to reformulate it in universal terms or, failing that, to get non-Jews to speak out. Isolationist sentiment was still strong in America and few Jews wanted to feed stereotypes of "the international Jew" mobilizing, or of Jews as warmongers, by blatantly contradicting what was seen as consensus opinion.

The rise of Nazism in Germany helped strengthen American anti-Semitism and highlighted the need to adapt in order to fit in, in a country increasingly showing itself less welcoming than it had seemed. If indeed a Golem correspondence with Superman was intended by Siegel and Shuster, it is unlikely that it was used as a celebration of a European past or to express a concern about anti-Semitism, whether in Europe or in America. Such concerns would have had to be sublimated and brought in line with contemporary American discourse, stymied by the constraints of identity politics. In 1938, the year Superman first appeared in print, this would begin to change, bringing American public opinion and official policy to a more critical stance against Hitler. Even then, National Periodical Publications,

Superman's publishers, would not yet "allow the character to take an implicit stand on the subjects of war and fascism."[14]

Gulie Ne'eman Arad writes that "[w]hile no historian can disown Auschwitz when writing about any facet of this period, to situate the analysis within a closed referential framework of its catastrophic ending, when the real became unreal by the reality of the unthinkable, is likely to engender a *supra*-historical interpretation."[15] Given the date of Superman's first appearance, and what was to come, it is understandable that he is read as a protector figure. However, there is little in *Action* #1 itself to support such explicitly anti-Nazi interpretations, which, while seemingly self-evident, are problematic.

There are many versions of the story of Superman's creation that would date the event as far back as 1931, but it is likely that the character as it appeared in *Action* #1 was created sometime during 1934.[16] There might, then, be a more appropriate key to interpreting Superman in the immediate context of his creation: to wit, the first term of President Franklin Delano Roosevelt.

Franklin Delano Roosevelt's first term and the creation of Superman

In the aftermath of the stock market crash in the fall of 1929, events would conspire to make life in America very hard indeed. Pledging himself to a "New Deal for the American people," Roosevelt seemed to be just what the country needed. Undoubtedly, he struck an impressive figure when he was targeted for assassination in February 1933. Having escaped the assassin's bullet, he stayed with Chicago's Mayor Anton Cermac, who had been hit, until he was assured that the less fortunate man would survive the night.[17] Especially when viewed in juxtaposition to incumbent president Herbert Hoover, who was perceived as having worked mainly to favor banks and business interests, who had refused to extend direct federal aid to the poor and destitute, who even went so far as to send military forces into the streets of Washington, D.C., to rout protesting World War I veterans hoping to expedite payments of promised bonuses for services rendered, which were due in 1945—perceived, in essence, as asking only for what was theirs by right to help them weather the storm—FDR was surely larger than life.

The New Deal was not a program carefully laid out from the beginning, but rather a hodgepodge of thought-through policies, compromises, shots in the dark, and other measures of varying consistency and success, aimed at warding off or counteracting the effects of the Great Depression. We know now that it did not completely succeed; the U.S. economy would limp on through recovery and recession until its entry in World War II jump-started American industry and revived the country.

During FDR's first term, however, and especially its now mythical first one hundred days, the New Deal seemed to be a juggernaut moving toward economic recovery, "a whirlwind of changes in the old order."[18] More importantly, he claimed to be championing the cause of the "forgotten man." Evidenced by the results of the election, FDR had won the support of the American people, and especially the working class and much of the country's ethnic minorities.

Taking off from a running start, Roosevelt's inaugural address on March 4, 1932, contained a searing indictment of those perceived to be the cause of the current situation:

> [Our] distress comes from no failure of substance. We are stricken by no plague of locusts. . . . Nature still offers her bounty and human efforts have multiplied it. Plenty is at our doorstep, but a generous use of it languishes in the very sight of the supply. Primarily this is because the rulers of the exchange of mankind's goods have failed, through their own incompetence, have admitted their failure, and abdicated. Practices of the unscrupulous money changers stand indicted in the court of public opinion, rejected by the hearts and minds of men.[19]

Business interests and bankers, people portrayed as greedy speculators and self-serving employers, took several hard hits in his presidential addresses, as well as from dissatisfied employees who felt encouraged by FDR's legislative agenda and his rhetoric. He promised and, to a lesser extent, delivered jobs to the unemployed, he listened to others beyond those of the moneyed elites, and he championed "social justice," extending his hand not only to the old-guard whites of the country, but to all—or at least most—of its citizens.[20] Through the making and implementation of policy, speeches, and his cozy "fireside chats," FDR bred an image of a president of the people, including the People of the Book. For many, if not most, American Jews, Roosevelt was regarded as a friend to whom the majority gladly gave their vote in the elections that gave him an unprecedented four consecutive terms in the Oval Office.[21]

American Jewry was, for a long time, optimistic about the possibilities afforded to them in the country. Such feelings were bolstered by FDR's appointment of several Jews to prominent positions in local and federal government. While anti-Semitism was not unheard of in the United States, it was rarely rampant, as had so often been the case in Europe, and it never exploded into pogroms.[22] A belief in the United States as a truly New World was consequently strong. Internal restraints, including the tendency of earlier waves of Jewish immigrants to remain isolated from newcomers (often because of their different national origins), and external ones, like overt anti-Semitism and discrimination, were perceived to have been replaced by a new social and geographical openness, even though these beliefs were not always entirely justified.[23] But such emancipation and integration was not without its cost.

The definition of an American in the 1700s, as it was formulated by Hector St. John de Crevecoeur, is telling: "*He* is an American, who leaving behind him all his ancient prejudices and manners, receives new ones from the new mode of life he has embraced, the new government he obeys, and the new rank he holds." Having done so, "[h]e becomes an American by being received in the broad lap of our great Alma Mater. Here individuals of all nations are melted into a new race of men . . ."[24] The same perception of what it took, and what it meant, to become American would continue to be promoted into the twentieth century. Just as immigrants were expected to "melt" into America in Crevecoeur's time, so too were they accepted into the American "Melting Pot" only on the condition that they accepted the mores and ideals of white America in the decades and centuries that followed.[25] Foreign cultures and ideas were to be checked at Ellis Island, as it were, and people coming from all over the world were to become a homogeneous whole, a country of Americans in race, creed, and culture, through assimilation and acculturation. When Jerry Siegel dreamed up Superman in the early 1930s, these conditions on becoming American were still in effect.

Eric A. Goldstein argues that the "Melting Pot" proposition was not always an easy one, and that its acceptance was never complete among American Jews.[26] However, whether or not they bought into the ideal wholeheartedly, few were comfortable in displaying too obviously parochial sentiments. We cannot know how strongly Siegel and Shuster felt about the events occurring in Germany,[27] nor to what extent they believed in the "Melting Pot" rhetoric. It can, however, be seen that they were ready to provide support for its validity—consciously or not—through the creation of Superman and the world he inhabited.

Pop culture between rhetoric and reality

Jonathan Sarna has remarked that "Jews sometimes like to claim that they created contemporary culture." He goes on, citing many such claims, before dismissing them:

[F]or years the array of arts in which Jews participated actually bore little relationship to Judaism, and were, in many cases, an effective means of escaping it. Fearing that if their work were "too Jewish" it would remain provincial, the most creative Jews in America hid or sublimated their faith. They changed their names and universalized the products of their creative genius in a bid to attract a wide audience.[28]

In a similar vein, Goldstein writes that "[f]ew immigrant groups embraced popular music, film, sports, and other forms of mass entertainment as enthusiastically as the Jews, who saw them as major vehicles for claiming their status as white Americans."[29] The production and consumption of pop culture by American Jews, then, seems largely geared toward the attainment of an American identity and the whiteness it conferred.

Whether or not they consciously embraced that aspect, Siegel and Shuster were voracious consumers of American pop culture. They were among the first people to call themselves "fans," and Siegel even has the honor of being credited as the creator of the first "fanzine."[30] He spent his teens in his room, either reading pulp stories or trying to write his own, or at the movies, consuming the Hollywood version of America (which, like the stories he would write, did not always reflect present realities). Shuster, too, embraced pop culture. The fad of physical culture turned him into an avid body-builder.[31] His artwork was inspired by the very white *Tarzan* comic strip, telling a "romantic daydream on the idea that the high-born English baby dropped in the jungle would naturally come to master not only the beasts but black men also." This vision was created by Edgar Rice Burroughs, a man who believed in the "innate virtue of the 'Anglo-Saxon'" race.[32]

In contrast to pop culture more immediately grounded in the harshness of the times, songs like "Yip" Harburg's "Brother, Can You Spare a Dime?" or "Skip" James' "Hard Time Killing Floor Blues," for example, Siegel and Shuster did not reproduce the view from out their window when they created Superman. In that respect, their story was more like Hollywood in its escapist presentation, as, according to film historian Richard Jewell, "very few feature films depicted the 'hard times' in realistic or penetrating fashion."[33] The Depression shaped Hollywood's output, but the moviemakers did not tackle it head-on. Siegel and Shuster, less concerned with accuracy and more concerned with being accepted and lauded in their own time,[34] similarly produced a piece of escapist science fiction that reverberated with the times, something that tapped into the anxieties of a wider population without being explicitly about what was going in America. Their creation reflected not only the uncertain status of Jews in America but also that of other groups of immigrants. It also demonstrated the uncertain status of the destitute and hungry masses of urban working-class unemployed and stricken rural farmers hoping for improvement, those who had recently suffered through the winter of 1932–1933, the worst in memory, and heard promises that all would soon be well.

The rhetoric of the New Deal and the "Melting Pot", and the American beliefs, values, and norms they promoted, were not consistent with the realities of contemporary American life, though. Despite what seems like wide support for the "Melting Pot" ideal—unsurprisingly strongest among old-guard whites into whose culture others were to assimilate—Americans were not one people. Blacks were still, at best, second class citizens in many places, and many of the attempts by the Roosevelt administration to improve their lot were killed in the cradle or soon talked out of existence. Jews in America were, at the time of Superman's creation, straddling a line dividing the country as American anti-Semitism reached unprecedented levels. While the worst was yet to come—with demagogues like Father Charles Coughlin, Fritz Kuhn, and too many others—this increase had been evident since the 20s, and was surely felt already by the early 30s. For many, the growing anti-Semitism strengthened the resolve to be perceived as white, and as such inspired them to act and express themselves in line with what was perceived as "American."[35]

While the effects of the Depression were often underreported in favor of gossip and sports news, a fair share of both the extravagances of organized crime and the steadily increasing petty crime resulting from poverty and corruption made headlines.[36] Jerry Siegel knew better than most what simple want could do to a man; the Depression settled into his home when, a few months after the stock market crash, his father was killed in a robbery.[37] News on policy and politics often came directly from FDR, who regularly informed people of what was going on in his popular and personal "fireside chats," and from a largely loyal and supportive press corps, which had strategically been won over by the president's charm and—admittedly selective—openness.[38] As a "man of the people" who championed the cause of the "forgotten man," many saw him as deserving of the support he asked for, even when it went against their immediate interests, and it is not unlikely that his words carried great weight in assuring Americans that things were not as bad as they seemed.

Superman's America—A reading of *Action Comics* #1

In fact, Depression realities are strikingly absent in *Action* #1. Superman's Cleveland[39] is a clean city, without breadlines, "Hoovervilles," or any other telling signs of widespread home- or joblessness. Rather, it is a simple hero-narrative that focuses on the same ills that were the topics of the president's speeches and chats.

In his inaugural address, FDR had said that "the only thing we have to fear is fear itself. . . . In every dark hour of our national life a leadership of frankness and vigor has met with that understanding and support of the people themselves which is essential to victory. I am convinced that you will again give that support to leadership in these critical days."[40] Underscoring this point in the first of his "chats" a few days later, he asked once more for Americans' confidence and help: "Let us unite in banishing fear. We have provided the machinery to restore our financial system; it is up to you to support and make it work. It is your problem no less than mine. Together we cannot fail."[41] The invitation had been extended and, in *Action* #1, Siegel and Shuster seem determined to do their part.

Situating *Action* #1 in its historical moment, what emerges is very much a typical cultural product of its time. Superman's portrayal differed little from that of contemporary fictional heroes such as Dick Tracy, Doc Savage, or the Lone Ranger. These characters were so similar in the recurrence of basic narrative elements that John Shelton Lawrence and Robert Jewett speak of their period of greatest influence as the "axial decade" in the development of a collection of tropes and conventions they label with the somewhat grandiose moniker "the American Monomyth"—a myth, in simplified terms, about a harmonious community threatened by evil, which is saved by a selfless hero who then recedes into obscurity.[42] What appeared in the summer of 1938 was in many respects so typical as to be expected— not only in terms of adherence to contemporary pop culture convention, but in historical precedent.

Susan Faludi argues that this type of "monomythic" narratives have recurred in the United States "at pivotal moments in our cultural life extending back to the Puritans," reverting to simple masculine hero-narratives that emphasize a discursive potency and mask a substantial impotence. As Faludi explains, Americans restore "our faith in our own invincibility through fables of female peril and the rescue of 'just one young girl.'"[43] In such stories, presented in the form of both fiction and history, albeit selectively read and amended, strong men save weak women who cannot do so themselves.

Leaving aside the discussion on whether or not it truly constitutes a "monomyth," the *Action* #1 story certainly seems an example of this type of storytelling in service of the New Deal. The way the kidnapping of Lois plays out—itself appearing as a throwback to the "captivity narratives" of frontier times[44]—makes the discourse of ambiguous masculinity and the relegation of women into victimhood explicit. Borrowing from Yvonne Tasker, we can speak of a weak, "verbal man," and a strong, "physical man," present in the narrative.[45] The feebly protesting Clark, reluctant to act, gets pushed aside and is emasculated by Lois, who calls him "a spineless, unbearable COWARD!" Superman, on the other hand, shakes the kidnappers' car like a man possessed and hunts them down as they flee. The difference between the two types of man is clear. It is the latter type of man that can save Lois, the death-row inmate, and the battered wife. It is that type of man that can do what is needed to "banish fear." It is that type of man that many, including Siegel and Shuster, wished they could be—but were not.

In the episodes about the woman who narrowly escapes the death penalty and the woman violently subjugated by her husband, it becomes obvious that as far as Siegel and Shuster were concerned, care and a helping
hand should be extended to all who were subjected to unjust treatment. The
first half of the Superman story focuses on the issues of "social justice" and
the "forgotten man," or woman in this case, that FDR promoted through
his rhetoric. As such, New-Dealers should not only work toward stabiliz-
ing the country's economy, but they should also extend their concern for
the well-being of the common man into the domain of the household, or at
least this is how Siegel and Shuster perceived the mission of the New Deal.

Further eliciting tried and true narrative models, Lois' kidnappers
embody much of what the New Deal ideology opposed, and they showed
it by directing their wickedness toward that "just one lone girl." They take
what they want, when they want, and care little for the consequences of their
actions. They are not, in any sense of the word, sympathetic. Similarly, the
episode with the Senator contains signs of support for FDR. Like Matson
and his cronies, the politician puts his own interests ahead of those of his
country. The Smoot-Hawley Tariff Act of 1930, which introduced tariffs
on imports at levels that were effectively prohibitive, and FDR's economic
nationalism, expressed at the World Economic Conference of 1933 in the
insistence that his country would pursue its own path to economic recovery
before considering any international agreements, marked a continuation of
the United States' long-held policy of isolationism.[46] Superman, it seems,
was not willing to let any man stand in the way of this policy, and so he
does his utmost to find out who is "behind corrupting Senator Barrows."[47]
In his championing of virtues espoused in New Deal policies and social
justice, Superman appears almost as a "cartoonified" FDR in a cape, a hero
that could translate comforting words into deeds.

Superman's alien origin, hastily added just prior to publication, provided
a "scientific explanation" for his powers. It also, inadvertently, underscores
the lack of diversity in *Action* #1: he comes from outside but sheds all
traces of outsiderhood, except those that can be used to serve his country. The American walking the clean streets of Superman's Cleveland is
similarly idealized, showing that the restrictions of the simple hero-narrative did not only apply to women. On occasion, FDR championed a more
inclusive nationalism which granted ethnicity a little wiggle room, but not
to the extent that even those Jews closest to him, "the president's Jews,"
in Arad's words, felt comfortable raising particularly Jewish concerns.[48]
While vaguely ethnic in appearance, rather than conforming so strictly as
to become the embodiment of whiteness, the Superman depicted in *Action*
#1 still has the features of Hollywood stars: broad shoulders, chiseled jaw,
and near-perfect posture, even when playing the bumbling Clark Kent.
Likewise, Lois Lane is a pin-up: slim, beautiful, and toothsome, while
remaining shy of being overtly sexual. She is not blonde, but her skin is

fair. Like the men, she is not on the whitest end of the scale, but remains well within the acceptable bounds of contemporary discourse. Looking to the other side of the color divide, however, there is a conspicuous absence of non-whites in the story.[49]

While the New Deal's protection in *Action* #1 is extended to a whole host of people, from the masses bound to be adversely affected if the United States were to become involved in European affairs to the downtrodden wife of a violent man, it is not expected to reach into the lives and homes of those who insisted on remaining outside mainstream America, or to stretch across the color line. While marginalized, neither women nor non-whites are vilified, however. That lot falls to others.

The decade leading up to the Great Depression was in many ways a time of a realized American Dream. When it all came crashing down, someone had to be blamed. So too, Superman, as hero, needed villains. With their story, Siegel and Shuster helped propagate and popularize (perhaps somewhat naively) a hegemonic image of a homogeneous America worth fighting for through a representation of New Deal rhetoric and the idea of America as cultural "Melting Pot" as social reality. Being Jewish and poor, they were outsiders in regards both to ethnicity and class. In that capacity, however, they did not sit idly by on the sidelines hoping for inclusion, but rather created a country where they already fit in perfectly. Their idealized comic book America simplistically pitted "real" Americans against those who did not belong, made un-American by not serving the "greater good."

The line was drawn through what Peter Herriot calls the meta-contrast principle, by which the differences between members of the in-group are minimized while the differences between the in-group and the out-group are maximized. The "Us" that was demarcated in *Action* #1 consisted of white, law-abiding, and hard-working Americans. Superman accentuated those who fit into this category by granting them his protection, and through embodying the virtues of the American as in-group prototypes, a set of characteristics believed to describe group members.[50] He respected the system, followed the rules, and contributed to the greatness of the country; he was part of the American community, as those who acted like him would be. "They," the non-Americans, worked only for their own good and profit, did not care for their neighbor, and had no respect for the rule of law; in short, they did not subscribe to the American values embodied in Superman's fight for truth, justice, and, as would later be made explicit, "the American Way."

In my reading of *Action* #1, Superman was introduced as a figure to look up to, to believe in, and to take comfort in. Trusting in him was trusting in the ideals that would allow America to weather the storms threatening to destroy it—both the one that was raging at full strength when he was created and, through constant adaptation to contemporary mores and situations, those it would face throughout his long publication history. As such,

Action #1's Superman was a figure that can be called, acknowledging that such a characterization is a description of a cultural function and not of a historical inspiration, an American Golem, not one made of European river-bed clay to protect the Jews, but from a far more familiar material—the proverbial salt of the earth—to protect law-abiding, hard-working, white Americans.

Notes

1   Jerry Siegel (w) and Joe Shuster (a). *Superman Chronicles: Volume One* (New York: DC Comics, 2006), 4–16.

2   Similar arguments have been made in, for instance, Bradford Wright, *Comic Book Nation: The Transformation of Youth Culture in America* (Baltimore: Johns Hopkins University Press, 2001); Matthew J. Smith, "The Tyranny of the Melting Pot Metaphor: Wonder Woman as the Americanized Immigrant," in Matthew P. McAllister, Edward H. Sewell, Jr., and Ian Gordon, eds, *Comics & Ideology* (New York: P. Lang, 2001), 129–150.

3   Yudl Rosenberg, *The Golem and the Wondrous Deeds of the Maharal of Prague*, trans. Curt Leviant (New Haven: Yale University Press, 2007). Ideas of Golems as artificial life date as far back as 16 centuries ago. The Rosenberg version, however, was the first to have the Golem be an autonomous and benevolent protector against persecution and Blood Libels that can be said to correspond to a superheroic configuration. See Curt Leviant, "Introduction," in Yudl Rosenberg, ed., *The Golem and the Wondrous Deeds of the Maharal of Prague* (New Haven: Yale University Press, 2007), xxviii–xxix.

4   Golems have appeared in such popular TV shows as *The Simpsons* and *The X-Files*. Both DC and Marvel, the "big two" superhero comics publishers, have both had characters explicitly equated with the Golem of the Rosenberg version.

5   Louise Simonson (w), Jon Bognanove (w, p), and Dennis Janke (i). [untitled]. *Superman: The Man of Steel* #80–82 (June 1988–August 1988), DC Comics.

6   See Simcha Weinstein, *Up, Up, and Oy Vey!: How Jewish History, Culture, and Values Shaped the Comic Book Superhero* (Baltimore: Leviathan Press, 2006), 21, 30–32, 50–51. Chabon masterfully weaves the two figures together in his highly influential novel *The Amazing Adventures of Kavalier and Clay*. The book, although a work of fiction, seems to have been highly influential in inspiring Golem interpretations.

7   Peter Sanderson, "Comics in Context #125: Miller, Front and Center," *IGN. com*, March 20, 2006, http://au.comics.ign.com/articles/696/696965p1.html (accessed November 21, 2011).

8   Leviant, *The Golem*, xxv.

9   Gulie Ne'eman Arad, *America, its Jews, and the Rise of Nazism* (Bloomington: Indiana University Press, 2000), 2.

10   Jonathan Sarna, *American Judaism: A New History* (New Haven: Yale University Press, 2004), 258–259.

11   Cf., for instance, Arad, *America, its Jews and the Rise of Nazism*, 87, 95, 113.
12   Gerard Jones, *Men of Tomorrow: The True Story of the Birth of the Superhero* (London: Arrow Books, 2004), 128.
13   For a detailed account which I cannot hope to do justice here, see Arad, *America, its Jews and the Rise of Nazism*.
14   Jones, *Men of Tomorrow*, 165.
15   Arad, *America, its Jews and the Rise of Nazism*, 2.
16   Jones, *Men of Tomorrow*, 109–115, 122–123; Les Daniels, *Superman—the Complete History* (San Francisco: Chronicle Books, 2004), 18.
17   Ronald Edsforth, *The New Deal: America's Response to the Great Depression* (Malden, MA: Blackwell Publishers, 2000), 124–125.
18   Edsforth, *The New Deal*, 142.
19   Reprinted in Richard A. Harris and Daniel J. Tichenor, eds, *A History of the U.S. Political System: Ideas, Interests, and Institutions*, vol. 3 (Santa Barbara: ABC-CLIO, 2010), 203–205.
20   Cf. Eric L. Goldstein, *The Price of Whiteness* (Princeton: Princeton University Press, 2006), 189; Edsforth, *The New Deal*, 285–287.
21   Cf. Arthur Hertzberg, *The Jews in America: Four Centuries of an Uneasy Encounter* (New York: Simon & Schuster, 1989), 282–300.
22   That is not to say that there was no violent anti-Semitism. For example, Leo Frank, a Georgia Jew, was accused of rape and murder and subsequently lynched in 1915.
23   Cf. Arad, *America, its Jews and the Rise of Nazism*, 15–16.
24   J. Hector St. John de Crevecoeur, *Letters from an American Farmer* (Carlisle: Applewood Books, 2007 [1782]), 54–55.
25   The term "whiteness" refers not only to skin color, but also to ethnic, cultural, and religious factors.
26   Goldstein, *The Price of Whiteness*.
27   In a press release written shortly after news about the Superman movie appeared in 1975, Siegel wrote that he was led to create Superman in the early 30s by FDR's "fireside chats," "being unemployed and worried during the depression [*sic*] and knowing hopelessness and fear." He also writes about "seeing and reading of the oppression and slaughter of helpless, oppressed jews [*sic*] in Nazi Germany." Reading about and seeing "gallant, crusading heroes" in pulps and movies, he claims to have "had the great urge to help . . . help the despairing masses, somehow." It is difficult, however, to ascertain from this how much the rise of Nazism informed his creation of Superman and how much his statement is informed by later developments. See Jerry Siegel, "Re: THE VICTIMIZATION SUPERMAN'S ORIGINATORS, JERRY SIEGEL AND JOE SHUSTER (Facsimile)" (*The Comics Journal*, 1975), 9, http://archives.tcj.com/275/siegel1975.pdf (accessed November 21, 2011).
28   Sarna, *American Judaism*, 330–331.
29   Goldstein, *The Price of Whiteness*, 153.
30   Cf. Jones, *Men of Tomorrow*, 37–38.
31   Many of the early Superman stories included tips on how to "Acquire Super-Strength!" See Siegel and Shuster, *Superman Chronicles*, 58, 82, 110.
32   Jones, *Men of Tomorrow*, 70–71.

33 Richard Jewell, *The Golden Age of Cinema: Hollywood, 1929–1945* (Malden, MA: Blackwell Publishers, 2007), 30.
34 Jones writes that "[f]or all his love of science fiction, [Siegel's] heart was ultimately not in advancing the cause but in finding an idea he could sell. He wanted to be noticed. He wanted to believe that an idea was out there somewhere that would make him suddenly significant, suddenly potent, suddenly adult." Jones, *Men of Tomorrow*, 38.
35 See Goldstein, *The Price of Whiteness*, 146.
36 See Edsforth, *The New Deal*, 39–40, 76–77, 93–94.
37 Jones, *Men of Tomorrow*, 38.
38 The first "fireside chat" was broadcast on March 12, 1933, just over a week after his inauguration, and heard by nearly half of America's population. See Edsforth, *The New Deal*, 135, 133, 123.
39 Superman's home is not named as Metropolis until *Action Comics* #16, reprinted in Jerry Siegel (w) and Joe Shuster (a), *Superman Chronicles: Volume Two* (New York: DC Comics, 2007).
40 Harris and Tichenor, *A History of the U.S. Political System*, 3: 203.
41 Franklin D. Roosevelt, "Fireside Chat 1: On the Banking Crisis (March 12, 1933)," *Miller Center of Public Affairs*, n.d., http://millercenter.org/scripps/archive/speeches/detail/3298 (accessed November 21, 2011).
42 John Shelton Lawrence and Robert Jewett, *The Myth of the American Superhero* (Grand Rapids: W. B. Eerdmans, 2007), 36–43. For the full myth, see p. 6.
43 Susan Faludi, *The Terror Dream: Fear and Fantasy in Post-9/11 America* (New York: Metropolitan Books, 2007), 200, 212–213.
44 See Faludi, *The Terror Dream*, for their significance in promoting the gendered hero myth.
45 See Yvonne Tasker, *Spectacular Bodies: Gender, Genre, and the Action Cinema* (London and New York: Routledge, 1993), 95–96.
46 Edsforth, *The New Deal*, 31–32.
47 Siegel and Shuster, *Superman Chronicles: Volume One*, 15. The story continues into the next issue, with Lois taking on the role of victim a second—but far from last—time.
48 See Arad, *America, its Jews and the Rise of Nazism*, 130–137, 163.
49 This is the case with all of the thirteen *Action Comics* stories, as well as *Superman* #1, collected in Siegel and Shuster, *Superman Chronicles: Volume 1*. The first distinctly non-white representation in a Superman story appears in *Action Comics* #25, cover dated June 1940. (Reprinted in Siegel and Shuster, *Superman Chronicles: Volume 2*, 112–125.)
50 Peter Herriot, *Religious Fundamentalism and Social Identity* (London: Routledge, 2007), 33–34.

CHAPTER SIX

"Dreams May End, But Love Never Does"

Marriage and Materialism in American Romance Comics, 1947–1954

Jeanne Emerson Gardner

In 1967, the Beatles told a generation of girls that love was all you need. However, 20 years previously, a different group of young men promulgated a very different message, full of complexity and ambiguity. They were the creators and publishers of romance comics, a hugely popular genre that originated in 1947 and accounted for almost 25 percent of the total comic market by the early 1950s.[1] Though romance comics never attracted the kind of critical attention garnered by their notorious contemporaries (the crime, horror, and war comics), within their supposedly "harmless" pages their overwhelmingly female adolescent audience could absorb some hard lessons about love.[2] For the most part, romance comics propounded traditional gender roles, championing feminine passivity and domesticity as the qualities required to win the love of a good man. By doing this, the comics reinforced and reiterated similar themes of "domestic containment" that could be heard in many other areas of postwar American society.[3] From the 10-cent comic book to officials at the highest levels of government came the message that "the most fundamental job of the American woman" was "being a good wife, a homemaker, a mother," as Secretary of Labor James P. Mitchell declared in 1957.[4] Yet women's perceived centrality in the domestic sphere was not without complications. In making the ethics and characteristics of female domestic consumerism a key point of conflict in many stories, romance comics reflected a national sense of uncertainty and confusion regarding gendered consumption and the material expression of social class in America after World War II.

Many profound social changes marked the postwar era, including sub-urbanization, the expansion of the cultural middle class, and an abrupt transition toward a consumer-driven economy. It was an affluent time, but also a period of acute national anxiety.[5] For example, many social commentators described a pervasive sense of crisis over postwar gender roles. Unsurprisingly, much of this anxiety was couched in economic terms. William H. Whyte and David Riesman argued that the masculine role of provider was diminished in the postwar economy, for increasingly men were not the independent entrepreneurs of America's fondest self-imaginings, but the salaried employees of a larger organization. Whyte argued that this made men acquiescent, static, and ultimately neurotic.[6] In Riesman's famous phrase, the modern man was "other-directed," constantly adjusting his behavior in conformity with the opinions of his peers, exhausting himself in a constant search for approval, lacking autonomy.[7] Meanwhile, women were feared to have too *much* economic power. While postwar female employment increased markedly among married, middle-class women (a development that romance comics roundly condemned), within the home housewives were perceived to be the authorities over household spending and consumption. While advertisers were perfectly willing to celebrate women's central role in domestic consumption (and then fulfill their needs with an ever-broadening array of products), other public figures propagated a backlash against the supposed economic dominance of the American wife. For example, in John Keats's caustic 1957 best-seller, *The Crack in the Picture Window*, unhappy and bored Everywoman Mary Drone sought fulfillment through consumption by nagging her husband into buying comfortless but fashionable new furniture, a television, dryer, dishwasher, and all kinds of other gadgets on credit. These expenses were "motivated by that ageless habit, common among ineffectual people, of keeping up with the Joneses," and eventually contributed to the Drone family's financial ruin.[8]

By increasing veterans' access to mortgages and credit, the federal government and a constellation of business interests (the "framers of the Consumer's Republic," in Lizabeth Cohen's term) encouraged all Americans to increase their consumption in order to boost the postwar economy.[9] But, as Barbara Ehrenreich put it, there was a widespread perception that within the family unit, "It was the husband's job to earn, but it was *her* job to spend. And in a consumer society centered on private life, her job often seemed more important."[10] It is clear that despite the valorization of the American housewife in her appliance-filled suburban home, lauded as a "tangible symbol of the American Way of Life" in the 1959 "Kitchen Debate" between Richard Nixon and Nikita Khrushchev, the moral dimension of gendered consumption in postwar America was far more nuanced and contested.[11] This is strikingly evident in a surprisingly large body of romance comic plots that centered on economic and lifestyle disputes between married couples.

In story after story, a woman's desire for a house, furniture, clothes, cosmetics, or entertainment drove a wedge between her and her husband, a theme of marital discord that has sounded since the Stoic philosophers excoriated the matrons of Rome for their extravagant pearl earrings. The very first romance comic, Joe Simon and Jack Kirby's *Young Romance* #1, offered a hint of what was to come. In a story called "The Farmer's Wife," the main characters' marriage is nearly destroyed by the young bride's demands to go to dinner parties and theatrical performances which her older husband is too tired to enjoy after a long day of work. The key elements of a story that reappeared in hundreds of different romance comics are all present here: the wife's desires conflict with the husband's, and her dissatisfaction builds over time until a dramatic rupture between the two occurs ("I'm tired too! Tired of sitting around this hat-box night after night!").[12] However, when faced with a permanent estrangement, the wife repudiates her desires and finds lasting happiness in acceding to her husband's wishes.

The first issue of *Young Romance* enjoyed spectacular sales and within 2 years over 120 copycat titles appropriated its winning formula and began competing for sales and display space in the nation's drug stores, newsstands, and five-and-tens.[13] Like *Young Romance*, which Simon described as a "comic book version" of the phenomenally successful *True Story* magazine, most romance comics contained several stand-alone stories presented as first-person confessionals.[14] Ostensibly, the "youthful, emotional, yet wholesome stories" were "by love-smitten teenagers," although Simon frankly admitted that while he "shamelessly" promoted each story in *Young Romance* as the true confession of a woman or girl, "in actuality all were authored by men."[15] Nevertheless, it is difficult to understate the central importance of the confessional format to romance comics, and not only in the marketing of titles like *Girl Confessions* and *Pictorial Confessions*, the "TRUE LOVE Stories" supposedly contained in *Hi-School Romance* or the "Glimpses into the intimate secrets of girls in love" promised by *Diary Loves*. On a narrative level, the confessional format privileged recounting the events of the plot over character development, which has led many commentators to dismiss romance comics on the grounds that the characters were "virtually indistinguishable from each other,"[16] and that they repetitively employed "hackneyed and clichéd" plots.[17] Yet while isolated stories do appear slight, a wider survey of the genre reveals that even among broadly similar tales, familiar situations could play out in many different ways.

For good and ill, the use of the confessional format also informed the way romance comics looked. The romance comics offered, in Simon's words, "more reading material and less art than usual," because the narrator's confession was usually presented via ubiquitous text boxes.[18] However, the images were still of critical importance for as National/DC artist Everett Raymond Kinstler pointed out, "Romance comics dealt with a range of emotions, some of them quite subtle and sophisticated," and "a great deal had to be implied through facial expressions and body language."[19] While in some cases the text boxes containing the narrator's recollections of past events were nothing but clunky redundancies, in the highest-quality romance comics the intersection of text and image could be a source of tension, dynamism, and humor. For example, in a story called "Together," the main character, Marie, meets an architect named Frank in the department store where she works as a salesgirl. She thinks, "He's nice! Oh, what's the use! I'll never see him again, so why dream!" while above the panel, the narrative text box simply says, "I saw him standing at the elevators, looking back at me."[20] The art tells a rather more complicated story, however. In the background, Frank is indeed pictured in front of an elevator glancing back at Marie over his shoulder. Marie stands in the foreground, but her face is not depicted. Rather, the illustration (and presumably Frank's gaze as well) emphasizes her enormous breasts and the curious twisting gesture of her hands, which draws the viewer's attention to her unadorned left-hand ring finger and suggests that she might be dreaming after all. The image also introduces a degree of sexuality to an interaction that the text deals with in a deceptively understated way.

"Together" is one of the many romance stories that justified the subordination of women's desires by recasting them as mere selfish materialism. In "Together," Marie eventually brings Frank to the brink of ruin with her passion for luxury and excess. Though at first glance it seems that theirs is a case of spontaneous mutual attraction, Marie's narration continually stresses Frank's financial appeal. On their first date, she concentrates not on his dimpled chin or blonde good looks, but on the fact that he "made a good salary and came from a fairly wealthy family."[21] Though Marie takes pains to explain that she loves Frank when she accepts his proposal of marriage, this information is relegated to a small text box in which she also confesses that she sees Frank as a "means of escape" from her despised job.[22] The rest of the page consists of Marie reminiscing about the material advantages of her marriage: she gets a "lovely apartment in the most fashionable part of town," "fun and parties all the time," and the ability to buy "all the things I'd ever wanted"[23] (see Figure 6.1). Yet the images that accompany Marie's fond, self-centered narration cast the marriage in a very different light, for they show Frank, with an anxious and hangdog expression, worried about expenses and the effect of their hectic social schedule on his work. The discordant note struck by the difference between text and image on this page heralds the marital strife to come.

As the story progresses, Marie's demands grow more and more brusque and Frank's acquiescence more emasculating. During one exchange, Marie

Figure 6.1 Enjoying the life of luxury. Uncredited (w) and Vince Colletta (a). "Together." *Girl Confessions* #33 (April 1954), Marvel Comics, 4. *Girl Confessions,* © and ™ Marvel Entertainment, LLC. All rights reserved and used with permission.

(her feet planted in an aggressively wide, masculine stance though clad in a pink pair of marabou-trimmed boudoir slippers) orders Frank to "Be home early! We have a date with the Carletons!" to which he replies meekly, "Oh, all right Marie!"[24] The comic implies that Marie has usurped the dominant role in the marriage and that his attempt to accommodate all her demands has made Frank passive, exhausted, and distracted, thus costing him his job. Deprived of his identity as provider, Frank is sent packing by Marie, who coldly informs him, "I've lost any respect I had for you!"[25] However after a short separation involving a stint back at the hated department store job, Marie sees the error of her ways. "I missed my one chance for a wonderful life, love, and happiness," she thinks sadly. "I was too wrapped up in the things I had always wanted! I ruined the life of a wonderful man, and my own life at the same time!"[26] Fortunately for Marie, when she bumps into Frank again, he is willing to forgive her and the couple decides to try again, "the *right* way," presumably with Frank reasserting his prerogative of control over their finances.[27]

"Together" was far from the only romance comic story that treated the pursuit of wealth with an attitude of great suspicion, as a path that led women into selfish, immoral, or even illegal behavior. In a story called "Love or Money," a girl who wants to "wear mink and drink Champagne at the Ritz" parlays her innocent high school "date bureau" into a gang-affiliated party girl service that teeters precariously on the fringes of prostitution.[28] The heroine of "How Mad Was My Heart" gambles away her savings and wages on horse races in an attempt to afford fancy clothes.[29] In "Love Demon," a young woman accepts a bribe in the form of a fancy house from her uncle, a corrupt contractor, to persuade her engineer fiancé not to inspect a shoddily built bridge.[30] It promptly collapses. However, by far the most common means through which romance comics portrayed riches as a moral hazard to women was by introducing a wealthy male character who tempted the heroine with his glamorous lifestyle and expensive gifts, only to ultimately be revealed as an untrustworthy and shallow cad with dishonorable intentions.

Typical of the breed is Neil, the playboy who charms the main character, Madge, away from her middle-class life with a loving husband and baby in the 1953 story "I Was a Toy of Love." Although Neil did lack the classic pencil-thin moustache that many artists used to visually signify untrustworthiness, he had most of the character flaws that romance comics typically assigned to rich but unsuitable love-interests. Drawing upon a longstanding American suspicion of luxury as a "source of both bodily and spiritual enervation," romance comics usually presented rich characters as sensual but unmanly, selfish, afraid of any hardship, and incapable of standing up for themselves or others.[31] Thus, the reader sees Neil cowering before the masculine fury of Madge's husband Rod ("Stay away from my wife, you yellow pup, or I'll kill you!") and hears his own sister refer to him as a "spineless parasite."[32] Neil even condemns himself out of his own mouth during an argument with Madge. When she suggests he "go out and get a job like a man," he replies, "And live in a cheap apartment? Skimp on everything just to exist? No thank you. I'm not made that way."[33] Neil refuses to legitimize his relationship with the "dirt poor" Madge via marriage out of fear that his wealthy grandmother will cut off his inheritance.[34] Eventually realizing that Neil cares for money more than he does for her, Madge walks out saying, "You'd rather sacrifice our love than lose a penny! I hope it chokes you . . . you weakling!"[35]

The text of "I Was a Toy of Love" dwelt on the physically compelling, even addictive, nature of Madge's passion for Neil: "It was as if I were drugged" by his kisses, she confesses.[36] Yet the *visual* emphasis of the story is material: as Rod's wife, Madge wears plain dresses and ruffled aprons while going about her everyday household tasks in a simple nursery and tiled kitchen, but as Neil's mistress she occupies a sumptuous boudoir, dresses in evening gowns and furs, and receives glittering gifts of jewelry. This was almost certainly due in part to the fact that romance comics could not go too far in their depictions of physical intimacy without attracting criticism.[37] (After the appearance of *Young Romance* #1, even comic publisher Martin Goodman worried that "love comics for kids" bordered on "pornography," and would "do irreparable harm to the field."[38]) But the addition of this material dimension to Madge's illicit love for Neil served other purposes besides camouflaging its sensual aspect. On one hand, the material differences in Madge's circumstances help the reader sympathize with her decision to leave her husband for a handsome man who drapes diamonds around her neck and says things like "Tell me what you want and I'll pick it up first thing in the morning."[39] Yet ultimately, Neil's wealth serves to emphasize that the root of their relationship is the selfish desire for pleasure. Madge comes to understand that real happiness lies in "becoming one" with her family.[40]

Many other romance comics reiterated this message. Sporting titles like "A Lesson for Bored Wives," "The Worst Mistake a Wife Can Make," and "Truant Wife," these stories featured women fleeing marriages that they found overwhelming or monotonous in search of ease, excitement, and the wealth that would supply it. Historian Alex Lubin has argued that though these comics could be said to present models of female independence by showing wives who were "discontent with the middle-class conformist society of the postwar years," and "shirked their domestic imperatives by exploring the outside world," their forays were ultimately presented as selfishness at worst, mistaken at best.[41] (For example, the "lesson" learned by the main character in "Lesson for Bored Wives" is that the "glamorous" lifestyle of her much-envied friend in New York is only made possible by the fact that she is the kept mistress of a married, "large, flabby man, at least fifteen or twenty years older" than she.[42]) Furthermore the comic stories that featured such "truant" women made it abundantly clear that such behavior undermined the values of marriage. Thus, as Lubin argues, the wives had to finally accept these values in order to be "redeemed" at the end of the story. It was by falling into the loving arms of their forgiving husbands and "living up to their marriage vows," that these characters tasted "the sweetest happiness in the world."[43]

However, to emphasize the punitive tone that many romance comic stories adopted toward their characters' aspirations and material desires is to greatly oversimplify the ambivalence toward female consumption that prevailed within the romance genre as a whole. Some stories embraced young women's material aspirations as simple common sense or even a sign of maturity. In the course of one 1951 example called "Love Must Wait," a young girl named Janice, desiring the independence and licit physical contact sanctioned by marriage, pressures her boyfriend Roy to elope with her despite the fact that he only has two hundred dollars to his name.[44] However, at the last minute she comes to the understanding that by demanding marriage immediately, she is not cementing their happiness but risking it. While on a bus rolling past a comfortable suburb on her way to the Justice of the Peace, Janice realizes that should they marry according to her plans, she and Roy wouldn't be able to afford such a nice house for years, and for the first time thinks of their future realistically: "What kind of chance am I giving my sweetheart? A home in a wretched furnished room? A wife who doesn't know the first thing about cooking or cleaning?"[45] By ending the story this way, the comic validates the pair's decision to return to their homes and put off their marriage until they are financially secure.

Janice's rationale for calling off the elopement offers a clue as to what kinds of material desires were accommodated in romance comic books. Characters' aspirations to the trappings of middle-class domesticity (such as a house in the suburbs) were usually presented as acceptable, but anything that smacked of upper-class luxury was not. Thus, Marie's appetite for furs, gowns, cocktail parties, and glamour is censured in "Together," while Janice's desire to share a respectable suburban home with Roy is praised. Once a couple was married, though, romance comics expected wives to adhere to their side of the marital "bargain," no matter what their expectations might have been prior to the wedding. Thus, a 1951 story presents the reader with the story of Ginny and Ed, who endure a situation similar to what Janice and Roy might have faced had they gone through with their planned elopement. However the story, entitled "Runaway Bride," faults Ginny for leaving Ed, her first husband, even though he was financially unable to provide for her and their son. When reduced to living in a cheap room with cracked walls and returning milk bottles to pay for food, she abandons him and soon makes a prosperous second marriage with a man whom her mother and friends consider "worthy of her" in a way that Ed was not.[46] Yet the story ends with Ginny in tears, blaming herself for failing Ed instead of the other way around, and "knowing all too late that when you spurn the gift of love, the penalty is paid with broken hearts!"[47]

As with Marge in "I Was a Toy of Love," the marked improvement in Ginny's standard of living is not presented as reason enough to sanction leaving her husband. But even when romance comics did *not* validate their characters' material desires, the stories often addressed them with a striking degree of sympathy—at least initially. Even a story like "Together" (as straightforward a cautionary tale as one could find about the consequences of untrammeled female materialism) attempted this balancing act, carefully presenting Marie's acquisitiveness and appetite for luxury as the result of a financially deprived childhood. Two particular examples, one from 1952 called "Wife Without Principles" and the other, "Dream's End," from 1954, further showcased the ambiguity and ambivalence surrounding romance comics' presentation of marriage and materialism.[48] Adopting Jennifer Scanlon's analysis of the fiction in the *Ladies' Home Journal*, when these comics are read "against the grain," and equal weight given to the conflicts as well as the happy resolutions, these stories are not nearly as simple, or as punitive, as they first appear. Though the stories valorize traditional marriage, they also expose its frustrations and unfairness. Women's desires for material things are here encompassed within their desire for a certain standard of living associated with the middle-class, the culture of which became, by gradual consensus during the postwar years, synonymous with American culture, as many historians, such as Beth Bailey, Wini Breines, and Matthew Costello, have noted. Yet though the women's desires are at least initially portrayed sympathetically, in the end these stories approved their acceptance of their husbands' priorities over their own. Romance comics attempted to perform this sleight-of-hand by emphasizing the material dimensions of wives' desires, thus reiterating the centrality of the stereotypical postwar female consumer in the American popular imagination while simultaneously drawing attention to her role in the perceived diminution of the postwar American man.

"Dream's End" is a particularly poignant story, for it traces the disintegration of a pulp fiction writer's marriage. As many comic book creators spent part of their careers in the pulp marketplace, it is difficult to avoid wondering if there is not a biographical element present. It opens with the soon-to-be-wed pair, Kip and Jane, standing in front of a showroom window looking at the "not very fancy" furniture that they will make do with until Kip "writes a great play or a famous novel," as Jane confidently expects.[49] Jane's confessional text boxes inform the reader that the two are "so much in love . . . we had stars in our eyes! Stars that blinded us from reality!"[50] The reality is that the two do not have quite enough money to marry on. Once installed in an inexpensive apartment, Kip confirms, "Our honeymoon and furnishing this place took up about all the money we had!"[51] Still, Jane's faith in their future is boundless until after their baby arrives. The birth leaves her weak, irritable, sleep-deprived, and driven frantic by the monotony of housework and the loud clacking of Kip's typewriter. One night, after Kip's deadlines interfere with their plans to go to a movie, Jane's anger boils over: "Ten years from now you'll still be writing for cheap magazines and we'll be living in a cheap apartment and still not making ends meet!"[52] In this resentful and aggrieved frame of mind, Jane attends a party thrown by a wealthy school chum and meets a man who offers her a job as a model. Jane turns the offer down ("I'm afraid Kip wouldn't like it!") but it dwells in her mind, stoking her discontent.[53] Eventually she walks out on Kip, taking their daughter with her, for an exciting new life of modeling and dating prosperous men. Jane is trying to decide which suitor to choose for her second husband when her daughter is suddenly taken dangerously ill. When Jane encounters Kip in the hospital, she has an epiphany: "Kip *hadn't* neglected me! He's just worked hard to provide for me . . . because he loved me!"[54] The couple reunites, with Jane begging to be taken "home" and claiming to "miss the sound of a typewriter!"

The story of Jane and Kip addresses issues that Scanlon identifies as "major complaints middle-class, European-American women had in the early twentieth century."[55] The root of these complaints was ambivalence about the expectation that a wife should subordinate her needs to the needs of others. The manifest inequality between heterosexual partners with regard to supposedly "shared" marital responsibilities meant, in practice, wives' "continual self-sacrifice and assistance."[56] The narrative raises such

Figure 6.2 Struggling with the realities of housework. Uncredited (w) and Russ Heath (a). "Dream's End." *Girl Confessions* #34 (June 1954), Marvel Comics, 4. *Girl Confessions*, © and ™ Marvel Entertainment, LLC. All rights reserved and used with permission.

problems between Kip and Jane, and like Ginny in "Runaway Bride," it seems to give Jane a genuine reason to leave. Her life does appear intolerable. In one particular illustration, she is pictured in her tiny kitchen with rain pouring down outside the windows, struggling to complete several household chores at once (see Figure 6.2). She has nowhere to hang the laundry except over the stove on which several pots and pans are boiling over, and her toddler is screaming and flinging toys from her high chair. Meanwhile, barely visible off in the corner of the panel, Kip is typing in the background with his pipe in his mouth, insulated and oblivious to Jane's domestic trials in the chaotic kitchen. When Kip suggests Jane go to the movies without him so he can meet a deadline, her response ("I'm going to the show . . . *alone as usual*!") indicates that this is not the first time he has broken their plans.

"Dream's End" almost encourages the reader to approve Jane's flight from such a joyless, drudgery-filled marriage, especially since the proffered alternative involves a glamorous career as a model and being pursued by wealthy and handsome men (in a departure from romance comics' stereotyping of rich cads, Jane's boyfriends are honorable and propose marriage to her). But in the end, the story treats Jane's return to Kip as a triumph of true love, even though there is no expectation that Kip's financial circumstances

will change and allow him to support his daughter and Jane any better than
he had before. The last text box goes as far as to validate Jane's willingness
to lower or abandon her marital and monetary expectations, proclaiming
"Dreams may end, but *love never does!*"[57] As in Scanlon's appraisal of
the fiction printed in the *Ladies' Home Journal*, "Dream's End" sought
to please its young readers with a happy ending, but also to shape their
perceptions about "realistic" feminine expectations and desires within a
marriage. But if the conflict in the story revolves around real problems that
resonate with and validate readers' experience, the simplicity of the resolution is ultimately unconvincing.[58] The story ends up being ambivalent and
ambiguous, and its ending rather contradictory.[59]

By connecting Jane and Kip's marital troubles to a lack of money rather
than focusing on her frustrated expectations and sense of conjugal neglect,
the comic attempts to introduce a moral dimension to their marital strife
and shift culpability to Jane. Thus, Jane's "dreams" for a better life are
framed as materialistic desires. "Fame and fortune!" she prophesies gaily
early on in their marriage, while later she grumbles to herself, "What a
fool I was to think we'd ever be rich."[60] Kip, for his part, comes in for a
bit of sympathy during their fight over the broken movie plans: "I do my
best! I know the pulps don't pay very well, but at least it's a living!"[61] The
implication is that Jane's desires are actually unrealistic, and she should
be satisfied with her husband's meager income instead of supplementing it
with a modeling job of her own or suggesting the switch to a better-paying
line of work.

"Wife without Principles" illustrates the extent to which romance comics' treatment of female characters' desires could drastically change over
the course of a story. In this case, the character's name is Sally and her
narration establishes immediately that owning a house is very important
to her because her childhood was precarious, poor, and transient following the death of her parents in a car crash. When she falls in love with a
man named Bill, Sally requests that they not marry until they can buy their
own home. In contrast to the agreeable Roy in "Love Must Wait," Bill
considers this a "tough condition" because it means that she will continue
working after their wedding.[62] In due course, however, they purchase a
perfectly standard-looking two-storey Cape Cod-style house of brick and
white clapboard, and marry a few days later. The first "cloud" over their
marriage occurs on the day that Bill receives a pay raise that he hopes will
allow Sally to quit her job, only to come home and find that she has ordered
a bedroom suite on credit and to make the payments she will have to keep
working. The illustration of Bill's grim face, regarding the new furniture
as Sally wheedles him ("You wouldn't want me to send these things back,
would you?") is repeated when his firm goes under and he loses his job.[63]
In contrast to Frank, the henpecked husband in "Together," Bill responds
to Sally's usurpation of his role as breadwinner with bitterness, grumbling

about having to receive "the daily handout."[64] The thought that Sally might enjoy her job or her life as a working woman is not one that Bill chooses to entertain.

Sally's devotion to her house is put to the test when Bill finally gets another job in a distant state, and immediately assumes she will be willing to sell it and move away with him. When she is reluctant to do so, suggesting that he wait until a job in their hometown opens up, Bill's reaction is to draw away from her angrily and ask, "So, you'd rather keep the house than have me keep my self-respect?"[65] Sally placates Bill and sends him off with promises to join him, but cannot quell the thought that "it just isn't fair, asking me to give up all this just because he wants to take a particular job."[66] She puts off joining Bill from day to day, and though she engages in a brief flirtation with her boss, Sally's primary attachment remains to her home, "the one thing I possessed that was real," until sitting alone in it one night she realizes that she has "given up real love for material things!"[67]

The illustration that accompanies this epiphany is striking, for it depicts a room that has changed quite dramatically from previous illustrations of the inside of the house. Sally's living room has metamorphosed from a cozy all-American suburban interior (complete with a Colonial-style secretary desk and oil lamp) to a scarlet-swagged expanse of lonely luxuriousness. She is pictured huddled on her sofa, a solitary figure adrift in a space that seems to have suddenly expanded to the size of a hotel ballroom. With one stroke, the comic attempts to recast Sally's attachment to the house that she not only dreamed of since her traumatic and deprived childhood but also selected, decorated, and to a large extent paid for by herself. By visually transforming the beloved home to an empty mansion, the story also transforms Sally's domestic devotion to excessive materialism that interferes with her conjugal bond. Hoping to rectify the situation, she flies into Bill's arms, only to learn that he has resigned himself to the failure of their marriage and reenlisted in the army out of despair. Though the two reaffirm their love, Sally finds herself scheduled to live in an army camp, a place that is never illustrated but which Bill verbally characterizes as "pretty much of a dump." She replies, "I won't even notice it, for I'll be far too busy being in love with you!"[68]

As in "Dream's End," the denouement of "Wife without Principles" is as abrupt, irrational, and unconvincing as the build-up to the marital crisis was incremental and plausible. As Scanlon and Janice Radway have argued, the popular fiction consumed by women (which must certainly include romance comics) appeals to them because it provides identification as well as escape and catharsis; to succeed it must "validate women's life experiences and their values."[69] Whether or not the young readers of romance comics took "the opportunity to put the magazine down and dream" of their own future marriages by imagining themselves in the familiar situations that the comics presented over and over again, some evidence exists to indicate that at least a few readers took the comics' claims to confessional accuracy with a degree of seriousness.[70] Many comics printed pages of letters to the editor in which readers recounted their personal romantic tribulations, suggested story ideas, and voiced critiques of comics they found insufficiently reflective of their own experience. For example, in one charming letter to Stan Lee at *My Own Romance*, a reader from Oregon wanted to know why every character was pictured in a convertible: "We live up north, where for about nine months of the year you'd freeze your nose riding around in one of those open jobs." (Lee's reply promised "sedans—with skid-chains—in future issues.")[71] Some titles did even more to promote the idea of reader responsiveness, such as *Lover's Lane* which published a regular feature called "How Did He Propose?" and offered winning readers 10 dollars for the privilege of pictorially dramatizing their "entrancingly different" marriage proposals.[72]

We may never know how much weight to give romance comics' claims to be "true-to-life," but it is indisputably true that romance comics committed sins of omission. They offered an incredibly narrow vision of postwar American life, focusing on conflicts of gender and class to the almost total exclusion of other cleavages in American society, including race, ethnicity, religion, politics, and sexuality. Yet in Scanlon's words, even the "standard, pat definitions of middle-class womanhood" that romance comics propagated "did not even easily apply to those who most nearly fit the bill," the girls for whom entering womanhood meant "agreeing to enter, or attempting to enter the apparent reality" that romance comics tried to illustrate.[73] In the stories that dealt with gender roles within marriage and consumerism, romance comics "exposed the wrongs of the institutions [they] promoted as right," by acknowledging the frustration of women's desires and aspirations and illustrating, almost in spite of themselves, that the traditionally sanctioned response of feminine accommodation was not always adequate to the problems that women faced.[74] This became more and more apparent as the feminist and sexual revolutions of the 1960s began to stir. Hobbled by the 1954 Comics Code, which mandated "Respect for parents, the moral code, and for honorable behavior shall be fostered[;] a sympathetic understanding of the problems of love is not a license for morbid distortion," romance comics could not change enough to keep up with the times.[75] Though they dressed up their characters in mini-dresses and go-go boots and filled their speech bubbles with jive slang, by the time the Beatles sang "All You Need Is Love," romance comics had entered their "long, lingering decline."[76] Facing competition from other media, particularly television and movies, and unable to connect with a new generation of readers, romance comics dwindled in number until 1977, when the last issue of the venerable *Young Love* appeared.

Notes

1 Jean-Paul Gabilliet, *Of Comics and Men: A Cultural History of American Comic Books*, trans. Bart Beaty and Nick Nguyen (Jackson: University Press of Mississippi, 2010), 33.

2 David Hadju, *The Ten Cent Plague: The Great Comic Book Scare and How It Changed America* (New York: Farrar, Straus, and Giroux, 2008), 161.

3 Bradford W. Wright, *Comic Book Nation: The Transformation of Youth Culture in America* (Baltimore and London: Johns Hopkins University Press, 2001), 127.

4 Susan M. Hartmann, "Women's Employment and the Domestic Ideal in the Early Cold War Years," in Joanne Meyerowitz, ed., *Not June Cleaver: Women and Gender in Postwar America, 1946–1960* (Philadelphia: Temple University Press, 1994), 90.

5 Wright, *Comic Book Nation*, 110.

6 William H. Whyte, *The Organization Man* (New York: Simon and Schuster, 1956), 366.

7 David Riesman, *The Lonely Crowd* (New Haven: Yale University Press, 1961), 22.

8 John Keats, *The Crack in the Picture Window* (Boston: Houghton Mifflin, 1957), 46, 86–87.

9 Lizabeth Cohen, *A Consumer's Republic: The Politics of Consumption in Postwar America* (New York: Vintage Books, 2004), 195, 200.

10 Barbara Ehrenreich and Deirdre English, *For Her Own Good: Two Centuries of the Experts' Advice to Women*, 2nd edn (New York: Random House, 2005), 263.

11 Elaine Tyler May, *Homeward Bound: American Families in the Cold War Era* (New York: Basic Books, 1999), 145.

12 Joe Simon (w) and Bill Draut (a). "The Farmer's Wife." *Young Romance* #1 (September–October 1947), Crestwood: [14–21], 6.

13 Michelle Nolan, *Love on the Racks: A History of American Romance Comics* (Jefferson, NC: McFarland, 2008), 42.

14 Joe Simon and Jim Simon, *The Comic Book Makers* (New York: Crestwood, 1990), 122.

15 Ibid., 122–123.

16 Bruce Bailey, "An Inquiry Into Love Comic Books," *Journal of Popular Culture* 10, no. 1 (Summer 1976): 246.

17 Trina Robbins, *A Century of Women Cartoonists* (Northampton, MA: Kitchen Sink Press, 1993), 109.

18 Simon and Simon, *The Comic Book Makers*, 123.

19 Hadju, *The Ten Cent Plague*, 163.

20 Uncredited (w), Vince Colletta (a). "Together." *Girl Confessions* #33 (April 1954), Zenith, 3.

21 Ibid., 3.

22 Ibid., 4.

23 Ibid., 4.

24 Ibid., 4.

25 Ibid., 5.
26 Ibid., 6.
27 Ibid., 6.
28 Uncredited. "Love or Money." *Teen Age Romances* #27 (November 1952), Saint John Publications, 1.
29 Uncredited. "How Mad was my Heart!" *Intimate Love* #6 (March 1950), Standard Magazines.
30 Uncredited. "Love Demon." *Pictorial Romances* #17 (January 1953), Saint John Publications.
31 T. J. Jackson Lears, *No Place of Grace: Antimodernism and the Transformation of American Culture, 1880–1920* (Chicago and London: University of Chicago Press, 1983), 28.
32 Uncredited. "I Was a Toy of Love." *Pictorial Romances* #19 (May 1953), Saint John Publications, 6, 8.
33 Ibid., 7.
34 Ibid., 11.
35 Ibid., 11.
36 Ibid., 1.
37 Gabilliet, *Of Comics and Men*, 33.
38 Simon and Simon, *The Comic Book Makers*, 125.
39 "I Was A Toy of Love," 7.
40 Ibid., 12.
41 Alex Lubin, *Romance and Rights: The Politics of Interracial Intimacy, 1945–1954* (Jackson, MI: University Press of Mississippi, 2005), 50.
42 Uncredited. "A Lesson for Bored Wives." *Pictorial Romances* #21 (September 1953), Saint John Publishing, 3.
43 Uncredited. "The Worst Mistake a Wife Can Make." *Pictorial Romances* #11 (January 1952), Saint John Publications, 11.
44 Uncredited. "Love Must Wait!" *Intimate Love* #11 (April 1951), Standard Magazines.
45 Ibid., 9.
46 Uncredited. "Runaway Bride!" *Intimate Love* #13 (August 1951), Standard Magazines, 9.
47 Ibid., 12.
48 Jennifer Scanlon, *Inarticulate Longings: The Ladies' Home Journal, Gender, and the Promises of Consumer Culture* (New York and London: Routledge, 1995), 138.
49 Uncredited (w), Russ Heath (a). "Dream's End." *Girl Confessions* #34 (June 1954), Zenith [Marvel Comics], 1.
50 Ibid., 1.
51 Ibid., 2.
52 Ibid., 4.
53 Ibid., 4.
54 Ibid., 6.
55 Scanlon, *Inarticulate Longings*, 143.
56 Ibid., 143.
57 "Dream's End," 6.

58 Scanlon, *Inarticulate Longings*, 144.
59 Ibid., 138.
60 "Dream's End," 2, 4.
61 Ibid., 3.
62 Uncredited. "Wife without Principles." *Pictorial Romances* #15 (September 1952), Saint John Publications, 2.
63 Ibid., 3.
64 Ibid., 5.
65 Ibid., 6.
66 Ibid., 6.
67 Ibid., 8.
68 Ibid., 9.
69 Scanlon, *Inarticulate Longings*, 139.
70 Ibid., 139, 141.
71 "Letters to the Editor" column, *My Own Romance* #24 (September 1952).
72 Uncredited (w) and Ruth Atkinson (a). "How Did He Propose?" *Lover's Lane* #3 (February 1950), 3. In *Agonizing Love*, ed. Michael Barson (New York: Harper Design, 2011), 29.
73 Scanlon, *Inarticulate Longings*, 142.
74 Ibid., 168.
75 Amy Kiste Nyberg, *Seal of Approval: The History of the Comics Code* (Jackson: University Press of Mississippi, 1998), 168.
76 John Benson, introduction to *Romance without Tears*, ed. John Benson (Seattle: Fantagraphics, 2003), 6.

CHAPTER SEVEN

Parody and Propaganda

Fighting American and the Battle against Crime and Communism in the 1950s

John Donovan

During 1954 and 1955, seven issues of *Fighting American* comic magazine were published by Headline Publications. The series focused on Johnny Flagg, a newscaster at the television station U.S.A. who was a vociferous advocate of keeping America strong, using his position in the media to expose criminals and communists who endangered America's freedom. Working side-by-side with his sidekick Speedboy (actually a page boy at the station), Johnny Flagg pursued and captured criminals on behalf of law enforcement and government agencies as the costumed superhero Fighting American.

Created by Joe Simon and Jack Kirby in 1954, Fighting American was envisioned by his creators as the "first commie-basher in comics" to directly battle the "red menace" of the Cold War.[1] The storylines were a direct reflection of the anti-communist fervor associated with Senator Joseph McCarthy, who sought to expose communist subversion and espionage in America while serving on the Senate Committee on Government Operations from 1953 to 1954. Fighting American also battled criminals who preyed upon the kind of innocent victims that were discussed during the hearings conducted by the Senate Special Committee to Investigate Crime led by Senator Estes Kefauver in 1950 and 1951. Even though Fighting American and Speedboy tackled serious challenges and issues related to crime, as well as confronting communist plots in America and around the world, the stories were never fully presented in a serious manner and were obviously parodies dealing with social, political, and foreign policy issues of the time. Still, the storylines found in those seven issues reflected the Cold War political and social concerns of those who perceived criminal and communist elements as threats to the United States, our allies, and the American way of life during the mid-1950s.

In early 1941, in the wake of the financial success of Superman and Batman, American comic writer/artist Joe Simon sought to create a similar character for Timely Comics. As Simon considered the situation overseas, he decided that the fascist menace posed against Europe (and the free world) made Adolf Hitler "a truly believable villain in comics . . . hated by more than half of the world."[2] With this political and military scenario in mind, Simon designed an American hero clad in red, white, and blue with a star on his chest and carrying a shield who could take on Hitler and his Nazi hordes. He originally wanted to name the character "Super American," but opted instead for the name Captain America. He also devised a sidekick named Bucky so Captain America could have someone to interact with during his adventures combating Nazism.[3] Working with artist Jack Kirby, Simon developed the characters, and soon the first issue of *Captain America* with a cover date of March 1941 was released. Simon has proudly described Captain America as "the first major comic book hero to take a political stand" and not just fight criminals.[4] In 1954, hoping to recapture the magic and success of Captain America in a Cold War context, Simon and Kirby created and developed Fighting American and his sidekick, Speedboy, as two new characters to fight the social, political, military, and ideological threats to American liberty posed by communism and crime in the United States and around the world.

The years after the end of World War II and leading up to the creation of Fighting American were filled with controversy as Congressional leadership publicly dealt directly with three topics that eventually would be greatly relevant to the Fighting American: communism, crime, and comics. In 1949, high-profile investigations into communist influence and actions in the United States were conducted by the Committee on Un-American Activities (HUAC) under the auspices of the U.S. House of Representatives. The HUAC investigations received a great deal of attention, and the publicity generated by the committee hearings raised public awareness about the dangers of communism. In August 1949, HUAC approved and released a pamphlet entitled *100 Things You Should Know about Communism* which contained an analysis of communism's possible impact on the United States and especially its religion, education, labor, and government. It outlined how Communists used their organizing skills to "operate a carefully trained force of spies, revolutionaries, and conspirators" in support of "a world revolutionary movement" using "disciplined agents operating under a plan of war."[5] After examining the strengths and weaknesses of Communism, the committee determined that its greatest strength is its "appeal to the lust for power" as a force using money, conspirators, and violence "toward control of the world." Its greatest weakness is that "Communism can dominate only by force." As such, the pamphlet argued, it must be "stopped by driving every Communist out of the place where he can capture power."[6] This danger of communist influence was certainly on the minds of millions of Americans—a number that doubtlessly included Simon and Kirby.

Like communism, another hot topic of social and political discourse during the Cold War was the menace of organized crime in America. In 1951, the Special Committee to Investigate Organized Crime in Interstate Commerce (under the auspices of the U.S. Senate) released its findings. Similar to the findings of HUAC on communism, the committee concluded that "the tentacles of organized crime reach into virtually every community throughout the country."[7] Additionally, just as Communists have a lust for power, the committee concluded that underworld characters participate in organized crime "for the purpose of increasing their power and wealth and gaining greater protection for their illegal activities."[8] In the context of the times, the threat of organized crime, as well as communism, in the United States was seen as a danger to our nation's values and Americans were told that it would require great vigilance on the part of all citizens to halt their corrupting influences.

Many Americans were also concerned about a third form of corruption, one that came out of the pages of comic books. As a result, the U.S. Senate Subcommittee of the Committee on the Judiciary to Investigate Juvenile Delinquency held hearings in April and June of 1954 to examine the role of comics in the development of juvenile delinquency. Comics that depicted and promoted violence and let criminals go unpunished were described in testimony and exhibits presented before the Subcommittee as "perverted magazines" that contain "instructions in crime, narcotic uses, and sex perversions, and moral degradation."[9] A report entered into the record during the testimony of Richard Clendenen, Executive Director of the Subcommittee, explicitly made the connection between efforts to stop the suppression of "indecent publications" with communism by asking "how long and how often can the American people be duped?" Just like the danger of "indecent" comics, "the objective of communism is to despoil your children, to rob them of their respect for law and the teachings of morality, to enslave them with sex and narcotics," adding that "when that happens, the seeds of communism will fall on fertile ground."[10] In evaluating the appropriateness and decency of comics for children, Clendenen also entered into the record criteria established by the independent Committee on Evaluation of Comic Books (CECB) from Cincinnati, Ohio. The CECB especially found objectionable any comics that used "propaganda against or belittling traditional American institutions," and "stories or frames which tend to affect the war effort of our Nation adversely."[11] Just like the insidious danger of communism and organized crime, comics had the power to influence and corrupt young minds, causing them to turn away from American values and principles. All three of these social and political issues were debated in U.S. newspapers and magazines of the day, and undoubtedly played a role in the mindset of Simon and Kirby as they developed a new hero for the Cold War: Fighting American.

Joe Simon, reminiscing about the creation of Fighting American in 1954, stated that he and Jack Kirby had "clobbered the Nazis with Captain America," and that they "saw perfect foils for our new super hero in these red bogeymen." After naming their new character Fighting American, Simon recalled that they gave him a "kid buddy, Speedboy" based on the fighting duo concept they developed years earlier with Captain America and Bucky.[12] Kirby also saw the idea of reinventing a Cold War Captain America character as a natural fit for the two creators because he and Simon "were patriots down to our very toenails."[13] In this spirit, Simon stated that the first stories were "deadly serious" as an attempt to take on the "red menace," and that he and Kirby were proudly creating "the first commie-basher in comics" for America's Cold War against the Soviet Union.[14]

Interestingly, despite Simon and Kirby's intentions in creating the comic, the first issue of *Fighting American* (cover dated April–May 1954) did not even mention Fighting American and Speedboy's war on communism or crime. The reader was enticed to purchase the comic with the copy around the title: "Where there's DANGER! MYSTERY! ADVENTURE! We find The NEW CHAMP OF SPLIT-SECOND ACTION! FIGHTING AMERICAN with SPEEDBOY, the wonder kid." The action on the cover gave no indication of the war on communism, either, as it showed the two superheroes jumping from a speeding red race car, with the unidentified driver's leg firmly in Fighting American's grip, while the driver took shots at them. A text box at the bottom of the cover lured the reader into the comic with the comments, "WHO is the FIGHTING AMERICAN? Learn his secret in this issue!"[15] Inside the book, the reader would encounter several of the major themes that would come to define the series.

The five main themes evident in *Fighting American* reflect the major concerns of Americans during the Cold War era. These themes include the elimination of domestic foreign spies in America, stopping American criminals from cooperating with organized crime, halting foreign military troops on American soil, preventing communist sabotage on American and foreign soil, and the promotion of American freedom and ideals. The first stories in *Fighting American* #1 not only told the origin of America's Cold War commie-bashing superhero team, but it also addressed the first of the five themes, the elimination of domestic foreign spies in America.

In "First Assignment: Break the Spy Ring!" Simon and Kirby introduce the reader to Johnny Flagg, a television newscaster broadcasting over Station U.S.A. He is a handicapped "war hero" who needs crutches to walk (it is never specified when or in which war Flagg was injured, but based on the age of the character the reader can safely assume it was probably World War II or the Korean War) and uses his platform to warn Americans about the "traitors and foreign agents" that he describes as "vermin in our midst!" Every night, he ends his patriotic broadcast by stating, "And, so, ladies and gentlemen, this is the voice of freedom—saying good night—and thanks—for keeping America strong!"[16] The story also introduces Flagg's younger brother, Nelson, who writes Flagg's material for him. Nelson Flagg is very reminiscent of the young and emaciated Steve Rogers (identified by doctors as too weak for military service), the Simon and Kirby character from World War II who would be transformed into Captain America in 1941. Later in the story, Nelson is confronted by a "government agent" who escorts him to a "huge, well-guarded building" in which Nelson encounters his brother, dying on an operating table. A military officer tells Nelson that Johnny Flagg "had many enemies," and that "some of them have finally carried out their threats!" Bruised and battered, Johnny looks up at Nelson from the operating table and tells Nelson that "I'm dying . . . this Cold War sometimes gets a bit too hot for some of us!"

Before passing away, Johnny reminds his brother that the individuals who attacked him are "after our freedom, Nelson . . . they're after all men who think for themselves! They've got to be stopped—stopped—st . . ." Standing over his brother, Nelson vows, "I'll do my best, Johnny! I'll spend the rest of my life tracking down the rats who did this to you! I swear it!"[17] The officer gives Nelson an opportunity to carry out his vow through a process that would allow the United States to "produce the type of man we need. The agent of the future . . . a highly geared, almost indestructible power . . . who we call . . . Project Fighting American!" By using a "revitalized and strengthened" version of Johnny Flagg's body, scientists are able to transfer Nelson's mind into his brother's body (now clad in the Fighting American costume). After the process is completed, Nelson exclaims to the scientists, "W-why, it's amazing! Am I really in my brother Johnny's body?" One of the scientists replies "You are! And as of now you're also Fighting American!"[18]

Assuming the identity of Johnny Flagg, Nelson appears on the television announcing that his potential assassins have failed, emphasizing that "I say once again to these traitors that neither threats nor bullets shall stay their being brought to justice!" Seeing that he is still alive, the ringleader of the communist cell who thought they had killed Flagg, Peter Piper (one of the first of many clever names used for a communist agent by Simon and Kirby to describe the attraction of communism to its followers, just like the rats who followed the Pied Piper), calls Flagg to challenge him to a showdown meeting. Flagg accepts and Fighting American quickly defeats the communist cell (we know they are Communists because one of the men calls Peter Piper "Comrade"). The story ends with Johnny Flagg appearing on his newscast telling viewers to "remember the name Fighting American!" A caption reminds readers of the patriotic project of the series, explaining, "Tonight, he cleaned up a vicious nest of evil! But, he will not stop there . . . not while the principle of life, liberty and the pursuit of happiness is under attack by the ruthless forces of greed and ignorance!" The comic's second story would also focus on the theme of eliminating foreign spies, and would also introduce Speedboy, Fighting American's sidekick. With these two stories, readers understood who both the main characters were and how their mission to weed out subversion would keep America free.

One of the best examples of this goal can be found in "Poison Ivan," from *Fighting American* #3. One day, Flagg and Speedboy are visited in their television office by the father of a boy in a local neighborhood. The father, with the boy in tow, is exasperated by his son's pro-communist comments and is hoping that Flagg can straighten him out. The boy refuses to talk to Flagg, calling him a "tool of the capitalist warmongers! What a phony! I wouldn't believe him if he took an oath on a stack of books by Karl Marx!" and runs out of Flagg's office with his father chasing after him. Speedboy, astonished by the exchange, says to Flagg, "Did you get a load of that! If that kid didn't sound like a dyed-in-the-wool commie, my name isn't Speedboy!" Flagg, changing into his superhero costume, replies, "There's a dyed-in-the-wool commie behind this, you can bet on that! Get set for action, fella, we're going to find him!"[22] By scouring the city neighborhoods, and talking with local kids, the duo learns about the deceptive propaganda being spread by Poison Ivan and Hotsky Trotski. Watching from a trash can (in which he has hidden), and realizing that the commie-bashing duo is on their trail, Poison Ivan vows, "Da! You'll see me soon enough, 'Mister Fancy Underwear!' You'll wish you was dead! By golly, I'll have you shanghaied to communist country—where everyone wishes he was dead!" The inevitable conflict between the superheroes and communists takes place during the last three pages of the story, in which Fighting American and Speedboy knock out and capture both Poison Ivan and Hotski Trotski. As he subdues Poison Ivan, Fighting American explains, "There! He's quiet now! When he begins wagging his tongue again—he'll do it from behind the bars of a federal prison!" Speedboy replies, "I suppose there's more of his kind around—spreading the poison of hate. Our job is far from done."[19] While there are strong anti-communist elements in this story, the tone of "Poison Ivan" is much less serious than it had been in the first issue. This was not accidental.

Joe Simon admitted in 1990 that in the wake of the April–June 1954 Army-McCarthy hearings (and McCarthy's subsequent condemnation by the U.S. Senate for his belligerent and unprofessional actions), he and Kirby became "uncomfortable with Fighting American's cold war" and focused more on having "fun with the characters."[20] We can see this new emphasis in the third issue, cover-dated August–September 1954. In effect, Simon and Kirby set out to create two noble superheroes to directly promote their own version of pro-American propaganda, but ended up leaning more toward using parody and silly situations for Fighting American to promote American values and ideals. This could be clearly seen in the second theme of the series, stopping American criminals from cooperating with organized crime and foreign spies.

One of the most interesting villains of the series was Doubleheader, a man with two heads, one of which is sophisticated with a high I.Q., and the other with a low I.Q. and low-class demeanor. In "Assignment: Find the King of the Crime Syndicate" (from *Fighting American* #2), Doubleheader's higher-I.Q. head has created a "telekinetic" hand-held energy device which allows him (and his "brother") to manipulate cards, dice, horse races, boxing matches, and other sporting events, the same kind of influence that the U.S. Senate Special Committee to Investigate Organized Crime in Interstate Commerce in 1950–51 feared was coming from the mob. Fighting American and Speedboy learn of Doubleheader's device, and track him down because, as Flagg states to Speedboy, "if the party who's perfected a thing like that is a shady party, he may have other tricks which could be dangerous to the nation . . ."

While the duo is unable to actually stop Doubleheader, they track signals coming from the device to a passing vehicle and copy down the license plate number of the car. Flagg later gives his secretary, Mary, the vehicle license number to find the owner of the vehicle, and she discovers that it belongs to a Casper Newberry. Realizing that she's heard the name before, she recalls that it belongs to a man who was questioned during "televised hearings of the Senate Crime Investigation Committee" about his income taxes and "connection with the crime syndicate." Hoping to uncover a big news story for her boss Johnny Flagg, Mary decides to pose as a reporter to interview Newberry at his place of business. Newberry turns out to be a front-man for Doubleheader, who decides to use Mary as a hostage to lure Flagg into a trap. When the superheroes show up, they defeat Doubleheader and his fellow criminals and turn them over to the FBI.[21]

Without one mention of communism, Simon and Kirby had added an element to Fighting American's mission. Now, he would also be interested in stopping criminals involved in organized crime who could, as he put it, "be dangerous to the nation." More importantly, perhaps, we also see significant changes in tone as Simon and Kirby become much more likely to use humor and parody as tools to address the other themes of the series. In "Assignment: Investigate the City of Ghouls," Fighting American and Speedboy use a pay phone to defeat a foreign military invasion of the United States (as well as some inexplicable "devil worshippers"). Later, they stop communist sabotage of the food production system based on a mysterious additive called Element "Z" when two spies turn into human balloons. Most importantly, though, we find stories that establish the difference between "freedom" and "communism" as a way to promote American ideals. A classic story called

"Stranger from Paradise" begins with Speedboy receiving a letter from a boy living in the Russian village of Paskutzva. The letter is filled with sarcastic attempts to attack America, all of which backfire and end up humorously poking fun at life in a communist dictatorship. For example, the writer tries to mock America's food bounty, wondering why anyone would want "ice cream sodas, hot dogs, pies, steak dinners—who wants anything but borscht! Who can get anything but borscht!"[22]

What many people consider the best story of the series, "Super-Khakalovitch," from *Fighting American* #6, is another example of an attempt to promote American ideas through a comparison of the freedom and wealth of the United States to the deprivation found in the Soviet Union. Super-Khakalovitch is introduced to the reader as being "faster than a meatball in a high wind, tougher than anybody's landlady, stronger than a year's supply of garbage. Watch out! He's zooming your way! It's . . . Super-Khakalovitch . . . boy 'has been'!" The description is accompanied by a full-page drawing of a domino-masked bearded character wearing a tattered gray uniform, with red shorts and green socks (with holes in the area of both big toes). On his shirt are the words "Hero of the People." His superpower is his tremendously strong body odor, so potent that a Soviet military official describes it as being worth "a hundred divisions to us right now!" Sent to the U.S. to attack the Fighting American, he begins by terrorizing hundreds of average people. In the ensuing battle between Super-Khakalovitch and Fighting American, we see Simon and Kirby's satire on the difference between life in America and life behind the Iron Curtain.

Confronting Super-Khakalovitch, the American superhero duo is quickly defeated because, as one caption states: "For three thousand years, not one member of the Khakalovitch clan has been known to take a bath. Thus has been developed the aroma which takes its toll of even Fighting American and Speedboy." But herein begins his inevitable defeat. Seeing the neatly tailored costume of the unconscious Fighting American, Super-Khakalovitch thinks to himself, "My superiors didn't tell me that he dressed like THIS! Loud, classy—fine material . . . who wants to kill him for the cause! I'll kill him for that uniform alone . . ." But before the villain can act, police show up on the scene with their guns blazing and he flees the area. A caption explains that once on the loose "Super-Khakalovitch [quickly discovers] America . . . land of plenty . . . of fine clothes [above a scene in which the villain steals new clothes from a tailor shop] . . . and sports cars [in a scene in which he steals a car from an auto dealership] . . . and food! Never in his life has Super-Khakalovitch eaten so well!" Unfortunately for the Soviet superhero, his spree is stopped when he is arrested as a traitor by "communist secret police" spies hiding in the United States. Meanwhile, Fighting American and Speedboy have recovered and are combing the city looking for Super-Khakalovitch. They discover that he has been captured by a communist cell, and when they confront one of the members, she tells them that

"Super-Khakalovitch has been taken to a Turkish bath." This, she explains, is "what the traitor deserves! When he is thoroughly washed, he will no longer be what has made him great—a DIRTY SLOB!!" Wanting to find out why he turned against the Reds, Fighting American and Speedboy rush to the Turkish bath to locate the villain, but they are too late to help him. Finding him sitting in a puddle of water, the duo helps the Red to his feet while Fighting American notices that he "smells as sweet as a rose! He's finished as a super being!" Super-Khakalovitch replies, "Help me—I'm so CLEAN, I can hardly walk! This also disqualifies me as a communist—." He left his mission because he "began living like an American! I was never happier!" Khakalovitch even wants to get a job so that he can buy what he wants with the money he earns. This is a huge change for him, since, he explains, "In communist paradise, one works hard . . . but all he can afford to buy is stale borscht!"[23] Throughout *Fighting America* but perhaps especially in this story, Simon and Kirby are able to combine propaganda and parody and brilliantly capture the economic and political competition that dominated the atmosphere of the Cold War.

In only seven issues, Fighting American and Speedboy confronted a multitude of criminals and communists. Created in the historical and political context of the Cold War, Simon and Kirby based *Fighting American* stories on concerns in the United States about communism and organized crime, with an underlying subtext that understood the controversial role of comics in shaping the minds of younger readers. Fighting American and Speedboy traveled around the world to foil communist plots and protect American interests and prestige. They confronted unique criminals such as Square Hair Malloy and Rhode Island Red, and communist characters such as Poison Ivan, Hotsky Trotski, and Super-Khakalovitch. The fighting duo even traveled behind the "Iron Curtain" to rescue a family from communist "tyranny," to India to prevent an uprising against United Nations programs, and single-handedly uncovered a plot by communist troops establishing a base in California to conquer America (even calling in air strikes by the U.S. Air Force to bomb and destroy the invasion force). While Simon and Kirby set out to create the first "commie-basher" in comics, they discovered that in the wake of the Army–McCarthy hearings, they were uncomfortable taking a serious propagandistic look at the time period, and opted instead to focus on humor and parody as a way to inculcate pro-American ideals in their Cold War era readers while also entertaining them.

Notes

1 Joe Simon (w) and Jack Kirby (a). *Fighting American* (NY: Marvel Comics, 1989), vi.
2 Joe Simon, *The Comic Book Makers* (NY: Crestwood/II Publications, 1990), 50.

3   Ibid.

4   Ibid., 52.

5   U.S. House of Representatives, *100 Things You Should Know about Communism*, prepared by the Committee on Un-American Activities (Washington, DC, 1949), 10.

6   Ibid., 20–21.

7   U.S. Senate, *Organized Crime in Interstate Commerce: Final Report of the Special Committee to Investigate Organized Crime in Interstate Commerce*, 82nd Congress, 1st session, Report No. 725 (Washington, DC, 1951), 2.

8   Ibid., 5.

9   U.S. Senate, *Juvenile Delinquency (Comic Books): Hearing before the Subcommittee to Investigate Juvenile Delinquency of the Committee on the Judiciary*, 83rd Congress, 2nd session (Washington, DC, 1954), 29.

10 Ibid., 35.

11 Ibid., 44–45.

12 Simon and Kirby, *Fighting American* (Marvel), vi.

13 Ibid., vii.

14 Ibid., vi.

15 Joe Simon (w) and Jack Kirby (a). *Fighting American* #1 (April–May 1954), Headline Publications, cover.

16 Joe Simon (w) and Jack Kirby (a). "First Assignment: Break the Spy Ring." *Fighting American* #1 (April–May 1954), Headline Publications, 1–2.

17 Ibid., 4–5.

18 Ibid., 6–7.

19 Joe Simon (w) and Jack Kirby (a). "Poison Ivan." *Fighting American* #3 (August–September 1954), Headline Publications, 4–8.

20 Simon, *The Comic Book Makers*, 1–6.

21 Joe Simon (w) and Jack Kirby (a). "Assignment: Find the King of the Crime Syndicate." *Fighting American* #2 (June–July 1954), Headline Publications.

22 Joe Simon (w) and Jack Kirby (a). "Stranger from Paradise." *Fighting American* #3 (August–September 1954), Headline Publications.

23 Joe Simon (w) and Jack Kirby (a). "Super-Khakalovitch." *Fighting American* #6 (February–March 1955), Headline Publications.

CHAPTER EIGHT

Grasping for Identity

The Hands of Shang-Chi, Master of Kung Fu

Peter Lee

While exploring the slowly emerging countercultural scene of Los Angeles in 1959, journalist Richard Mathison observed the current state-of-mind among Beatniks. "Zen," Mathison wrote, "has replaced existentialism as the latest plaything of faddists." Its appeal was simple in objective ("the goal is 'to find myself'") and easily accessible to all ("anyone can give Zen a try without training").[1] Although Mathison's meditation ends with a perplexing puzzle concerning mind over matter ("How am I ever going to get out of this position?"), the movement caught on as individuals sought to answer their own universal questions concerning self-identity.[2] More serious than Mathison, one critic worried in 1959 that "the version of Zen that the Beats had adopted bore little resemblance to the real thing," suggesting that "the cool, fake-intellectual hipster searching for kicks, dropping bits of Zen and jazz jargon to justify disaffiliation from society . . . is in fact just callous exploitation of other peoples."[3]

Despite concerns over the legitimacy of certain building blocks used to construct new communities, philosophies, and identities, the younger post-war generations continued to reach across chronology and geography for inspiration. In spite of critics' contentions that such trends were not the real deal, zealots participated in Zen with enthusiasm, broadening their horizons as they fished in uncharted cultural waters of America. By the 1970s, those involved in consciousness movements and political activism were often marching to different ethnic beats. One symbolic chime that attracted the interest of both conventional and counterculture audiences alike was the emerging fascination with kung fu.

The kung fu craze in American culture, like the zest for Zen, originated in the Far East. However, while kung fu also sprung from philosophical sensibilities, American culture emphasized its physical side. Film scholar Verina Glaessner argues that the western world welcomed kung fu as a breath of fresh air, replacing the "all-pervasive, torturous, self-hatred, middle-aged disillusionment and sheer moral blackness that marked much of Hollywood's staple action output in the early 70s. The Chinese cinema was young. And it offered a world of diagrammatic moral clarity."[4] Glaessner adds that the kung fu films were timely, arriving right at the time when social consciousness was emerging in American film. Kung fu movies had a cross-audience, appealing to the "same ghetto audience that carried the wave of 'black' Hollywood action films," leading to the production of "black karate thrillers."[5]

More recently, scholar Sheng-mei Ma sees the kung fu fanaticism of the 1970s as a violent symbol of protest utilized by the counterculture against a generally parochial public.[6] But with defiance came absorption: while "black karate thrillers" and a Nordic Chuck Norris filled the big screen, television's *Kung Fu* starred a white actor, David Carradine, as a mixed-race Shaolin priest. From this standpoint, Sheng-mei Ma writes that kung fu's symbolic message is applicable to the 1970s generation at large; the various rights and consciousness groups understood that the "myth of triumph in spite of adversity is inherent in the kung fu genre, subject to borrowing by any individual or any group identifying with the besieged hero."[7] While Bruce Lee, hero of live-action film and legend in the afterlife, epitomizes kung-fu on celluloid, Lee himself was outlived by his comic book counterpart, Marvel's self-styled "master of kung fu," Shang-Chi.

Originally a way to cash-in on "chop-socky cinema," Marvel's *Master of Kung Fu* thrived in the 1970s. At the time of Shang-Chi's birth, Marvel, and the industry at large, was best known for superheroes with super-angst, waxing philosophical while warring persistently. Having no super powers and living in London—geographically apart from Marvel's New York-centered universe—the series had minimal connection to the rest of Marvel's continuity (save for a two-issue confrontation with Doctor Doom). As such, the series was a self-contained chronicle, leaving readers to explore Shang-Chi's character without weaving the narrative into an already-established framework. Shang-Chi's orphan status daunted creators as well: the original writer and artist left shortly after the series began. Fortunately, writer Doug Moench and artist Paul Gulacy soon came on board (in issues #20 and #18 respectively) to give the series its voice and distinctive look.

Enter the Master

Master of Kung Fu opens with the titular character's introduction, translating his name from the Marvel dialect of Chinese: "Call me Shang-Chi, as my father did. . . . I learned many things from my father: that my name means 'The Rising and Advancing of a Spirit,' that my body could be forged into a living weapon through the discipline of kung fu . . . Since then, I have learned that my father is Dr. Fu Manchu, the most insidiously evil man on Earth . . . and that to honor him would bring nothing but dishonor to the spirit of my name."[8] Yet no matter how fast Shang-Chi's spirit rose, it eluded his dexterous grasp. Shang-Chi would spend 109 issues of his series, five "giant-size" issues, one annual issue, and most issues of a black-and-white magazine, *Deadly Hands of Kung Fu* (running 33 issues), crafting his identity. Spurned by his father and betrayed by his friends, Shang-Chi's violent quest became a metaphor for the ethnic consciousness of various minorities and especially Asian-Americans during the 1970s.

Shang-Chi's origin issue, *Special Marvel Edition* #15 (December 1973), set the tone for the years to come. Based on Arthur Henry Sarsfield Ward's early twentieth-century fiction written under the nom de plume of Sax Rohmer, Shang-Chi is an obedient youth sent by his "honorable" father, Fu Manchu, from China to London to assassinate an ailing Dr. John Petrie. Petrie and the now wheelchair-bound Sir Denis Nayland Smith are the original protagonists from Rohmer's work. As such, the eternally young Fu Manchu (thanks to an anti-aging serum, the "elixir vitae") decides that these aged antagonists should not live out their golden years. Shang-Chi doesn't see how a bedridden Petrie can bother his father, but he dutifully complies, killing the old doctor with one blow. Smith enters and proves that the Oriental "devil doctor" is responsible for his crippled state. "The yellow devil!" Smith curses. "The inhuman yellow fiend! Will he never recognize an end to it?" While Smith contemplates the never-ending battle, a distraught Shang-Chi flees London to visit his unnamed American mother who unearths some family skeletons. She "could not love [Fu Manchu] . . . but I could hunger for his power—power I could transmit to a child of mine by him!"[9] Galled by his dad's evil ventures and his mom's easy virtue, Shang-Chi renounces his family ties. The next issue, Fu Manchu acknowledges that the feeling is mutual and sends his adopted African son, "Midnight," to kill Shang-Chi.

The first issue played upon holdovers from a more politically incorrect past. The Orientalist perspective is presented through Fu Manchu, his occult surroundings, and his feline gait (Shang Chi's mother acknowledged her attraction to his "cat-green eyes"). Fu's own signature dress is reminiscent of Boris Karloff's robes in the film *The Mask of Fu Manchu* (MGM, 1932) where Karloff's features were concealed behind yellow-face on the silver screen. The immortal film is paid homage to in the comic; Smith mentions 1932 as the year which Fu Manchu gained eternal youth, even though several silent features about Fu Manchu predate Karloff's production.[10] The movie's Mandarin madman also shared the same ambitions as his comic book counterpart: to "lead hundreds of millions of men [and] sweep the world!"

In a larger context, Fu Manchu had precedents, with the sickly yellowed Asians who populated four-colored publishing and other mediums of popular culture decades before Shang-Chi was conceived. One 1933 study concerning motion pictures on childhood development quoted a college student who relayed the effects of watching decades of the "yellow peril" on celluloid. She maintained an impression that "all Asiatics" concealed "murderous intents behind their bland features, their humble attitude— merely a disguise until the time was ripe to seize you and kill you, or, worse yet, to make you a slave." She added:

> I never passed by our Chinese laundry without increasing my speed, glancing apprehensively through the windows to detect him [the Chinese proprietor] at some foul deed, expecting every moment one of his white slave girls to come dashing out of the door. If I heard some undue disturbance at night outside, I was certain that [the Chinese owner] was at his usual work of torturing his victims. *I have not been able to this day to erase that apprehensive feeling whenever I see a Chinese person, so deep and strong were those early impressions.* [italics in original][11]

Literal representations of the yellow peril persisted into comics. The first issue of the long-lived *Detective Comics* featured stock Asian villains, all with slanted eyes, long fingernails, and broken English. Despite some sympathetic portrayals during World War II, characters such as the Blackhawks' Chop-Chop (as shown in *Military Comics*) still featured bucked teeth and wielded meat cleavers. Marvel's 1950s series *Yellow Claw* starred a Sax Rohmer rip-off who colluded with Nazis and Commies with the same global domination scheme in mind.

However, by the 1970s, such artistic license was rendered unspeakable. Emerging from the Civil Rights movements, Asian-Americans were also undergoing a cultural shift in American society; the hyphenated label was coined in 1968, followed by their reputation as a "model minority" that quickly assimilated into American culture.[12] That same year, the Blackhawks' title was in the red and was cancelled; despite several revival efforts, the World War II series, along with Chop-Chop (by then named "Wu Cheng"), could not make the switch from a military comic to a modern one.[13] In 1974, Frank Chin published *Aiiieeeee! An Anthology of Asian American Writers*, dedicated to Asian-Americans "who got their China and Japan from the radio, off the silver screen, from television, out of comic books, from the pushers of white American culture that pictured the yellow man as something, that when wounded, sad, or angry, or swearing, or wondering, whined, shouted, or screamed, 'Aiiieeeee!'" Chin hoped to turn the exclamation of exasperation into fighting words.[14]

Chin's high-brow literary collection had little use for kung fu, especially a comic book created by white men. Nevertheless, Marvel insisted that Shang-Chi's birth was more than cashing in on a fad. Editor Roy Thomas recalls the creation of the series over "cheeseburgers and chocolate mousse" with writer Steve Englehart. Englehart claims that his own interest stemmed from social factors, referring to himself in the third person: "Recently, an interest in Oriental philosophy swept America and two of the most swept were Steve and [artist] Jim [Starlin]. They started haranguing Roy for a chance to do a strip about a master of the martial and mental arts."[15] The team took advantage of Marvel's license of Fu Manchu from Rohmer's estate and developed the series as a generational conflict between father and son.

Shade of gray: Social relevance

Conflict over the series wasn't confined to the battle between Fu Manchu and Shang-Chi. Early on, readers commented on not only the plot lines, but the very look of the characters. In particular, the skin tones of stock Asian characters had some readers seeing red. In older films, flickering images in black-and-white translated yellow to white; moviegoers recognized Asians as "yellow" through other media or verbal cues. After decades of taking such color schemes for granted, however, color became an animated discussion among fans. In *Master of Kung Fu* #27, reader Jim Vicko sent a missive announcing that he was "annoyed at the artistic representation Orientals are given." Vicko points to Fu Manchu's pale yellow shading, all the more stark, when contrasted with Shang-Chi's bronze tones. In response, Marvel claimed technological limitations: when printing images of Asians, a pre-determined color scheme allowed only three hues: pink pigmentation (usually reserved for Caucasians), "the color we use on Fu Manchu and others, and the bronze shade we use on Shang-Chi himself. As you can see, there's not exactly a wide variety to choose from, and therefore we have settled on what seem the only possible color, under the circumstances."[16] Marvel didn't elaborate on its circumstantial evidence—namely, that Shang-Chi's mixed parentage might have played a role in his physical appearance. However, the company's choice was symbolically apt: Fu Manchu, having lived through the various incarnations of the "yellow peril," exhibited and internalized both his occidental and oriental legacy. Fu Manchu's stereo-type was not merely skin deep.

However, readers were not as thick skinned and refused to let the issue lie still. When Fah Lo Suee, Fu Manchu's daughter, surfaced in issue #26, she confirmed her 1932 film legacy as a woman who lost her reputation and caused men to lose their lives. As one victim swooned in death, "For deep within her unwavering stare I glimpsed everything which is at once depraved and irresistible . . . every dark sin and bright lust capable of man."[17] More captivating for the white men she wowed was her Caucasian coloring, despite her full Chinese heritage (she, too, drinks the anti-aging serum, although, she remains up to date in modern fashion and puffs her hair into an afro). However, by 1975, enough letters prompted Marvel to revise its editorial policy regarding color: "all future Asian characters would be colored in the same flesh tones as our Caucasian characters" except for those already established (i.e. the yellow Fu Manchu and the bronze Shang-Chi).[18] Writer Doug Moench justified such whitewashing, arguing that Asians' skin tones were more akin to those of whites. His first character to fit that policy was Leiko Wu, Shang-Chi's espionage-affiliated girlfriend. However, despite having spilt ink over the issue of color, confusion circulated over Wu's own ethnic identity. Early print runs gave her red or brown hair; with her pale skin, Wu was Asian in name only.[19]

While readers raged over the four-colored pulp pages, Shang Chi's own quest for an identity haunted the character throughout the book. Out of his element in England and alienated from his father, Shang-Chi was culturally isolated in metropolitan London. However, Shang-Chi's search for identity did not necessitate fitting in anywhere. Rather, his quest was a more introspective one, involving a search for inner peace. Shang-Chi often wished to be alone, even subtly rejecting his own comic book's title. However, by default, Shang-Chi remained steeped in violence, working unofficially for Denis Nayland Smith. In doing this, Shang-Chi does not really embrace western culture, but instead merely opposes everything his father stood for.

Unfortunately for Shang-Chi, his working with Smith complicated his search for identity. One of Fu Manchu's oversized minions, Tak, tactlessly calls Shang-Chi a "half-breed fool" in the first issue, confirming that Shang-Chi is not wholly Asian. Indeed, in a later issue, pale-skinned locals in Hong Kong would call the bronze hero "white," a label not referring to a surface reading. Another karate enthusiast, the "Cat," also declares Shang-Chi a "Britisher" due to his speaking the Queen's tongue with an English accent—a rare audio cue in a visual medium. While the Cat is unopposed to the mingling of the races (as his blonde girlfriend can attest), he accuses Shang-Chi of cultural contamination in one exchange from issue #39:

CAT: "You have been polluted by the western world!"

SHANG-CHI: "I have learned from the western world. I have found things of great value—and things I never wished to learn. These least things are the most valuable."[20]

Shang-Chi did not elaborate, but, as the series progressed, he incorporated some occidental idiosyncrasies. Originally content to meditate in a park and eat foliage, Shang-Chi slowly came out of his shell. For a time, he wore a superhero bodysuit rather than his signature red *gi* until Marvel's editorial staff instructed readers that loose clothing was standard attire for masters of kung fu.[21] More permanently, Shang-Chi develops close friendships with MI-6 agents Clive Reston, himself a descendant of Sherlock Holmes and James Bond, and Black Jack Tarr, a war veteran with a handle-bar mustache who affectionately addresses Shang-Chi as a "Chinaman." Although decades older than Shang-Chi or Reston, Tarr's gruff exterior belied a modern disposition; Tarr partakes in Zen meditation. "Zen stuff I can understand. Practiced it myself for a while. Takes the edge off a person. Lets you fit in smooth with everything else."[22] Shang-Chi, meanwhile, would learn to like rock 'n' roll and would even quote Mick Jagger, neither of which the British-born Clive Reston tolerates.[23]

Of course, no one could stand Dr. Fu Manchu who has managed to keep up with the times, having no problems incorporating the latest technological wonders, mind-altering drugs, and genetic engineering in his continual quest to revive the mythological Orient and dominate the world. His London skyscraper is gutted out to resemble an Asian interior, complete with booby traps, clashing gongs, and lurking assassins. One fan, Bill Wu, was resigned to the fact that the Asian characters were Asian-esque: "I can only repeat that no matter how good the intention of comics' writers, such roles do act as racial representation. Until we also see good Chinese mandarins in contrast to the deviant Fu Manchu, and good Asian women in contrast to his . . . daughter."[24]

Identity and imitation

Fu Manchu's continual presence in the series would serve as a constant reminder of unsavory Asian stereotypes. As such, Moench and Gulacy attempted to resolve Fu Manchu's conflict with his son in an epic six-part story in *Master of Kung Fu* #46-51. The plot involves Fu Manchu becoming a nuclear power and planning to destroy the moon, thereby unleashing meteorological maelstroms that will wipe out the majority of the human race. Ever the scientific mathematician, Fu Manchu synchronizes the moon's rotation with his nuclear detonations, allowing China to be spared the ensuing celestial annihilation. With him leading the Chinese, Fu Manchu would realize his dream of "saving the world by restoring the ancient and simple glories of Old China," a term he does not define, but would include his modern military might. To inaugurate this expansion of the Middle Kingdom to all corners of the globe, Fu Manchu uses genetic splicing to fuse the spirit of a deceased ancestor with his own DNA to create a new son, Shaka Kharn, as a replacement of Shang-Chi. This plan is not entirely without some admirers. As early as issue #30, reader Ralph Machio suggests that counterculture support for Fu Manchu's project was entirely plausible: "It appears Fu Manchu is attempting to re-create the past in a very meaningless present [by] using his power to return [the world] to a time when there was purpose and direction."[25]

MI-6, Shang-Chi, and Fah Lo Suee, rebelling against her father, are not impressed by the anti-establishment sentiment inherent in Fu Manchu's plan. In a preemptive strike, the heroes assault his base of operations and pursue him to the moon. There, Shang-Chi encounters Shaka Kharn and easily beheads him (the unfinished Kharn dies without a skin covering, but his skeleton is tinted yellow). However, at the pivotal moment, Fu Manchu is poised to unleash his nuclear arsenal. There, he justifies himself: "The world is *finite*, my son, but the *greed* of the western world is *infinite!*"[26] He also alludes to western collusion and a sense of Asian racial solidarity because the CIA and MI-6 supposedly have "possession of gases and poisons fatal only to those who possess Oriental genes." Shang-Chi doesn't believe him. Instead, too far away to leap to earth's defense, Shang-Chi opts for a modern means and shoots his father. Fu Manchu manages to escape, but is exiled into space.

Shang-Chi returns to Earth, and tells Nayland Smith he is done with the games of "death and deceit." He turns to the future, his own future, unencumbered by race or ideology. His lover, Leiko Wu, joins him. At first Smith dismisses Shang-Chi easily, but then his entire staff quits as well. The younger people run off to find their own lives, leaving Smith alone—a relic from the Yellow Peril era with no place in the modern age. The issue also marks a new direction for artist Paul Gulacy as well; apart from some cover art, this was his last issue.

Shang-Chi's rejection of Smith's games of "death and deceit" did not last long, however. Given the comic book's title, martial arts mayhem was a requirement, and Shang-Chi had to keep showcasing his skills, lest he fall by the wayside of aspiring imitators who seemed to be coming out of the woodwork as the martial arts became more popular in the real world. Marvel's *Deadly Hands of Kung Fu* in particular owed its existence to the practicing of the martial arts; along with comics, its pages contained discriminating movie and book reviews, interviews with actors, biographies of karate connoisseurs, pin-ups, and instructions for budding martial artists to imitate the masters. In addition, comic books were filled with karate ads. Not unlike the Charles Atlas ads and beauty tips that pervaded the medium for decades, martial arts advertisements for course books, records, and testimonials abounded, urging All-American youths to gain mental and physical discipline. This was all especially apt for teenagers and those struggling with self-doubt and uncertainty in 1970s. "A new you!" the copy for one typical set of karate lessons declared. "Once you learn the skills of Karate, and our Total Self-Defense System—you'll possess a New Self-Confidence that will generate a new you!"[27] Kung fu advertisements extended beyond comics; in *Popular Mechanics*, the publishers mingled scientific wonders with a sensei's wisdom: "kung-fu can make you a giant in both mind and body!"[28]

Indeed, to market kung fu successfully required broadening its appeal beyond ethnic or gender boundaries. As such, like the "black karate thrillers" on the silver screen, comic book companies crafted kung fu comics with multi-ethnic audiences in mind. Scholar Frank H. Wu remembers that, in his own childhood in suburban Detroit in the early 1970s, kids mimicked karate moves as a means of taunting him; yet kung fu itself easily crossed ethnic lines.[29] DC's *Richard Dragon: Kung Fu Fighter* featured a white delinquent who teams up with a black monk (who later became the "Bronze Tiger") in Japan to battle international baddies and later forms his own kung fu school.[30] Marvel's *Iron Fist* starred a white martial artist who acquires a super-powered punch from an Asian spiritualist.[31] Marvel also introduced other karate enthusiasts in *Deadly Hands of Kung Fu*, including the Sons of the Tiger, a trio of unrelated, multiethnic students avenging the death of their kung fu master against the "Silent Ones." The Sons gave way to the White Tiger (a name held by several ethnic characters, none of them white) and the Daughters of the Dragon (Misty Knight, an African-American, and Colleen Wing, a woman of mixed Asian and white heritage).[32] In fact, Marvel's growing martial artist population edged Shang-Chi from *Deadly Hands of Kung Fu* for a period. Even Wonder Woman, in a brief celebration of liberated womanhood, traded her magic lasso for martial arts taught by an Asian guru, I-Ching.[33] While none of these martial artists lasted as long as Shang-Chi's series, they do demonstrate the democratization of kung fu as an Americanized activity for all. Of course, comic creators emphasized the physical side over the martial arts' philosophical foundations. Shang-Chi himself recognized the western overindulgence in the combative side of karate. "This sudden fad of foreign violence, with little regard for foreign philosophy, saddens me," the master muses as he enters an American-taught martial arts school at one point.[34]

One of DC's martial artists demonstrates Shang-Chi's observation concerning the superficial portrayal of the martial arts. The thirtieth-century team the Legion of Super-Heroes had Val "Karate Kid" Armorr among its ranks since the mid-1960s.[35] By the mid-1970s, Armorr was given Japanese ancestry, although this origin did nothing to alter his appearance. (One police officer in the 1970s does comment, though, that Armorr "looks like a foreigner—you know, one of those Bruce Lee types!"[36]) Armorr also embarks upon a search for his identity and abandons the staid future for the wilds of modern America in his own title. The editor queried, "Should *Karate Kid* have more martial arts action—or more super-heroics a la *The*

Legion?"[37] The comic was unable to resolve this question, and, after several changes in direction with little introspection, Karate Kid's quest ended 15 issues later. The last issue returns Armorr to the future (albeit an alternate reality) set in another series, *Kamandi*, about another wayward youth trying to discover himself in an unfamiliar land.

What made Shang-Chi different from the rest of his Chop-socky competitors was his namesake, his spiritual growth, rather than the physical action. One fan wrote that another comic, *Yang*, starred a Chinese fighter, but was merely a "poor adaptation of TV's *Kung Fu*." While the fan may have found Shang-Chi more similar to David Carradine's Shaolin sojourner, Marvel editor Roy Thomas argued differently: "Shang-Chi is *not* Caine. Though he was obviously instructed in philosophy, he must have been affected by the evil pall that always surrounds his father. Thus, while basically good, he most definitely has shortcomings—he is not as perfect as Caine, nor is he meant to be." Rather, it was Shang-Chi's progression, the "'rising and advancing of his spirit,' that we are chronicling."[38] To differentiate the two, Shang-Chi encounters a look-alike version of *Kung Fu*'s Caine. This version of Caine is content to sit under a tree and wax philosophical; his identity is already established. Unlike Shang-Chi's inner turmoil, "Caine" lectures Shang-Chi that "a man who is not at peace *within himself* will not be at peace with *anything else*," appropriate words for a kung fu master instructing another as to how to find his niche in American culture.[39] One letter writer noted Shang-Chi's relevance to youth culture. "Shang is the kind of hero most young people can identify with because he, like so many of us, was brought up believing the world was one way, only to go out and discover it was something wholly different." He explains that readers had the opportunity to explore various forms of oriental philosophy, from Shang's "violence as the last resort" to Fu Manchu's goal to become the world's "conqueror at all costs."[40]

However, with Fu Machu lost in the cosmos and Shang-Chi free of familial ties, Shang-Chi now had the opportunity to move on. Even Nayland Smith, who loses his entire staff at the end of issue #51, has a change of heart. His lifelong mission complete, Smith contemplates retirement, telling his former associates that he has "doubts about what my life has become . . . what it means . . . what's happened to Petrie, Shang-Chi, to all of us . . . we've all been changed . . . It's not a pleasant feeling, Clive, convinced you've been the 'good guy' for so many years—and then opening your eyes to find that something has changed and your convictions are suddenly all wrong."[41]

However, the past and the present catch up with Moench's characters. Smith learns that MI-6 is infiltrated with saboteurs, madmen, and assassins who try to kill their former agents. Going against the Establishment himself, Smith implores Shang-Chi to aid him, giving the Master of Kung Fu another opportunity to demonstrate his handiwork. Free from his father's Orientalist trappings, Shang-Chi agrees. However, whether being besieged by World War I flyers or Japanese ninjas, Shang-Chi's world was one of uncertainty. Shang-Chi trots across the globe, returns to Hong Kong, and even ventures into the United States. Even in the melting pot of 1970s America, however, the natives of New York quickly single him out, if only for his English accent and red pajama outfit. His former colleagues in MI-6 never stray far away, and it is clear that his spiritual quest was secondary to martial arts action.

Indeed, by issue #76, Shang-Chi acknowledges that despite his father's passing, Fu Manchu's identity hovers over him; he cannot escape his roots. Sitting down with an aged, yellow-faced old man, Shang-Chi sighs, "How can my entire life be a lie? I am not a fighter, yet I fight—again and again." He pauses and then goes on, at length, "But I wish only to engage in quiet pursuits—the search for harmony, universal peace, solitary tranquility."[42] The old man has no solutions. Instead, he denies Shang-Chi all of the above, turning out to be a thief, and Shang-Chi defends himself, as he is faced with another deception, another death.

That Shang-Chi could not escape his father's legacy became a literal truth in issue #80. At a meeting with Smith, the weathered spymaster states the obvious: "I don't believe any of us here in this room ever fully conceded that Fu Manchu could die." Learning that his father may have actually compromised MI-6, Shang-Chi wearily waxes poetic about the inevitable: "Welcome to nowhere, but possibly everywhere. Welcome to nothing, but beware of everything. Welcome to the Great Game, but remember: the rules change with every turn of the dice." Seeing his friends' confused expressions, Shang-Chi flatly states, "My own name . . . the meaning of it, the rising and advancing of a spirit . . . has come to seem strange to me . . . foreign . . . alien." In other words, Fu Manchu's return was more of a revisit. "This is not another game," Shang-Chi realizes. "It is the same one, never ending."[43]

Fu Manchu meets an ending at the conclusion of this story arc and again in issue #118. However, even in another short-lived death, his legacy taunted Shang-Chi well into the 1980s. By then, superheroes had beaten out the other kung fu titles and sales declined to the point of cancellation. (Moench had left the book by this point after the death of artist Gene Day, leaving behind a revolving carousel of creators.) In the last issue, Shang-Chi, if not finding himself, at least makes peace with his forefathers. Journeying to Fu Manchu's hideout in Hunan, he severs ties with his western allies. At his father's mountain retreat, he performs atonement in front of his ancestors. "Though I cannot call you 'honorable father,'" Shang-Chi admits, "I acknowledge you as my father and pray for your soul's rest."[44] Shortly before retiring, Shang-Chi overhears a group of scheming locals. He leaps head first into combat, convinced they are leftover assassins from his father's compound. However, this time, the deceit originates in entirely Shang-Chi's own mind; the "assassins" are merely a group of actors rehearsing. By the last page, Shang-Chi retires to a fishing village where he prepares for a simple life. Even then, his identity is mixed; Shang-Chi trades his traditional fighting togs for a white t-shirt and jeans.

In 1983, the Master of Kung Fu had retired, but he returned in full force 7 years later (although the story begins right where Shang-Chi's last issue ends) in an 80-page extravaganza entitled *The Return of Shang-Chi, Master of Kung Fu*. However, aside from guest appearances in other superhero titles in which Shang-Chi acquired a tattoo, utilized wisecracks, and adapted actor Jackie Chan's cheeky charm, Shang-Chi remained relatively quiet for many years.

Peace and endings

Both Moench and Gulacy revisited Shang-Chi in 2001. Ignoring the 1990 special and other miscellaneous appearances, Moench scripts a violent tale that takes place a few years after the Master of Kung Fu's retirement. Shang-Chi's solitary life is disturbed when he learns that Leiko Wu—now Reston's wife—is kidnapped by none other than his father, back to haunt the world one last time. Despite the real time advancement of 20 years since his last appearance, Shang-Chi's father still had the grandiose desires to dominate the world and restore "Old China" with himself as sovereign. Now nameless (Marvel lost the copyright to Rohmer's characters; Nayland Smith does not appear), Shang-Chi's father still embodies the past, having retained his yellow skin, slanted eyes, Mandarin robes, and, repeating his own history, has concocted another son in a laboratory. In a twist, Black Jack Tarr, now head of MI-6, is also warding off a takeover from younger, gung-ho group of agents (the men rely on big guns, the women on minimalist attire). Shang-Chi's father fails and dies; Shang-Chi returns to retirement.

While the story is ultimately inconsequential—Moench and Gulacy seem content to tread the same plots as they had decades before—the tale demonstrates that Shang-Chi cannot escape the Orientalist tapestry woven around him; his father is a permanent thread into the past. But perhaps that is appropriate. In 1971, writer Tom Wolfe posits that there was no Asian-American equivalent of the NAACP, mainly because they were not interested. Despite the flurry of activity in San Francisco in 1968 that created a category of people on paper, the Asian-American rights movement "boiled down to not much more than a few student and young faculty intellectuals." While they netted a "few mild reforms and perhaps some more poverty program money," Wolfe asserts that the "young Chinese were not much more interested in [civil rights activism] than their parents were."[45] Wolfe believes that the Chinese-Americans, out of ethnic pride, never saw themselves as a disadvantaged minority. Rather, as their terminology for the western majority indicates, they saw whites as the true "barbarians," of mainstream America.

As such, Shang-Chi's final retreat to an isolated fishing village demonstrates his acceptance with his past. There, in a timeless setting, the lack of external conflict resolves his internal struggle: there is no need for a master of kung fu. Shang-Chi's sole request is that Black Jack Tarr discontinue his "Chinaman" nickname. However, other than this note of political correctness, nothing has changed. Indeed, Fu Manchu's legacy permeates Orientalist readings of modern incidents: scholar David Shih sees analogies between the public debate concerning nuclear scientist Wen Ho Lee's alleged espionage and the yellow peril of old.[46] However, unlike his father's feline fingernails, Shang-Chi's hands no longer reach out to the outside world; his quest for his identity ends in an ageless village. Abandoning the genre that gave him birth, Shang-Chi prefers isolation rather than assimilation; he finds his identity alone.

Notes

1 Richard Mathison, "Today's Bohemian Has All Answers for Zen," *The Los Angeles Times*, January 17, 1959, 14.
2 See Howard Brick, *Age of Contradiction: American Thought and Culture in the 1960s* (Ithaca: Cornell University Press, 1998), 114–115.
3 Quoted in Joseph Heath and Andrew Potter, *Nation of Rebels: Why Counterculture Became Consumer Culture* (New York: Harper Business, 2004), 263.
4 Verina Glaessner, *Kung Fu: Cinema of Vengeance*. (Thetford, UK: Bounty Books, 1974), 9.
5 Ibid., 14.
6 Sheng-mei Ma, *The Deathly Embrace: Orientalism and Asian American Identity* (Minneapolis: University of Minnesota Press, 2000), 53.
7 Ibid., 62.
8 See, for example, Doug Moench (w), Paul Gulacy (p), and Dan Adkins (i). "A Fortune of Death!" *Master of Kung Fu* #22 (November 1974), Marvel Comics, 1.
9 Steve Englehart (w), Jim Starlin (a), and Al Milgrom (i). "Shang-Chi, Master of Kung Fu!" *Special Marvel Edition* #15 (December 1973), Marvel Comics.
10 Marvel preferred Karloff's portrayal of Fu Manchu. In an article surveying the Fu Manchu's screen history, Marvel published three pages of images from Karloff's film, and only one photograph each from other films, including Christopher Lee's 1965 *The Brides of Fu Manchu*. See David Anthony Kraft, "Fu Manchu, Sax Rohmer, and Shang-Chi," *The Deadly Hands of Kung Fu: Special Album Issue* (1974), Marvel Comics, 29–33.

11 Henry James Forman, *Our Movie Made Children* (New York: The Macmillan Company, 1933), 162.

12 Helen Zia, *Asian American Dreams: The Emergence of an American People* (New York: Farrar, Straus, and Girroux, 2000), 46 and 47.

13 Sheng-mei Ma, "The Nine Lives of Blackhawk's Oriental: Chop Chop, Wu Cheng, and Weng Chan," *International Journal of Comic Art* 3, no. 1 (Spring 2001): 120–148.

14 Quoted in Frank Chin, "Introduction," in Jeffrey Paul Chan, Frank Chin, Lawson Fusao Inada, and Shawn Wong, eds, *The Big Aiiieeeee! An Anthology of Chinese American and Japanese American Literature* (New York: Meridian Books, 1991), xi.

15 "Missives to the Master" [Letters column]. *Special Marvel Edition* #15 (December 1973), Marvel Comics.

16 "Missives to the Master" [Letters column]. *Master of Kung Fu* #27 (April 1975), Marvel Comics, 18.

17 Doug Moench (w), Keith Pollard (p), and Sal Trapani (i). "Daughter of Darkness." *Master of Kung Fu* #26 (March 1975), Marvel Comics.

18 Doug Moench (w), Paul Gulacy (p), and Dan Adkins (i). "Wicked Messenger of Madness." *Master of Kung Fu* #33 (October 1975), Marvel Comics.

19 The issue of color does not appear in the black-and-white *Deadly Hands of Kung Fu.*

20 Doug Moench (w), Paul Gulacy (p), and Dan Adkins (i). "Fight without Pity." *Master of Kung Fu* #39 (April 1976), Marvel Comics.

21 Doug Moench writes, "Editorial policy and commercial mandates ('don't-mess-with-success') dictate that the more familiar—and, by now, popularized—pajamas-*gi* is here to stay." "Missives to the Master" [Letters column]. *Master of Kung Fu* #43 (August 1976), Marvel Comics.

22 Doug Moench (w), Sal Buscema (p), and Mike Esposito (i). "Assault on an Angry Sea!" *Master of Kung Fu* #32 (September 1975), Marvel Comics.

23 *Deadly Hands of Kung Fu* was more mature in content. Free from the requirements of the Comics Code, the black-and-white print reflected a world with racial slurs ("chink!") and drug use, However, Marvel, which had famously chronicled the dangers of substance abuse in its mainstream titles, refused to show Shang-Chi lighting up a joint to elevate his consciousness, though fashionable as it was among his younger readers. "Shang-Chi, believing as he does in the purity of the body and spirit, would have reacted the same way to the offer of drugs, a cigarette, a cigar, or any kind of pollutant which in some way, no matter how small, could lead to the bruising of his soul," the editor explained. "Enter the Letters" [Letters column]. *Deadly Hands of Kung Fu* #6 (November 1974), Marvel Comics.

24 "Missives to the Master" [Letters column]. *Master of Kung Fu* #30 (July 1975), Marvel Comics, 19.

25 "Missives to the Master" [Letters column]. *Master of Kung Fu* #30 (July 1975), Marvel Comics, 19.

26 Doug Moench (w), Paul Gulacy (p), and Mike Esposito (i). "Part VI (Fu Manchu): The Dreamslayer!" *Master of Kung Fu* #50 (March 1977), Marvel Comics.

27 "Karate: The Total Self-Defense System." Advertisement. *Richard Dragon: Kung-Fu Fighter* #1 (April–May 1975), DC Comics.

28 "Kung-Fu International." Advertisement. *Popular Mechanics*, May 1974, 71.

29 Frank H. Wu, *Yellow: Race in America beyond Black and White* (New York: Basic Books, 2002), 1–7.

30 Jim Dennis (w) and Leopoldo Duranona (a). "Coming of a Dragon!" *Richard Dragon: Kung-Fu Fighter* #1 (April–May 1975), DC Comics.

31 Roy Thomas (w), Gil Kane (p), and Dick Giordano (i). "The Fury of Iron Fist!" *Marvel Premiere* #15 (May 1974), Marvel Comics.

32 See, for example, Bill Mantlo (w), George Perez (p), and Jack Abel (i). "An Ending!" *Deadly Hands of Kung Fu* #19 (December 1975), Marvel Comics; Chris Claremont (w), John Byrne (p), and Dave Hunt (i). "If Death be my Destiny!" *Marvel Team-Up* #64 (December 1977), Marvel Comics; Chris Claremont (w) and Marshall Rogers (a). "Daughters of the Dragon." *Deadly Hands of Kung Fu* #32 (January 1977), Marvel Comics.

33 Denny O'Neil (w), Mike Sekowsky (p), and Dick Giordano (i). "Wonder Woman's Last Battle." *Wonder Woman* #179 (November–December 1968), DC Comics.

34 Steve Englehart (w), Alan Lee Weiss (p), and Al Milgrom (i). "Shang-Chi, Master of Kung Fu." *Deadly Hands of Kung Fu* #2 (June 1974), Marvel Comics.

35 Jim Shooter (w, p) and Sheldon Moldoff (i). "One of Us is a Traitor!" *Adventure Comics* #346 (July 1966), DC Comics.

36 Paul Levitz (w), Ric Estrada (p), and Joe Staton (i). "My World Begins in Yesterday!" *Karate Kid* #1 (March–April 1976), DC Comics.

37 "The Story Behind the Story" [Column]. *Karate Kid* #1 (March–April 1976), DC Comics.

38 "Missives to the Master" [Letters column]. *Master of Kung Fu* #18 (June 1974), Marvel Comics. *Yang*, printed by Charlton Comics, was set at the turn of the century, and is filled with clichés: children refer to their parents as "honorable fathers," or, if their intentions were less-than-honorable, they were at least honest about it. Yin calls her dad "master of evil" who sells his countrymen to slavers building railroads in America. The hero is a priest-turn-fighter, schooled in "karate" and the other Oriental martial arts. See Joe Gill (w) and Warren Sattler (a). "The Slave." *Yang* #1 (November 1973), Charlton Comics.

39 Steve Englehart (w), Paul Gulacy (p), and Al Milgrom (i). "Retreat." *Master of Kung Fu* #19 (August 1974), Marvel Comics.

40 "Missives to the Master" [Letters column]. *Master of Kung Fu* #19 (August 1974), Marvel Comics.

41 Doug Moench (w), Jim Craig (p), and John Tartaglione (i). "Glass Orchids." *Master of Kung Fu* #61 (February 1978), Marvel Comics.

42 Doug Moench (w), Mike Zeck (p), and Gene Day (i). "Smoke, Beads, and Blood." *Master of Kung Fu* #76 (May 1979), Marvel Comics.

43 Doug Moench (w), Mike Zeck (p), and Gene Day (i). "The Pride of the Leopards." *Master of Kung Fu* #80 (September 1979), Marvel Comics.

44 Alan Zelenetz (w), William Johnson (p), Alan Kupperberg (a), and Mike Mignola (i). "Atonement." *Master of Kung Fu* #125 (June 1983), Marvel Comics.
45 Tom Wolfe, "Bok Gooi, Hok Gooi and T'ang Jen: or, Why There is not National Association for the Advancement of Chinese Americans," *New York Magazine*, September 27, 1971, 35.
46 David Shih, "The Color of Fu-Manchu: Orientalist Method in the Novels of Sax Rohmer," *The Journal of Popular Culture* 42, no. 2 (2009): 304–317.

CHAPTER NINE

"Paralysis and Stagnation and Drift"

America's Malaise as Demonstrated in Comic Books of the 1970s

Matthew Pustz

The military defeat in Vietnam, "stagflation," the Arab oil embargo, Watergate, and even the kidnapping of Patty Hearst led many Americans in the 1970s to believe that their country was on a downward slide. Historian and cultural critic Christopher Lasch famously identified this "mood of pessimism" in his best-selling book *The Culture of Narcissism: American Life in an Age of Diminishing Expectations* (1979), arguing that this feeling had permeated American society.[1]

Films from the 1970s are filled with strong expressions of this sense of despair, but another, perhaps unexpected place to find this dark attitude is in the pages of mainstream comic books of this period. For example, a story in the first issue of the Marvel humor comic *Spoof* illustrates this gloomy attitude. The basic plot of the story involves a television program called "Darn Shadows" (a parody of the horror-themed soap opera *Dark Shadows*) that is struggling in the ratings. Apparently, another channel is showing something scarier that is taking away the program's audience. At the end of the story, we find out that the show that is scaring people so much is . . . the news. An oversized panel shows Walter Cronkite reading the news as depressing, frightening headlines float around his head.[2] Even advertisements in comic books of the 1970s sometimes reflected this sense of despair. A Twinkies ad from 1977 featuring Iron Man pits the superhero against Kwirkegard, "a philosophically sinister villain." When he aims his "existential depression ray" at New York City's water supply, he makes the entire population of the city feel so dejected that they cannot get out of bed the next morning. Although Iron Man announces that he is "too sad even to fight," he manages to pull himself together so that he can motivate an army of Twinkie-eating kids to help him defeat Kwirkegard.[3]

This feeling of doom and despair had become a common theme in comic books of the 1970s. In this way, they illustrate how Americans of this decade came to suffer from "malaise," a mood that was identified as one of the major problems of the period by writers like Lasch. The broad themes of malaise were outlined by President Jimmy Carter in his nationally-broadcast, prime-time address of July 15, 1979. The original purpose of the speech was to talk about the energy crisis, but after months of study and research Carter was convinced that America was suffering from a bigger, more profound problem that was ultimately spiritual or psychological in nature. Carter would identify this problem as a "crisis of confidence." The United States, he explained, was faced with a "fundamental threat to American democracy," a threat that "strikes at the very heart and soul and spirit of our national will."[4]

Carter listed five major symptoms of this crisis. First, he explained that Americans have lost faith in their ability to have a positive impact on the government. They essentially feel powerless to initiate change or stop the country's downward spiral. Second, Americans have diminished expectations for the future, the President argued, claiming that, "For the first time in the history of our country, a majority of our people believes that the next five years will be worse than the past five years." Another symptom, Carter explained, was that "too many of us now tend to worship self-indulgence and consumption. Human identity is no longer defined by what one does, but by what one owns." Making matters worse was that, on some level, Americans realized that buying things didn't make them happy and certainly did not "satisfy our longing for meaning." Finally, Carter suggested that Americans had lost faith in government specifically and had developed a general distrust of all manner of institutions, including churches, schools, and the news media. "This is not a message of happiness or reassurance," the President concluded, "but it is the truth and it is a warning."

President Carter blamed this crisis on forces beyond the control of his administration. He told Americans that "these changes did not happen overnight. They've come upon us gradually over the last generation, years that were filled with shocks and tragedy." The assassinations of the 1960s rocked Americans' faith in democracy and their faith in themselves, he explained. The Vietnam War raised doubts about the nation's military invincibility. Watergate made Americans doubt the integrity of political leaders. Stagflation (the combination of high inflation and high unemployment) led to doubts about the American dream, while the energy crisis made Americans realize that the nation's natural resources were limited. Looking back at the decade, two additional causes for this "crisis of confidence" are clear. First, Americans spent much of the decade reeling from problem after problem; at times, the crises seemed never-ending and impossible to solve. Beyond that, many Americans—especially by 1979—were frustrated with the Carter administration and its often ineffectual leadership style. This would especially be demonstrated in the months that followed the speech as the President struggled to address the Iran hostage crisis confidently and effectively.[5]

Evidence for this sense of malaise can be found throughout comic books of the 1970s. Malaise-themed stories, starring well-known characters like Superman and the Hulk as well as more obscure heroes like Deathlok, Machine Man, and the Inhumans, demonstrate that President Carter was right, that America was suffering from a "crisis of confidence," but also that the malaise he identified was deeper and more pervasive than he imagined, lasting throughout the decade. We can see America's malaise demonstrated in the comic books of the 1970s in four primary ways. First, superheroes in this period frequently suffered from their own "crisis of confidence" and often ended up abandoning their costumed secret identities. Second, it was common to find superheroes suffering from a lack of direction—much like Americans who were uncertain about the future. Third, superheroes in the 1970s were frequently faced with overwhelming power, problems and threats that seemed impossible to overcome. The final demonstration of malaise is personified by superheroes who lost their powers—clearly, a connection to the Americans who felt like their power to change the government or control their own little part of the world had also disappeared.

According to President Carter, the central problem of the "paralysis and stagnation and drift" that would define the 1970s was a profound "crisis of confidence" that caused Americans to lose hope for the future. Superheroes suffered from the same problem throughout this decade. Some heroes thought about quitting as a response to threats that were too big to overcome. For example, the Atlas Comics hero Phoenix decides that the alien invasion he's been trying to prevent is simply too much for him to stop. "Now there's nothing left to fight for!" he thinks to himself. "No matter how many of the aliens I kill, thousands more appear to take their place! No power on Earth can stop them!"[6] As a result, he gives up on the human race—"doomed from the day it first drew breath," he explains—and makes a plan to destroy himself.[7] The crisis of confidence suffered by Machine Man is also created by his profound doubts about humanity and especially its fearful reaction to him. One night while patrolling the city, he encounters one act of violence and cruelty after another, all motivated by money, and so he wonders about the flaw in human nature that apparently causes people to value pieces of paper over life. He shouts, "Everywhere there is greed and hatred. Everywhere grow monuments to man's inhumanity to his fellow man!"[8] Later, he wonders why he should even bother trying help.

"Humans are greedy. They hunger for power. Mankind not only doesn't deserve my help, they don't even want it!"[9]

Other heroes question their role because of mistakes they have made. After being involved in a battle that destroyed an innocent family's house, Daredevil decides in issue #128 of his own title to give up his costumed identity because he worries that he is hurting people more than helping them.[10] Of course, he puts the costume back on by the end of the issue, but he's plagued by the same problem a few years later when his girlfriend blames her father's suicide on Daredevil. So, once again, he decides that he will hang up his mask and tights.[11] Iron Man's mistake is alcoholism, and it causes a serious crisis of confidence in Tony Stark. In fact, he realizes that all of his problems have been caused ultimately not by some outside force or supervillain but rather by himself. As a result, he decides to stop being Tony Stark to focus on his Iron Man identity, but this doesn't work out right either as he puts lives at risk because he's often drunk. "Now I can't even make being a superhero work!" he cries. "And what does that leave?"[12]

The most sustained crises of confidence come about because of more specific trauma. While the Teen Titans are guarding Dr. Arthur Swenson, a Nobel Peace Prize winner and supposedly "the most important man in the world," he is assassinated. The young superheroes believe that it's their fault and hence begin to doubt their role as crime-fighters. When asked to sign an autograph for a young fan, for example, Kid Flash can't do it. "I'm not a superhero anymore," he explains. "I don't deserve to be!"[13] Even the elder heroes of the Justice League blame them and Superman demands that "this reckless use of your powers requires a responsible rectification! You must be your own judge and jury!"[14] And so the Titans decide to give up their superhero identities and join up with the mysterious Mr. Jupiter, a rich philanthropist who is putting together a secret project "to combat the new problems of tomorrow."[15] On the cover of the next issue, Wonder Girl announces, "We . . . we will never wear our uniforms again!"[16] Eventually, they do put their costumes back on, but only for special situations where the fate of the world hangs in the balance. The cause of the Titans' crisis of confidence was identified by President Carter in his malaise speech as the feeling of hopelessness that resulted from the assassinations of Martin Luther King Jr. and Robert Kennedy in 1968. The murder of Dr. Swenson is clearly meant to remind readers of these events.

The most significant crisis of confidence is also tied to another event mentioned by Carter: Watergate. The Secret Empire storyline in *Captain America* during 1973 and 1974 is filled with allusions to Richard Nixon, so when the star-spangled hero unmasks the group's leader who proceeds to commit suicide rather than be taken into custody, readers clearly understood that he was supposed to be the former president. Captions explain the effect of this on Captain America: "A man can change in a flicker of time. This man trusted the country of his birth. He saw its flaws, but trusted in its basic framework, its stated goals, its long-term virtue. Trusted. This man now is crushed inside. Like millions of other Americans, each in his own way, he had seen his trust mocked! And this man is Captain America!"[17] In response, he feels that he must give up his costumed identity, in part because he has "seen everything Captain America fought for become a cynical sham!"[18]

Captain America's crisis continued for another handful of issues until he put his traditional costume back on once again. The idea of "Captain America," he realizes, represents the hopes and aspirations of America, not the reality of what the government and politicians do. He realizes that it's his job to try to make sure that the reality of life in the United States matches up with these ideals. Captain America explains, "If I paid more attention to the way American reality differed from the American dream, if I hadn't gone around thinking the things I believe in were thirty years out of date, then I might have uncovered Number One [the leader of the Secret Empire] and stopped him before it was too late! I guess what I'm saying is there has to be somebody who'll fight for the dream, against any foe, somebody who'll do the job I started—right!"[19] His resolution implies that Watergate didn't totally destroy Captain America's (and Americans') confidence in the United States, but rather that it reminded citizens how fragile the country and its ideals really are. There's a sense here that having a crisis of confidence like this can ultimately be productive.

Generally, though, when President Carter talked about malaise, it wasn't a positive experience. Particularly troubling was America's loss of direction or purpose. Americans simply didn't quite know where their country was headed in the 1970s. This national lack of direction was depicted in an extended allegory in the pages of Marvel's *Inhumans*. Originally introduced in *The Fantastic Four*, the Inhumans are the ruling family of a city of superpowered individuals, the genetic structure of their ancestors having been manipulated by aliens to create a race of warriors. After a series of attacks on their capital city, Black Bolt, the king of the Inhumans, decides to travel into space with the rest of the royal family to find a new, more peaceful world to call home. After crashing on an apparently lifeless planet, the group is shocked to encounter a huge, robotic beetle that houses a complete, mobile city. The beetle expels torrents of water to flatten a path in the sandy soil so that it can make its way to the next watering hole, which will allow it to have enough water to get to another watering hole, and so on. The beetle-city is clearly meant to be a metaphor for the directionless state of affairs in the United States. Its empty progress reflects the feelings of many Americans that their country was on a road to nowhere. The criticism that the comic seems to be leveling against this ideology of "progress" comes out even stronger when the leaders of the city decide to respond to protests against the government by amputating one of the beetle's legs that housed the "squalor section" where the protesters lived. Without that leg, though, the beetle-city ends up moving in circles, making their belief in progress even more pointless. The final panels of the story show the beetle's repetitive path through the dust—and perhaps America's repetitive path, too.[20]

This broad focus on the problems of society is rare, though, in the comic books of the 1970s. It's much more common to find malaise-themed comics that focus on individual heroes who have lost their bearings and have become aimless and lost. The Hulk, for example, spent much of the 1970s suffering from this symptom of malaise. In *Secret Identity Crisis: Comic Books and the Unmasking of Cold War America* (2009), Matthew J. Costello describes the character as having "retreated into the privacy of his alienation in the early 1970s."[21] This is different than what the character experienced in the 1960s when, although he was often hounded by the military, the Hulk maintained a certain amount of control and agency. For years during the heart of the 1970s, though, he wanders aimlessly, battles seemingly random enemies, and experiences existential doubt. Sometimes, after a battle, the Hulk is literally thrown to some new, arbitrary location where, inevitably, there is someone or something to fight. For example, a rocket carrying the Hulk home after a battle on another planet is shot down, randomly crashing in Appalachia where he is forced to battle the Missing Link.[22] Later, after another adventure in space, Hulk randomly returns to earth in a place called "Loch Fear" where he must inevitably battle the local monster.[23] After helping to save Glenn Talbot, Hulk is thrown not just into a random location but rather into a random universe, this time one that looks like something out of a sword-and-sorcery comic.[24] Sometimes it's the Hulk himself who is traveling without direction or purpose. After defeating the Missing Link, he haphazardly leaps to Canada where he intervenes in a battle between Wendigo and Wolverine. A caption explains, "Like a great green billiard ball, the Hulk caroms aimlessly across the countryside."[25]

Frequently during this period, the Hulk's actions simply lack purpose. A caption in issue #183 explains, "Why [does the Hulk save the train that he began to destroy]? That's not an easy question to answer, friend. Reflex action? Instinct, perhaps? Some small portion of the man inside him momentarily rising to the surface? Who can truly say? Certainly not the Hulk."[26] The 1970s version of the Hulk is a hero filled with anguish and questions. He doesn't understand the world and why things happen the way that they do. Hulk expresses his confusion in, among other places, the opening pages of issue #219: "Why must Hulk always lose the ones Hulk cares for? Why must Hulk always be alone? Why? Why? Bah! Why does Hulk even bother asking? Maybe Hulk is better off alone! Hulk is tired of asking stupid questions, tired of smashing stupid rock. Hulk is tired of everything!"[27]

Fortunately, Hulk does get a brief reprieve in issue #190 during a story that emphasizes the deep malaise suffered by the hero during the 1970s.

The action begins in a typical way, with the Hulk battling the Soviet army. Suddenly, he spots a rainbow. There, he finds a gold-skinned man named Glorian who promises to take Hulk to a better place, where he can be at peace, where he can feel at home. A caption explains, "Home: the word fills the emerald behemoth with a strange sense of serenity. Since the day of his gamma-ray-spawned 'birth,' he has sought this nebulous place called home. Maybe this time he will actually find it!"[28] Glorian takes the Hulk to a world filled with beauty—"pretty flowers, pretty birds, pretty sky," as Hulk describes it[29]—and with his friends: the hobo Crackajack Jackson and Jarella, the hero's long-lost love. They help to make the Hulk happy, but it's his sense of control in this paradise that's more important. His feeling of malaise is relieved; he's content and his aimless, restless wandering looks to be over. Tragically, though, Hulk's paradise is violated by the Toadmen, an alien race looking for slaves. As he looks out the window of the spaceship taking the defeated Hulk to the Toadmen's home world, he knows what he's lost. "The single tear that tracks the monster's cheek goes unnoticed by all," a caption explains.[30] The Hulk's story in the 1970s—that of a powerful figure who responds to his malaise with confusion, anger, and sometimes sorrow—illustrates some of the effects of malaise plaguing American society more generally.

We can see other effects of malaise in the decade's ultimate aimless hero, Deathlok. Introduced in Marvel's *Astonishing Tales* in 1974, Deathlok is a cyborg assassin created out of the body of a deceased soldier named Luther Manning. A computer has been implanted in Manning's skull, making Deathlok the victim of manipulation that goes way beyond that suffered by the Hulk. He is literally programmed, with limitations put on his behavior by the government scientists who created him. The series begins with Deathlok's attempt to circumvent this programming and put his original life back together. He quickly finds out that this is, of course, impossible. When he finds his wife, she's disgusted by him and his decaying flesh. More importantly, she doesn't even recognize him as Luther Manning anymore. He comes to the conclusion that suicide is the only way out, but the computer in his brain won't let him kill himself.[31]

Later, after battling cannibals and robot tanks in his apocalyptic future world, Deathlok comes to the conclusion that all of his actions have been manipulated. "I feel like I've been had," he explains to the computer in his brain. "Like all along we been fighting the wrong war—a kind of hopeless, gut-stinkin' puppet war!"[32] Later, even after he has defeated the man who turned him into a cyborg, the manipulations of Deathlok continue. Eventually, he shows up in 1970s where he's turned into a pawn of two villains, the Fixer and Mentallo, who want to sell Deathlok's services as an assassin to various criminal or terrorist organizations. As a demonstration, they program him to shoot Jimmy Carter during his inauguration. Deathlok doesn't want to do this, but he has no choice—he's been programmed again.

Figure 9.1 Deathlok personifies the malaise of the 1970s. Marv Wolfman (w), Ron Wilson (p), and Pablo Marcos (i). "Day of the Demolisher!" *Marvel Two-in-One* #27 (May 1977), Marvel Comics, 15. Deathlok, © and ™ Marvel Entertainment, LLC. All rights reserved; images used with permission.

He angrily explains the situation, "I'm stuck in this dead carcass and I'm still bein' forced to do things I don't wanna do—still bein' controlled by someone other'n me"[33] (see Figure 9.1). A few years later, in Deathlok's final appearance for the decade, he can no longer question his programming as his humanity has been obliterated. While attacking a secret government installation, he explains, "Humanity is a meaningless concept. This unit is now totally automated . . . programming is all."[34] Visually, we can see that his humanity has been taken away, his half-human head replaced by something that is completely cybernetic. In the person of Deathlok, we can see other effects of malaise: dehumanization, loss of choice, reluctant acceptance of manipulation, loss of power, and the disappearance of free will.

One of the most important elements of malaise was this feeling of powerlessness, and this was demonstrated in two different ways in the comic books of the 1970s. First, superheroes frequently were faced with overwhelmingly powerful adversaries who they had little hope in defeating. In some ways, this is not surprising, given the conventions of the superhero genre. To build drama, writers have frequently created threats for the heroes that have seemed impossible to overcome. But in the 1970s, the forces that superheroes had to deal with were often of another magnitude entirely. One of the best examples of this can be found in the work of Jack Kirby, where the powerlessness of humanity was a central theme of two long story-lines that he orchestrated during the 1970s. The Fourth

World titles—*The New Gods, Mister Miracle, The Forever People,* and *Superman's Pal, Jimmy Olsen*—functioned together as a single, interlocking narrative about an eternal battle between Good (personified by the deities of New Genesis) and Evil (led by the nearly omnipotent Darkseid). Human beings were part of this battle, but only really as pawns to be manipulated by both sides. The action of the four series was driven by Darkseid's search for the Anti-Life Equation, a formula hidden in the minds of human beings which supposedly had the power to destroy the universe. Throughout the series, it seemed inevitable that Darkseid would acquire the secret. The humans in the story lacked the power to resist Darkseid and the citizens of New Genesis often seemed to be too constrained by their dedication to "good" to effectively respond to their counterpart's aggressive quest.[35] In fact, when the series resumed in the late 1970s without Kirby, Darkseid has acquired the equation and the New Gods have apparently given up. "All hope is lost," announces Highfather Izaya. "The fate of the universe is sealed."[36]

A few years later, while at Marvel, Kirby introduced more concepts that would render humanity irrelevant. *The Eternals* was a series that created an entirely new cosmology based on the visitation of the Earth by a group of god-like beings called Celestials. Their experiments in the distant past resulted in the creation of three intelligent species: the Eternals, a race of super-powered immortals, the Deviants, a biologically unstable monster race, and human beings. The humans don't know about this history, they certainly aren't aware of the age-old conflict between the Eternals and the Deviants, and they are oblivious to the ways in which they have been manipulated by both sides. As the story begins, we learn that the Celestials are returning to judge whether their experiment has been a success or a failure. The few humans who learn the truth of their origins are completely powerless to stop this evaluation, but so are both the Eternals and the Deviants. The Celestials are so powerful that they make even god-like beings completely ineffectual. A caption explains that they "tower over time itself."[37] Kirby's art, with magnificent, outrageous mystical machines looming over both humans and Eternals in double-page spreads, helps to create this mood of human insignificance. In light of the Celestials, nothing else in the world really matters. In Kirby's *Eternals*, human beings are completely powerless.

One of the most vivid depictions of coping with overwhelming power came near the end of the decade in the pages of *The Avengers*. Known among fans as the Korvac Saga, this 11-issue long epic involves three separate plots. The first focuses on the search for a villain named Korvac who has traveled back in time to kill the past-self of a member of the Guardians of the Galaxy. Meanwhile, the Avengers are mysteriously disappearing. At the same time, a government agent named Henry Peter Gyrich appears at the group's headquarters to evaluate its security measures. If he is not pleased, he has the power to essentially shut down the government-funded team. Each one of these storylines demonstrates a different aspect of overwhelming power. Gyrich eventually decides that the Avengers are sloppy when it comes to government secrets and, because of this, he revokes their security clearance. The group is powerless to stop him; they cannot touch him because of his government affiliation. It is also powerless to prevent the disappearances which we soon learn are being engineered by an Elder of the Universe named the Collector who wants to protect the Avengers so he can use them in a battle with a cosmic entity called the Enemy. The heroes are also unable to stop Korvac from consolidating his power through his transformation into a being of perhaps universal omnipotence.

It is this transformed Korvac—now calling himself Michael and living in the Forest Hills Gardens neighborhood of Queens—that has become the ultimate overwhelming power that the Avengers must face. When the heroes finally confront Michael and find out that he's the Enemy that the Collector was warning them about, they are faced with a battle where they hardly stand a chance. Michael sees himself as "the hope of the universe;" he believes that he is the being that will bring order to the chaos of reality—and he might have the power to do that.[38] The heroes attack, but Michael proceeds to kill one Avenger after another. Even gods like Thor and Hercules can't stand up to him. "You are but ants," he explains, "and I am a colossus!"[39] Despite this, the Avengers manage to hurt Michael, and he eventually looks to his mate Carina for reassurance and love. But she hesitates, and Michael is heart-broken and allows himself to be killed. Now filled with rage, Carina lashes out at Iron Man, Vision, and the Guardian of the Galaxy named Starhawk, murdering all of them before Thor is finally able to defeat her.

The only other survivor of the battle is Moondragon, and her psychic powers reveal the tragedy of the battle. She knows that the Avengers and their allies were in the wrong. Michael, she explains, "was not evil! He sought not to rule us, nor even to interfere with our madness! He wished only to free us from the capricious whims of Eternity!"[40] The Avengers are to blame, she explains, for the destruction of the one force that could have brought order, justice, and fairness to the universe. In fact, so benevolent was Michael that when he died he allowed his life force to enter the Avengers and restore them to life. The sense of malaise here is strong, as the Avengers were virtually powerless in a battle that (according to Moondragon) they should not have been fighting in the first place. Ultimately, the power that should have emerged victorious was defeated by the Avengers' inability to understand the love and benevolence that Michael represented. Being faced with overwhelming power is not enough here; the team is also faced with ideas and implications that it could not hope to fathom because the perspective of Michael was literally beyond their comprehension. In many ways, this is what malaise was all about: a feeling of being powerless in the face of change while also not really understanding the forces that were transforming the world.

This feeling of powerlessness is also manifested in stories that showed superheroes losing their powers. While this is a standard plotline for the superhero genre, this trope seemed to happen with a great deal of frequency and prominence in the 1970s. Some of the most well-known superheroes of the period spent significant amounts of time with reduced powers or with no powers whatsoever. For example, Wonder Woman willingly gave up her powers in the late 1960s and spent much of the early 1970s (from issue #178 to #203) as simply Diana Prince, martial artist and clothing boutique owner. In *Adventure Comics* #402, Supergirl was given a drug that, for the next few years, would unpredictably take away her powers for seemingly random amounts of time. After a battle with the Black Widow, Spider-Man thinks that he's losing his powers; not surprisingly, this leads him to an existential crisis. "After all these years, when I've secretly wished I could be normal like everyone else, now that there's a chance of my wish coming true, is that what I'm really afraid of?" he asks himself.[41]

As with the Spider-Man story, most instances of power loss are filled with anxiety as the heroes begin to doubt their usefulness as they become weaker. This, of course, is a big part of malaise. As Americans came to the conclusion that they didn't really have the power necessary to effect political change in a meaningful way, they came to have doubts about the potential of democracy to solve their nation's problems. When they came to see that the United States didn't have the power to control what happened in the Middle East or didn't have the power to win the war in Vietnam, Americans came to have serious doubts about America's place in the world. The Fantastic Four seemed to be particularly susceptible to this kind of anxiety. When Reed Richards comes to the conclusion that he's losing his stretching powers, he reacts with shame and fear. He hangs his head as he leaves the training room where he confirmed the truth of his condition to himself. In the next panel, his hand is over his face as he worries what this could mean to him and his team. "If that had been a real battle in there, I might have failed the others at a crucial moment—put their lives in danger, as well. I must tell them—tell them everything—but have I courage enough for that?"[42]

Two years later, when Mr. Fantastic's stretching power finally does give out, Reed becomes depressed, and it takes his wife, the Invisible Girl, to snap him out of it. "Listen, mister," she explains, "if your stretching powers were all you contributed to the FF we could replace you with a rubber band, but that's not true . . . and you know it!"[43] This does not alleviate Mr. Fantastic's anxiety, though, and his doubts about his place on the team linger, especially once his body gets taken over by the Molecule Man. "I can't let you continue risking your lives because of me, and I can't keep on being a fifth wheel!" he explains to his colleagues as he announces that he's quitting the team.[44] This, of course, is the end of the Fantastic Four—or at least until Reed is able to get his stretching powers back in issue #197.

Another long storyline focuses on the reduction of Superman's powers. The story begins in *Superman* #233 when a scientist performs an experiment that turns all the Kryptonite on Earth into iron. A side-effect of the experiment creates a weird Superman doppelgänger made out of sand; the double has somehow managed to siphon away some of Superman's powers. He first encounters the effects of this when his x-ray vision won't penetrate the hull of an airplane. Later, when he's passing over the site of the experiment, Superman feels "dizzy, exhausted, like the strength is being drawn from my limbs!"[45] Over the course of the next ten issues, Superman must come to terms with this loss of power and, in a way, he learns how Americans can come to accept and even value the country's diminished influence.

First, though, Superman's loss of power makes him feel overwhelmed. For example, in issue #237, he contracts a space disease, Lois Lane is kidnapped by South American rebels, a horde of army ants is getting ready to attack a small town, and his duplicate is still running around free. "So many problems," he says to himself. "I can't think where to begin!"[46] Later, he actually fails in his attempt to stop a burning building from collapsing, and for the first time people begin criticizing him. They're making jokes and poking fun at his rapidly diminishing super powers. Here we see Superman's second reaction to powerlessness: bitterness. "So soon, they've forgotten all I've done . . . my years of service . . . of sacrifice!" he explains. "I guess I'm being bitter—and I don't care! I've a right to bitterness . . . no man has a better right!"[47] Fortunately, I-Ching, the blind Asian man who helped Wonder Woman with her loss of powers, shows up to help Superman cope with his diminished abilities. At first, Superman is excited about the challenge of not having powers, but he soon changes his mind and decides that he wants to give up. I-Ching is able to convince him that this would be the coward's way out. Eventually, a confrontation with his duplicate convinces Superman that it's good for him to have powers and abilities that are less than what he is used to. "I've seen the dangers [of] having too much power . . . I am human, I can make mistakes! I don't want—or need—more [power]," he explains.[48]

Coming in 1971, before Watergate and before the Vietnam War ended in defeat for the United States, Superman's acceptance of this loss of power prefigures an important trend of the decade. "Alongside all the disco, the kidnapped heiresses, and the macramé," historian Rick Perlstein explains, "another keynote of 1970s culture was something quite more mature: a willingness to acknowledge that America might no longer be invincible, and that any realistic assessment of how we can prosper and thrive in the future had to reckon with that hard-won lesson."[49] Like Americans in that brief moment when they seemed to be willing to accept limits, Superman comes to a realization that being less powerful is a good thing, in part because it will give him more challenges and hence more sense of accomplishment, but mostly because it will prevent any sort of abuse of power. But comic book fans and writers rejected this version of a diminished Superman. The versions of Superman that appeared in other DC titles of the time— *Action Comics, World's Finest,* and *Justice League of America*—was just as powerful as always. More importantly, even in *Superman,* his reduction of power was forgotten once writer Denny O'Neil left the book. This, too, prefigures a trend that would characterize much of the 1970s: Americans' anger and resentment over their loss of both personal and national power. Americans did not especially like the limits of the age of malaise, even if they may have been more realistic and perhaps even better for the country and its people. The rejection of the malaise-influenced, diminished Superman helps to explain why the country would eventually reject President Carter— the prophet and product of limited expectations and limited power—for Ronald Reagan, a political personality who represented a rejection of those limitations and promised to return the United States to its "rightful" place in the world.

The pervasive sense of malaise in the 1970s was so powerful that dozens of superheroes of the period had to overcome its challenges. As the Superman storyline suggests, the ways in which malaise was resolved in comic books can give us some insight into how malaise was resolved in the real world. For example, at the end of the 1970s, the Fantastic Four (with the exception of the Human Torch) began to lose their powers at an accelerated rate after being bombarded by a Skrull weapon that caused rapid aging. Once the team got back to Earth, it was up to Johnny Storm to save them. With the help of a now-elderly Reed, Johnny is able to construct a machine that is supposed to restore them to their proper ages and rejuvenate their super powers. But it does more than that. As Mr. Fantastic explains to the Torch, "Not only did you reverse the Skrull aging ray, somehow you've almost made us younger than before—younger, stronger, more vital than ever!"[50] The fact that this issue was cover dated January 1980 is not insignificant. Many people hoped that the transition from the 1970s to the 1980s would involve shifting from a worn-out, weakened, malaise-ridden decade to one that, like the Fantastic Four, would be shiny and new, without the doubts of the previous 10 years but also almost magically more powerful and more vigorous than the years that had come before.

Unfortunately, fixing the problems of America—including reliance on foreign oil, economic and fiscal changes that were pushing manufacturing jobs out of the United States, and political conflicts over values and culture—was not going to be as simple as what the Human Torch does to save his teammates. But that's what many Americans wanted, and that's one reason why Ronald Reagan, a candidate who exuded optimism and confidence in America, a candidate who seemed unable to suffer from malaise or any kind of crisis of confidence, would be elected in 1980 to lead this transformation out of malaise and into something very different.

Notes

1 Christopher Lasch, *The Culture of Narcissism: American Life in an Age of Diminishing Expectations* (New York: Warner Books, 1979), 17.
2 Roy Thomas (w) and Marie Severin (a). "Darn Shadows!" *Spoof* #1 (October 1970), Marvel Comics, 6.
3 "Iron Man in 'City Crisis'" (advertisement). Amazing Spider-Man #166 (March 1977), Marvel Comics, 29.
4 President Carter's malaise speech is reprinted in a variety of places, including William H. Chafe, Harvard Sitkoff, and Beth Bailey, eds, *A History of Our Time: Readings on Postwar America* (New York: Oxford University Press, 2008), 325–330. All quotes of the speech come from this version.
5 For a detailed examination of the malaise speech and its reception, see Kevin Mattson, *"What the Heck Are You Up To, Mr. President?": Jimmy Carter, America's "Malaise," and the Speech That Should Have Changed the Country* (New York: Bloomsbury, 2009).
6 Gary Friedrich (w), Ric Estrada (p), and Frank Giacoia (i). "A Man for All Centuries!" *Phoenix* #4 (October 1975), Atlas Comics, 2.
7 Ibid., 3.
8 Marv Wolfman (w) and Steve Ditko (a). "Where Walk the Gods!" *Machine Man* #12 (December 1979), Marvel Comics, 7.
9 Ibid., 11.
10 Marv Wolfman (w), Bob Brown (p), and Klaus Janson (i). "Death Stalks the Stairway to the Stars!" *Daredevil* #128 (December 1975), Marvel Comics, 2.
11 Roger McKenzie (w), Gil Kane (9), and Klaus Janson (i). "Crisis!" *Daredevil* #151 (March 1978), Marvel Comics, 10.
12 David Michelinie (w), John Romita Jr. (p), and Bob Layton (i). "Demon in a Bottle," *Iron Man* #128 (November 1979), Marvel Comics, 6.
13 Bob Kanigher (w) and Nick Cardy (a). "The Titans Kill a Saint?" *Teen Titans* #25 (February 1970), DC Comics, 5.
14 Ibid, 18.
15 Ibid., 20.
16 Nick Cardy (a). "A Penny for a Black Star." *Teen Titans* #26 (April 1970), DC Comics, cover.
17 Steve Englehart (w), Sal Buscema (p), and Vince Colletta (i). ". . . Before the Dawn!" *Captain America* #175 (July 1974), Marvel Comics, 32.
18 Steve Englehart (w), Sal Buscema (p), and Vince Colletta (i). "Captain America Must Die!" *Captain America* #176 (August 1974), Marvel Comics, 32.
19 Steve Englehart (w), Frank Robbins (p), and Frank Giacoia (i). "Nomad: No More!" *Captain America* #183 (March 1975), Marvel Comics, 31.
20 Doug Moench (w), Gil Kane (p), and Don Perlin (i). "A Trip to the Doom!" *Inhumans* #7 (October 1976), Marvel Comics, 6.

21 Matthew J. Costello, *Secret Identity Crisis: Comic Books and the Unmasking of Cold War America* (New York & London: Continuum, 2009), 146.

22 Len Wein (w), Herb Trimpe (p), and Jack Abel (i). "Re-Enter: the Missing Link!" *Incredible Hulk* #179 (September 1974), Marvel Comics.

23 Len Wein (w), Herb Trimpe (p), and Joe Staton (i). "The Lurker Beneath Loch Fear!" *Incredible Hulk* #192 (October 1975), Marvel Comics.

24 Len Wein (w), Sal Buscema (p), and Joe Staton (i). "The Sword and the Sorcerer!" *Incredible Hulk* #201 (July 1976), Marvel Comics.

25 Len Wein (w), Herb Trimpe (p), and Jack Abel (i). "And the Wind Howls . . . Wendigo!" *Incredible Hulk* #180 (October 1974), Marvel Comics.

26 Len Wein (w) and Herb Trimpe (a). "Fury at 50,000 Volts!" *Incredible Hulk* #183 (January 1975), Marvel Comics, 3.

27 Len Wein (w), Sal Buscema (p), and Ernie Chan (i). "No Man Is An Island!" *Incredible Hulk* #219 (January 1978), Marvel Comics, 1–2.

28 Len Wein (w), Herb Trimpe (p), and Marie Severin (i). "The Man Who Came Down On a Rainbow!" *Incredible Hulk* #190 (August 1975), Marvel Comics, 11.

29 Ibid., 18.

30 Ibid., 31.

31 Rich Buckler (w, p) and Pablo Marcos (i). "Dead Reckoning!" *Astonishing Tales* #27 (December 1974), Marvel Comics, 32.

32 Bill Mantlo (w), Rich Buckler (p), and Klaus Janson (i). "Reflections in a Crimson Eye!" *Astonishing Tales* #33 (January 1976), Marvel Comics, 30.

33 Marv Wolfman (w), Ron Wilson (p), and Pablo Marcos (i). "Day of the Demolisher!" *Marvel Two-in-One* #27 (May 1977), Marvel Comics, 15.

34 Mark Gruenwald (w), Ralph Macchio (w), John Byrne (p), and Joe Sinnott (i). "Blood and Bionics." *Marvel Two-in-One* #54 (August 1979), Marvel Comics, 14.

35 Jack Kirby (w, a). *Jack Kirby's New Gods* (New York: DC Comics, 1998). The other Fourth World titles are also collected in similar trade paperback editions.

36 Gerry Conway (w), Don Newton (p), and Dan Adkins (i). "The Secret Within Us . . ." *The New Gods* #19 (August 1978), DC Comics, 6.

37 Jack Kirby (w, p) and John Verpoorten (i). "The Day of the Gods," *Eternals* #1 (July 1976), Marvel Comics, 31.

38 Jim Shooter (w), George Perez (p), and Pablo Marcos (i). "First Blood." *Avengers* #168 (February 1978), Marvel Comics, 15.

39 Jim Shooter (w), Dave Wenzel (p), Pablo Marcos (i), and Ricardo Villamonte (i). "The Hope . . . And the Slaughter!" *Avengers* #177 (November 1978), Marvel Comics, 7.

40 Ibid., 27.

41 Stan Lee (w), John Romita (p), and Jim Mooney (i). "Beware . . . the Black Widow!" *Amazing Spider-Man* #86 (July 1970), Marvel Comics, 19.

42 Roy Thomas (w), Rich Buckler (p), and Joe Sinnott (i). "All the World Wars at Once!" *Fantastic Four* #161 (August 1975), Marvel Comics, 3.

43 Len Wein (w), George Perez (p), and Joe Sinnott (i). "Aftermath: the Eliminator!" *Fantastic Four* #184 (July 1977), Marvel Comics, 11.

44 Len Wein (w), George Perez (p), and Joe Sinnott (i). "The Rampage of Reed Richards!" *Fantastic Four* #188 (November 1977), Marvel Comics, 30.

45 Denny O'Neil (w), Curt Swan (p), and Murphy Anderson (i). "Superman Breaks Loose." *Superman* #233 (January 1971), DC Comics, 13.

46 Denny O'Neil (w), Curt Swan (p), and Murphy Anderson (i). "The Enemy of Earth." *Superman* #237 (May 1971), DC Comics, 8.

47 Denny O'Neil (w), Curt Swan (p), and Dick Giordano (i). "To Save a Superman." *Superman* #240 (July 1971), DC Comics, 6.

48 Denny O'Neil (w), Curt Swan (p), and Murphy Anderson (i). "The Ultimate Battle!" *Superman* #242 (September 1971), DC Comics, 22.

49 Rick Perlstein, "Fact-Free Nation: From Nixon's Dirty Tricksters to James O'Keefe's Video Smears: How Political Lying Became the New Normal," *Mother Jones*, May/June 2011, 26.

50 Marv Wolfman (w), John Byrne (p), and Joe Sinnott (i). ". . . And Then There Was—One!" *Fantastic Four* #214 (January 1980), Marvel Comics, 30.

CHAPTER TEN

The Shopping Malls of Empire

Cultural Fragmentation, the New Media, and Consumerism in Howard Chaykin's *American Flagg!*

Matthew J. Costello

Between 1986 and 1988, Stanford University was engulfed in a controversy concerning its year-long Western Civilization requirement. The Black Student Union charged that the course, which explored central texts in the Western tradition from Genesis to Freud, was racist and sexist. A similar conflict arose at Dartmouth College. This debate about curriculum, which seemed to concern only students and faculty, garnered national attention and generated a heated public debate about the content of civic education. The Reverend Jesse Jackson and U.S. Secretary of Education William Bennett both visited the Stanford campus and publicly contributed to the debate. Bennett had been a lightning rod for debates about "the canon" for most of the decade, serving first as chair of the National Endowment for the Humanities before moving to the Department of Education. The public concern made bestsellers of such unlikely choices as Straussian political philosopher Allan Bloom's *The Closing of the American Mind* and educational theorist E. D. Hirsch's *Cultural Literacy: What Every American Needs to Know*. Ultimately, Stanford altered its Western Civilization requirement to include non-Western writers and encouraged inclusion of "women, minorities and persons of color."[1]

The debate over education was merely one moment in a broader concern with the splintering of American society and culture in the 1980s.

While a renewed patriotic rhetoric was fostered from Washington, where the 1984 re-election campaign of Ronald Reagan announced that it was "morning in America," the public at large was concerned with the breakdown of social order, domestically and globally. An aggressive Cold War posture by the Reagan administration, including vast military expansion, sought to replace the more reactive 1970s policy of détente and demonstrate greater control over world politics. Still, the world seemed uncontrollable. The United States saw increasing violence in the Middle East, had its military driven from Lebanon after a devastating bomb attack, continued to struggle with Hezbollah and Iran over hostages, and fought proxy wars in Central America and real ones in Granada and Panama. The Soviet Union was mired in Afghanistan and seemed to be losing control of Eastern Europe, where a Polish military coup in 1981 failed to block public support for the Solidarity movement. Scholars of international politics during the decade were concerned with the problem of imperial decline.[2]

Domestically, widespread protests against expanding nuclear arsenals and the government's activities in Central America and poor civil rights record demonstrated strong opposition to President Reagan's policies among significant segments of the population. Fears of domestic unrest were fed by dramatic increases in urban violence,[3] fueled by growing income inequality and the new threat posed by crack cocaine. The economy sputtered into the 1980s, saw some growth in mid-decade, and then sputtered out again in recession. Unemployment hit 10.8 percent in 1982 before declining, but household debt expanded rapidly (over 17% between 1980 and 1985), indicating continued cash-strapped households participating in the new materialism of the decade.

This new materialism was one aspect of a retreat into privacy that also included the anti-government sentiment that fueled the 1980 election of Ronald Reagan. "Government is not the solution, government is the problem," declared Reagan in his first inaugural. This message privileging the private over the public resonated with the American mood. Sociologist Robert Bellah and his colleagues noted the weakening of the American language of community. America had become a "society predicated on individual identities and feelings," with little means of even discussing communal institutions.[4] The celebration of private wealth was the most visible sign of this new individualism. Income tax cuts and financial deregulation put more money in the hands of upper class consumers, who displayed their new wealth even while income inequality grew rapidly. "Greed is good," declared Gordon Gekko, Oliver Stone's junk bond trader in the film *Wall Street* (1987). Conspicuous consumption was the goal, whether by newly minted junk bond millionaires, material girls on MTV, or television families such as those on *Dallas* and *Dynasty*. "It is the decade of money fever," wrote Tom Wolfe. "It's almost impossible for people to be free of the burning itch for money. It's a decade not likely to produce heroic figures."[5] All of this indicated that American society, politics, and ideologies were becoming increasingly incoherent.

This fragmentation was reflected in and fostered by the emergence of the new media, largely cable television and the personal computer. In 1981, IBM began selling a PC and CNN began broadcasting; in 1982, MTV launched and, in 1984, Apple released the Macintosh. The new media would provide venues for the dissemination of ideas to specific target audiences, blending news, entertainment, art, and advertising in novel ways. MTV in particular obscured the border between art and commerce to such an extent that some suggested the acronym stood for Money Television.[6] Market segmentation in these media would divide American society.

To understand this incoherent and unbounded American cultural landscape, scholars have increasingly turned to theorists of postmodernism, who argued against overarching order to social and intellectual phenomenon and rejected meta-narratives as discourses of power that obscured the reality that meaning was relative, often determined by one's position in society. Rejecting such totalizing formulas as Marxism, liberalism, or religious concepts of the world, postmodernism could support a view of society as decentered and multicultural, composed of many voices and visions. It could also be a clear target for those who saw such cultural pluralism as evidence of moral relativism and decay.[7]

Into this world of sundered meanings, balkanized societies, and irrelevant politics, Howard Chaykin introduced Reuben Flagg. Flagg was a postmodern hero, mixing celebrity and politics, heroism and hedonism, patriotism and paranoia. A post-imperial video-star become mall cop, Flagg had a patriotic love for a country in which he had never dwelt, and reluctantly and inadvertently fought against the agents of imperial power and postcolonial challengers in an attempt to recreate the America he loved, but had never known. Chaykin offers a satirical view of America in the 1980s by creating a dystopian future in which the United States and Soviet governments have relocated to Mars and the Moon, leaving the Earth to fragment politically and socially. Uniting through a media and commercial conglomerate called the Plex, the former imperial powers continue to exercise nominal authority through their imperial outposts, the Plexmalls, and through their police, the Plexus Rangers. Chaykin's dystopian vision links consumerism, political fragmentation, and reactionary ideologies as products of weakened and corrupted governmental power, casting the 1980s as an era of growing disorder—political, ideological, and social.

American Flagg! reflects, satirizes, and participates in the postmodern fragmentation of meanings of the 1980s. The book ran for 50 issues from 1983 to 1988 and was published by First Comics, a small, independent publisher that catered to the direct market.[8] Unable to command sufficient rack space from magazine sellers to remain profitable, major comic books producers Marvel and DC had begun selling directly to specialty stores in the late 1970s, passing the costs for overproduction on to the retailers. The comic book market thus became divorced or even fragmented off from the larger magazine market, with the target audience a smaller but very dedicated fan base. First Comics was one of the initial upstart companies producing for this newly defined market niche, with *American Flagg!* as its major commercial and critical success of 1983–1985.

Chaykin's approach to storytelling blends genres and crosses boundaries between high and low culture. While offering a sophisticated satire of the 1980s, Chaykin frequently plays for cheap laughs. His names are frequently puns, such as Medea Blitz or Acadia Driftwood, or outright insults, such as John Scheiskopf. While not a superhero comic, the bread and butter of the medium, the book is replete with fanciful costumes and action sequences that one finds in the more mainstream superhero books. The depictions of violence and the frequent sex, however, are excessive compared to more mainstream books, crossing the boundaries of what was considered socially acceptable.

Chaykin's page renderings (see Figure 10.1) offer a visual portrayal of the breakdown of order that is the main theme of his text. He tells his stories through a cascade of bright visuals that deviate from the traditional page layouts of comics. Panels often overlap; the action bleeds from one panel past the gutters and penetrates the next, driving the action at a frenetic pace. Panels are connected by an overlapping index, such as a digital clock counting down to some anticipated event, or by sound effects. A single image may cut through several panels. In this way, the linearity of the narrative is broken, chopped up, and reconfigured by the reader in a myriad of ways, rendering meaning highly variable. Dialogue often stretches throughout a panel, with two different conversations occurring simultaneously, forcing the reader to engage both conversations piecemeal, recombining them in novel ways. Chaykin thus pushes the graphic medium to new levels of complexity, uncommon in its contemporaries. Steve Erickson recalls encountering *American Flagg!* in the context of comics of the 1980s:

> Several things were almost always happening at once, which gave some of the ongoing action and commentary an almost subliminal effect. *American Flagg* was a graphic explosion, and if you were truly intent on catching everything, you wound up reading a given issue three times— but catching everything was probably never the point. Once you learned to give yourself up to the stories' pell-mell pace and not worry about every detail, the comic actually came more into focus; the less you tried to make sense of every single thing, the more the whole thing made sense.[9]

Figure 10.1 Postmodern page layouts. Howard Chaykin (w, a). "Hard Times." *American Flagg!* #1 (October 1983), First Comics, 15. © Howard Chaykin; used with permission.

Chaykin's book partakes of the fragmented social orders and sundered meanings that postmodern methodologies sought to parse. Part of the new media of the 1980s, Chaykin extends the range of graphic storytelling through his page layouts and panel constructions. By blending political satire with lowbrow comedy, adventure comics with excessive sex and violence, Chaykin disrupts boundaries between genres and media. *American Flagg!* is in many ways paradigmatic of the nonlinear, decentered texts of the postmodern turn of the 1980s. But the very fragmentations it embodies—of politics, ideology, and identity—are also the targets of its satire.

American Flagg!: Fractured politics, ideological breakdown, sundered meanings

American Flagg! opens in 2031, 35 years after a collapse of political authority on Earth led the United States government to relocate to Hammerskjold
Center on Mars. The USSR succumbed to an Islamic revolution, leaving an
outpost at Gagaringrad on the moon. Defecting, Gagaringrad becomes a
broadcast center called the Plex. Hammerskjold Center and the Plex unite
to form the Tricentennial Recovery Commission, seeking to return to Earth
by 2076. From Gagaringrad, they beam news and entertainment programming to the Earth, and manage the Plexus Rangers, a global police force,
and the Plexmalls, commercial, media and transport hubs that are the central administrative agencies in all major cities (see Figure 10.2).

Earth, meanwhile, has broken into a collection of new political entities
with some old animosities. The two strongest powers on the planet are
the Brazilian Union of the Americas and the Pan-African Union. Some
local conflicts continue, though, between Zionists and Arabs, and the Irish
Republican Army and (the People's Republic of) Britain. Canada remains
a backwater, not yet brought into the Plex; Havana is the center of illegal
activity in the Western Hemisphere. The United States, having seen the
East coast hit with nuclear weapons and California disappearing in some
undefined crisis, is now based in the Midwest with Chicago as the central city. While there is order in the Plexmalls, outside rage the gogangs,
rival motorcycle and political clubs who engage in random violence and
mayhem.

In the first story arc, "Hard Time," Reuben Flagg comes to the Chicago
Plexmall as a Plexus Ranger, having been fired from his television show,
Mark Thrust. He is met by Chief Ranger Hilton "Hammerhead" Krieger,
who has Reuben gear up to help stop the riots by the Chicago gogangs
that always follow the broadcast of popular video program, *Bob Violence*.
Reuben discovers that the program is laden with subliminal messages inciting the violence. Flagg disrupts the broadcast, and the violence stops. The
Plex sends an undercover agent, John Scheiskopf, to Chicago to investigate the disruption of *Bob Violence*. Scheiskopf discovers that Kreiger is
running a pirate video station, QUSA. When Krieger tries to bribe him,
Scheikopf kills Krieger. Reuben discovers this and in a battle apparently
kills Scheiskopf. Krieger's will bequeathes the station to Reuben, who continues to run it.

Over the next 15 issues, Reuben discovers that the Brazilian Union is
buying the American Midwest from the Plex, and that Brazil, the Plex, and
the Rangers are linked in some way to a neo-nazi terrorist organization, the
American Survivalist Labor Committee (ASLC). Reuben travels to Brazil
to find the source of the subliminals, and while there he meets Ranger Ivor

Figure 10.2 The Collapse of 1996. Howard Chaykin (w, a). "Hard Times." *American Flagg!* #1 (October 1983), First Comics, 17. © Howard Chaykin; used with permission.

Overholt, an old acquaintance who had sadistically tormented him during their days as cadets at the Ranger Academy. Flagg now discovers that the subliminals were actually planted by the ASLC which is in league with the Plex and has infiltrated the Plexus Rangers, in the form of Ranger Overholt, his homosexual lover Chief Ranger Emmet Golem, and Ranger Pelham Riverdale. Reuben exposes their plot to buy the United States and avoids their efforts to kill him, instead killing all three. Returning to Chicago, Reuben finds that Scheiskopf is still alive, nurtured back to health by the ASLC and outfitted with prosthetic legs by neo-nazi surgeon, Titania Weiss. Scheiskopf has taken over the Chicago Rangers, declared Reuben a criminal, and placed his own ASLC allies in charge of the Mall. He has a plan to murder all of the residents of Chicago so that the ASLC can move in. Reuben exposes the plan, stops the sale of the United States to the Brazilian Union, and mobilizes his allies to stop Scheiskopf, finally killing him and putting an end to the threat of mass murder in Chicago.

The political machinations of the Plex, Brazil, and the ASLC occur in a context of disjointed politics, ideologies, identities, and meanings that reflects the cultural fracturing of the 1980s. The weakening of both the United States and Soviet empires serves as the backdrop for *American Flagg!* The decline of effective governance is a major source of the political fragmentation that characterizes Chaykin's future, and he locates his vision of future imperial collapse in the politics of the 1980s. The prolonged Soviet occupation of Afghanistan finds its outcome in the Islamic Revolution Chaykin envisions for 1996. United States concern with Latin America in the 1980s reemerges in 2031 as rivalry with the Brazilian Union of the Americas. The political fissures of the 1980s inform the world of *American Flagg!*, and the legacy of those conflicts persists into its future. Cold War artifacts can still pose threats, such as when an abandoned Soviet weather satellite, intended to disrupt the 1996 American elections that never happened, is accidentally triggered, causing rampaging blizzards in the American Midwest, displacing thousands of refugees (called "dispers") into the Chicago Plexmall.

Mirroring the breakdown of global order, domestic politics in Flagg's United States has also collapsed, and the nation has become ideologically balkanized along the fault lines of the 1980s. This decade saw the collapse of the New Deal coalition and the liberal consensus that had characterized American politics through the 1960s. In the face of civil rights backlash evidenced by the Supreme Court Decision in Bakke v. The Regents of the University of California, tax revolts, and the general "crisis in confidence" addressed in President Carter's famous 1979 speech, the left was in disarray.[10] The right, often seen as a new conservative majority, was equally fragmented, being composed of a coalition of anti-tax libertarians, anti-civil rights Southern states-rights advocates, and disillusioned Democrats who feared weakness against the USSR and cultural breakdown.[11]

Chaykin pushes this fragmentation to an extreme, of course; the Chicago of *American Flagg!* has 75 registered political clubs. The ideological position of these clubs, however, seems purely reactionary. The most prominent is the neo-nazi Gotterdamocrats, who are allied with the clandestine ASLC. Reflecting the Reagan Democrats who would become the neoconservatives of the 1990s, the ASLC is composed of former Democrats who went underground just before the collapse of 1996. Numbering around 2 million, they espouse a fascistic ideology, opposing the "Italo-Brit-Zionist Conspiracy." Finding an ally in John Scheiskopf, they intend to release poison gas in Chicago, killing the entire population of "mongrels and half-breeds," and taking over the city.

Against the extremist ideologies of the ASLC and the Gottterdamocrats stands the ill-defined American patriotism of Reuben Flagg. Chaykin, a self-described "old lefty," was raised in 1950s Brooklyn in a leftist, Jewish household. He identifies the politics of *American Flagg!* as mushy and Reuben as a bleeding heart hero.[12] Chaykin is right about Reuben's "mushiness," but he portrays him as more than a mere bleeding heart. Reuben was raised on Mars by American parents, old lefties like Chaykin, and never came to Earth until his appointment to the Chicago Plexmall. His parents, he notes, taught him to love America and all it stands for, although what America stands for is never clearly defined. The closest he comes to such a definition is when he tells Mandy Krieger, "The American spirit—the honest, openhanded driving force of solidarity—has been corrupted. Betrayed by the banks, by big business, by slimy fat cats who use patriotism like a tart uses cheap perfume . . . betrayed by the Plex." Aside from a facile populism, there is little of substance here. From the story, Reuben's ideological commitments seem to be fairly centrist and pragmatic, promoting individual freedom and compassion for those in need while opposing extreme ideologies such as those of the ASLC and the tyrannical machinations of the Plex. Reuben's ideology represents the pragmatic liberalism of mid-twentieth century consensus historians such as Richard Hofstadter and Daniel Boorstin. His major allies who share his vision of pragmatic traditionalism, the Witnesses, also reflect this liberal consensus ideology. They specialize in information retrieval, oppose violence, and merely seek to maintain some semblance of order. Reuben's major Witness ally reinforces the traditionalism of Reuben's ideology—William Windsor Smith, the last king of Great Britain.

While the pragmatic liberalism of Reuben leads him to do the right thing and he becomes the hero of the series, he is neither a very committed hero nor a very competent one. When he first appears in the Chicago Plexmall, he is asleep on the moving walkway. After he rails against the corruption of the American spirit, Mandy asks Reuben what he will do about it. He indicates some vague future actions and says, "In the meantime, things will stay pretty much as they've been." Reuben, clearly upset about the corruption he has discovered all around him, has no idea what to do about it; the vague pragmatic liberal populism of his ideology does not give him much direction other than to see what comes up. Nor does it keep him focused on his heroic goals. He is easily distracted by the many voluptuous women who want to sleep with him, frequently forsaking duty for sex. His own convictions even fall prey to his libido. When he discovers that Dr. Titania Weiss, a beautiful surgeon with whom he is about to become intimate is in fact a neo-nazi, he rips off her swastika necklace but still has sex with her. His Jewish heritage fills him with recriminations and self-loathing after the fact but did not stop him at the time. He fails to recognize that the Plex is the real threat to his beloved America, instead battling against those with whom the Plex conspires—like the neo-nazis and the ASLC. Reuben cannot even operate QUSA effectively, but must turn it over to the Witnesses. Chaykin seems to suggest that the vague ideology of the left in the 1980s is inadequate to define a clear sense of mission or course of action.

From fragmented politics and ideologies arise fragmented identities and meanings, and Reuben clearly represents the splintered identities of the 1980s. He was born and raised on Mars, never visiting America until he is stationed there as a Ranger. Still, he has a passionate love for the country. He finds the hammer and sickle a repulsive symbol, but speaks and even swears in Russian. He is frequently paired with C. G. Markova, who was raised in Gagaringrad by Russian parents who loved the United States so much that they named their daughter after pop singer Crystal Gayle. Both Markova and Reuben blend Russian and American heritages, rendering their nationality an odd amalgam of Russian, American and post-crisis Plex. Reuben takes the sundering of identity further still; his very status as a person is suspect. A video celebrity, Reuben had starred for several years as *Mark Thrust, Sexus Ranger.* When he is fired and replaced by his own video image, the real Reuben is transferred to the Chicago Plexmall as a Plexus Ranger. The show, however, continues to be broadcast, and Reuben the Ranger is frequently dwarfed by billboards and broadcasts of the image of Reuben as Mark Thrust.

The character of Gretchen Holstrum/Peggy Krieger further suggests fragmented identities. Peggy Krieger was married to Hammerhead Krieger with whom she had a daughter, Amanda. When Hammerhead was reassigned to Caracas for 3 years, Peggy had an affair with C. K. and bore him a daughter, Medea Blitz. When Hammerhead returned and discovered the infidelity, he threw Peggy out. She traveled the country working as a sales person. In New Orleans, she met Ranger Emmet Golem, who would become so obsessed with her that, unable to have Peggy Krieger, he enters into a long-term affair with homosexual transvestite Ivor Holt, who, when in drag, resembles Peggy. While hitching a ride out of New Orleans with a female trucker named Gretchen Holstrum, Peggy is caught in an accident that leaves Gretchen dead and Peggy with amnesia. All of the doctors assumed she was Gretchen Holstrum, and plastic surgery and psychiatry convinced her as well. She moved back to Chicago and ran the Love Canal franchise in the Plexmall. As the ASLC plot becomes more apparent, Gretchen becomes increasingly confused, until the final reveal of the plot, and her own actions in killing the representative from Brazil who was trying to buy the United States. It is at this moment that she becomes aware of her true identity. Until Reuben brought all of these machinations before the public, there was nothing to believe in, and no reason for her to try to be herself. Now that the truth was coming out, so too was the true identity of Peggy Krieger. Her own connections to most of the players in the story are individualized, personal, and sexual. These connections, however, have no meaning under the fragmentary rule of the Plex. Only when Reuben's actions suggest that there may be something more can Peggy come back to reality.

New media, shopping malls, and social control

Chaykin links social and cultural incoherence to the rise of new media. The reality of *American Flagg!* is a mediated reality. Chaykin represents this visually through the use of FasFax news broadcasts to offer updates on the ongoing story. These broadcasts blur the lines between celebrity, politics, and commerce. The news anchors are marginalized, with interview subjects taking center stage. The reporter is thus displaced by the subject, and the story is narrated not by a dispenser of information, but from the perspective of the actors, leaving truth fragmentary and perspectival rather than defined, reinforcing the growing social disorder that is chronicled in text (see Figure 10.3 for one such update). A profile of the Chicago Mayor and representatives from Brazil is permeated with adjectival double entendres in an advertisement for a meat substitute. The political interviews never occur, instead offering mere celebrity images of the Mayor, the Brazilians, and Reuben. There is, in fact, no news in this news broadcast.

The merger of politics and celebrity, information and entertainment was not new to the 1980s, but it seemed qualitatively more significant during that decade. Musicians became politicized to aid Africa. Ronald Reagan's appropriation of Bruce Springsteen's song "Born in the USA" infuriated the singer and led him to become heavily involved in politics.[13] An ABC-TV movie that graphically portrayed the effects of nuclear war, *The Day After*, was used by nuclear freeze advocates and may have influenced President Reagan.[14] Actor Ed Asner, star of the hit television drama *Lou Grant* and president of the Screen Actors Guild, was an outspoken opponent of the administration's Central America policy, which was likely the cause for the cancellation of his program while it was still highly rated.[15] Most notably, former film and television star Ronald Reagan sat in the White House.

Like President Reagan, Reuben Flagg was a former actor. More a celebrity than soldier, Reuben blends the worlds of entertainment and politics; while he is trying to block the sale of the Midwest to Brazil and saving Chicago from the fascist ASLC, his program still runs and *Mark Thrust* billboards adorn many Plexmalls. People recognize him and respond to his celebrity, and he often needs to adopt a disguise. The Plex broadcasts also cross boundaries between entertainment, politics, and commerce. The Plex sells guns to the rival gogangs and then films their gang wars to broadcast

Figure 10.3 FasFax News. Howard Chaykin (w, a). "Southern Comfort!" *American Flagg!* #4 (January 1984), First Comics, 6. © Howard Chaykin; used with permission.

on its popular *Firefight Live* broadcast. It broadcasts an animated show, *Bob Violence*, largely as an advertisement for other weapons it sells. Its news broadcasts mix slanted information with celebrity profiles and advertisements for brothels, drugs, guns, and other goods, all with strong sexual overtones. Not only contributing to the fragmentation of meaning, this message of jumbled genres is also a form of social control. The Plex produces a climate of fear by subsidizing the violence the Rangers are meant to contain, but channels the frustrations and fears of the populace into consumerist avenues, controlling them by satisfying desires for sex, drugs, and violence. Reuben is not above using the media to his own political ends. He foils the plot by the ALSC in part by using QUSA to broadcast subliminals into Plex programming to disrupt the fascists' control of the Chicago Plexmall.

The world of *American Flagg!* is held together by the Plex, a communications conglomerate housed on the moon and Mars, but with outposts in many remaining world cities known as Plexmalls. Combining consumerism and political control, the Plexmalls represent twin pillars of the declining order—the co-optation of the population with the pleasures of consumption, and physical coercion. While the world outside the Plexmall is rife with gang violence, poverty, and social chaos, inside the Plexmalls is what remains of government, police authority, and the indulgence of almost any desire. While Chicago is plagued by weekly gang riots, inside the Plexmall all is orderly.

The concept of the shopping mall as an oasis of civic order is an idea that was discussed before *American Flagg!* In the view of pioneering mall architect Victor Gruen, malls would serve as civic centers for the new decentralized, suburbanized nation of planned communities. Historian Lizabeth Cohen describes how this vision spread through the 1950s and 1960s, although she notes the malls continued to be more about consumerism than civil society.[16] She claims that as public forums, the malls were more exclusionary and authoritarian than downtown city centers, since the malls were increasingly defined by the courts as private spaces, governed by their owners and managers.[17] They did, however, become central locations in suburban and increasingly in urban areas for teenage "mall rats" to socialize, senior citizens to "mall walk," and all to participate in the mass market. By 1973, Americans spent more time at the mall than anywhere else save home, school, and work.[18] In 1985, one survey reported 78 percent of respondents had visited a mall within the last month.[19] The 1980s were the high point of mall construction in the United States, with more square footage built during the decade than in any previous period; over 16,000 new malls opened in the decade according to the International Council of Shopping Centers. Mall culture was celebrated in the 1980s in films such as *Fast Times at Ridgemont High* and in such songs as Frank Zappa's "Valley Girl."

Chaykin pushes the phenomenon of mall culture further, seeing the mall not as the civic center of a utopian suburban democracy, but as an active component of empire. Gruen had envisioned suburban decentralization as a necessity of national security in the atomic age, and the mall would serve as the civic center of this decentralized utopia.[20] For Chaykin, the decentralization has come not as a defense against nuclear war, but from the breakdown of imperial power, and the mall serves as the last outpost of empire, the only entity to maintain some semblance of order in the chaos of post-1996 world. In all the cities of *American Flagg!* there is a Plexmall. There one finds airports, stores, broadcast centers, governmental authority, and the Plexus Rangers, the agents of order in the world. Locating the army of empire in the Plexmall defines them largely as mall cops, and given the continued level of violence outside the Plexmall, they are about as effective as mall cops. The Plexus Rangers are not supposed to make any real meaningful contribution, merely to hold back the forces of chaos. They are an imperial garrison whose existence demonstrates imperial power that may or may not be real.

In addition to presenting tangible evidence of the power of the Plex empire in the Plexus Rangers, the Plexmalls also serve imperial control in Gramscian fashion by commodifying and co-opting anything that could possibly be a source of threat to Plex authority. Exercising its authority, the Plex has trivialized everything into an ephemeral consumable. Broadcasting its popular video shows, *Bob Violence* and *Firefight Live*, the Plex turns urban decay and the gang violence that plagues the decrepit cities of Earth, like Chicago, into entertainment. The one franchise store that is clearly identified is the Love Canal, a brothel, and the dangers of its product are easily treated with a morning after prophylactic and antibiotic called Mañanacillan. Sex and violence are thus turned into commodities, tamed by the Plex and channeled through the mall into a means of control. Chaykin signals the power of commercializing pleasures by offering a trademark symbol after all product and franchise names, demonstrating that these goods—drugs, weapons, brothels—are all proprietary domains in the Plex. The plots to undermine the Plex all seek to subvert its control of sex and violence, signaling their centrality to Plex control. The subliminal messages planted into the *Bob Violence* broadcast, inciting the gogangs to riot, are one example of this. In "Northern Lights, Double Cross" in issues #15–18, Reuben must travel to Canada, a place not yet under Plex control, to pave the way for a new Plexmall, extending control to this region. Once there, he must break up an attack by the Pan African Union on Plex authority that consists of flooding the Plex with fake Mañanacillan, laced with an enzyme that destroys the human immune system. Aside from the clear allegorical reference to the emerging AIDS epidemic in the mid-1980s, this story highlights the significance of channeling sex through the Plex for its control and authority. By aiming the threat at these particular goods, Chaykin highlights how the Plex's incorporation of basic human drives such as sex and violence into purchasable commodities is a key element of its control.

Not only does the Plex convert physical human drives into commodities it can manipulate, but it also co-opts all counter authorities into itself, rendering them incapable of posing a challenge. Chief Chicago Plex Ranger Hammerhead Krieger and Chicago Mayor C. K. Blitz had formerly been gogang members who flouted Plex authority. Along with Hammerhead's wife, Peggy, they had built an illicit video broadcast station. Co-opted by the Plex into becoming agents of imperial authority, they become the government and police force of Chicago, and the broadcast station is reduced to running illegal sporting events (basketball games) featuring the blackmarket team owned by Blitz. Even the symbols of the governments the Plex supposedly represents—the United States and the Soviet Union—have been reduced to commodities. Reuben gets angry when he finds that Amanda Krieger has purchased the very popular hammer and sickle earrings, declaring them an abomination that she must take off. The Plex tries to commodify not only national symbols but also nation states themselves, as the Plex plots to sell the Midwest states to Brazil, literally turning the very nation the Plex is supposed to represent into a commodity for sale.

The fragmented society Chaykin describes is held together only by the machinations of weak political entities whose goals do not coincide with the interests of citizens. The Plex, the ASLC, and the Brazilian Union are incapable of implementing their various plots when opposed by one man. On the other hand, Reuben's actions may foil their plots, but he cannot alter the fundamental structure of power that keeps the Plex operating. He continues to be a Plexus Ranger, an employee of the very entity he believes is corrupt. With its control of the media and commerce, its ability to transform all opposition into another proprietary domain within itself, the Plex has sufficient power to maintain itself, if not to extend itself. Social and ideological divisions do not make for any effective organization against the Plex. The Plex thus endures, and the citizens of the Plex accept this, as long as they have access to the media, goods, and services that the Plex provides, much like the private individuals of the 1980s who retreat into consumerism.

Conclusion

American Flagg! was published in 50 issues over 5 years. The last 25 issues did not have the same involvement of Chaykin, and he stopped writing entirely after issue 32. In later issues, Reuben travels to London, California, and finally to Mars to confront the Plex itself. The stories, however, never achieved the same quality as the first 20 issues, and readership declined precipitously.

Over the course of his run, Chaykin created a postmodern vision of the future in which politics, ideology, and even identity are incoherent, broken into ever smaller pieces, with borders that remain unclear. His page layouts and overlapping dialogue mimic this obscure and disordered reality. He replicated a growing vision of information overload, engendered by the emerging 24-hour news cycle and increasing emphasis on the consumer as constructor of a meaningful narrative. He presents a story that in both substance and method reflects the political and cultural trends of the 1980s. Political fragmentation is growing as the superpowers weaken. Political ideology dissolves into mushy socially tolerant liberalism that fails to provide meaningful direction, or into socially conservative reactions to political and ideological society. In Reuben Flagg, Chaykin creates a post-modern hero, unsure of his own beliefs and easily distracted from public duty by private desire. His own identity is a blend of nationalities, of celebrity, and office. He is as incoherent as the society in which he exists, and as conflicted and complex as the era in which his comic book was published. If, as Tom Wolfe suggested, the 1980s could not produce heroics, the best we could hope for is a Reuben Flagg patrolling the shopping malls of empire.

Notes

1 Robert M. Collins, *Transforming America: Politics and Culture During the Reagan Years* (New York: Columbia University Press, 2007), 180–181; John Ehrman, *The Eighties: America in the Age of Reagan* (New Haven: Yale University Press, 2005), 200–202.
2 See, for example, Robert O. Keohane, *After Hegemony: Cooperation and Discord in the World Political Economy* (Princeton and Oxford: Princeton University Press, 2005 [1984]).
3 Witte reports a 60 percent increase in murder rates for those under 18 between 1980 and 1990.
4 Robert Bellah, Richard Marsden, William Sullivan, Ann Swidler, and Steven Tipton, *Habits of the Heart: Individualism and Commitment in American Life* (New York: Harper, 1985), 138.
5 Tom Wolfe, "Interview: Master of His Own Universe," *Time*, February 13, 1989, http://www.time.com/time/magazine/article/0,9171,956958,00.html#ixzz1MXrdmhEO (accessed November 21, 2011).
6 John Pettegrew, "A Post-Modernist Moment: Commercial Culture and the Founding of MTV," *Journal of American Culture* 15, no. 4 (1992): 57–65.
7 Collins, *Transforming America*, 147–192; James Patterson, *Restless Giant: The United States from Watergate to Bush v. Gore* (London: Oxford University Press, 2005), 254–255; Todd Gitlin, "Hip Deep in Postmodernism," *New York Times Book Review*, November 6, 1988, http://www.nytimes.com/1988/11/06/books/hip-deep-in-post-modernism.html?src=pm (accessed November 21, 2011).
8 There was also a 12-issue second volume, *Howard Chaykin's Amerikan Flagg!*, which was written and drawn by other creators. The first 15 issues of *American Flagg!* have been collected in *American Flagg! Definitive Collection, volume 1*. It is to this volume that I will make references. Unfortunately, it does not have page numbers. For material after the first 15 issues, I will refer to the original comic books.
9 Steve Erickson, "American Flagg," in Sean Howe, ed., *Give Our Regards to the Atomsmashers: Writers on Comics* (New York: Pantheon Books, 2004), 70–77.

10 Bradford Martin, *The Other Eighties: A Secret History of America in the Age of Reagan* (New York: Hill and Wang, 2010), xi; Collins, *Transforming America*, 7–28; Ehrman, *The Eighties*, 169–170.

11 Ehrman, *The Eighties*, 171–174; Patterson, *Restless Giant*, 130–132.

12 Gary Groth, "I Have a Hard Time with Vigilantes: An Interview with Howard Chaykin," *The Comics Journal* 109 (July 1986): 83.

13 Martin, *The Other Eighties*, 95–118.

14 James Mann, *The Rebellion of Ronald Reagan: A History of the End of the Cold War* (New York: Viking, 2008), 41–42; Daniel McCarthy, "Revising Ronald Reagan." *Reason*, June 2007, http://reason.com/archives/2007/05/09/revising-ronald-reagan (accessed November 21, 2011); Martin, *The Other Eighties*, 12.

15 Sam Tweedle, "The Ups and Downs of Lou Grant: A Conversation with Ed Asner," *Confessions of a Pop Culture Addict*, December 28, 2010, http://popcultureaddict.com/interviews/edasner/ (accessed November 21, 2011).

16 Lizabeth Cohen, *A Consumer's Republic: The Politics of Mass Consumption in Postwar America* (New York: Vintage Books, 2003), 257–278.

17 Ibid., 286.

18 Ibid., 270.

19 Collins, *Transforming America*, 158.

20 Timothy Mennel, "Victor Gruen and the Construction of Cold War Utopias," *Journal of Planning History* 3 (2004): 116–150.

PART THREE

Comic Books and Historical Identity

CHAPTER ELEVEN

Transformers and Monkey Kings

Gene Yang's *American Born Chinese* and the Quest for Identity

Todd Munson

For an American child of immigrants, what could be more important than "fitting in"? Negotiating with the ambivalent rhetoric of "e pluribus unum" can prove an arduous task, even if one's ethnic makeup is similar to that of the Anglo-Saxon founders. For others, the path to assimilation in the United States has been even more problematic. In his *Orientals: Asian Americans in Popular Culture*, Robert G. Lee notes the specific challenges Asians have faced, where the belief that "Asians are an alien presence in America, no matter how long they may have resided in the United States, nor how assimilated they are" still holds sway.[1] Min Zhou and Jennifer Lee note that for Asian American children in particular, there is a "constant negotiation between the traditions of their immigrant families and the marginalization and exclusion they experience from the larger society."[2]

Gene Luen Yang, himself a second-generation Chinese-American, wittily embraces the challenge of embracing both American and Chinese identity in his award-winning graphic novel *American Born Chinese* (First Second, 2006). Yang has said the theme of *American Born Chinese* "is to explore the minority experience, and how different internal and external pressures play a part in that experience."[3] His bildungsroman of a second-generation Chinese-American moving from San Francisco to the ethnically homogeneous suburbs embraces both the "model minority" stereotype of contemporary Asian Americans, while also self-consciously harkening back to the buck-toothed, slant-eyed "Yellow Peril" trope of the nineteenth century. As such, the novel deftly encapsulates the ambiguity of the Asian American immigrant experience in the twenty-first century: as implacably rooted in the racist past, but also embracing a contemporary, transnational sensibility that transcends "Chinese" or "American." This essay will examine *American Born Chinese* within the historical context of Chinese immigration to the United States, focusing in particular on the controversial character of Chin-Kee, and Yang's concept of "transformation" as it relates to the peculiarly hybrid nature of the Asian immigration experience.

American Born Chinese unfolds in a trilogy of interweaving narratives. The first begins in the realm of myth, with a retelling of the Chinese legend of Sun Wukong, the Monkey King. The subject of Wu Cheng'en's sixteenth-century novel *Journey to the West*, the character has remained popular in Chinese popular culture ever since, prompting Yang to compare the Monkey King to a "Chinese Mickey Mouse."[4] Though there are salient differences in Yang's version of the tale, he follows the same basic narrative trajectory as the original. The Monkey King contentedly rules Flower-Fruit Mountain until he is denied entrance to a party in Heaven, ostensibly because he is not wearing shoes. When pressed, however, the guard reveals the true reason behind his refusal: "you may be a *king*—you may even be a *deity*—but you are still a *monkey*."[5] Upon his return, the Monkey King is aware for the first time of "the thick smell of monkey fur" that greets him, and the next day decrees that all his monkey subjects must wear shoes. He masters a series of martial arts disciplines that transform him into a fully grown human being (albeit with his original head), and conquers a group of deities sent to punish him for his arrogance. At last, the highest deity of all, Tze-yo-tzuh (the Buddha in the original), urges the Monkey King to accept his original nature as a monkey; when he resists, Tze-yo-tzuh buries him under a mountain of rock. After five centuries, the Monkey King finally frees himself with the help of Wong Lai-tso, a humble monk charged with delivering three packages to the West (in a twist from the original, and in order to reflect Yang's own Christian belief, the three packages are delivered to the Christ child). The Monkey King accepts Wong Lai-tso as his master, and comes to terms with his monkey identity—symbolized by his rejection of shoes.

In the second (and central) narrative, young Jin Wang leaves behind his childhood home in San Francisco's Chinatown for life in the suburbs. Teary-eyed, and clutching his beloved Transformers figure, he recalls in first-person flashback a happy childhood spent watching Saturday morning cartoons, and staging "epic battles" with his Chinese friends "that left our toys smelling like spit."[6] Jin Wang's first day at school does not go well: his new teacher mispronounces his name, a classmate questions whether his family eats dogs (the teacher replies, unhelpfully, that they "probably stopped that sort of thing as soon as they came to the United States"[7]), and he is teased for bringing Chinese food for lunch. Fortunately, his isolation is brought to an end two months later when a Taiwanese boy named Wei-Chen Sun joins his class. His large eyeglasses, distinctively non-American clothing and hairstyle, and halting English all mark him as a recent arrival to the United States. Jin Wang makes no effort to befriend Wei-Chen, and at first rejects the latter's friendly overtures—that is, until Wei-Chen shows him a transforming robot he has brought to school, a toy that changes into a robot monkey. The sharing of the toy, a connection to Jin Wang's own childhood in Chinatown, is enough to cement their relationship.

In the next chapter of this narrative, 4 years have passed. Jin Wang—now in seventh grade—develops a crush on his classmate Amelia, but is too shy to say anything to her. In order to win Amelia over, he perms his hair in a curly style of a popular Caucasian classmate, Greg. When she and Wei-Chen are accidentally locked in a closet after school, Wei-Chen uses the opportunity to describe his friend's good points. Jin Wang "rescues" them from the closet, and is jolted by a sudden burst of confidence (represented visually by lightning bolts shooting from his permed hair) to ask her out. Their first date goes well—a second jolt of lightning-borne confidence enables Jin Wang to put his arm around Amelia at the movies—but their relationship is cut off shortly thereafter by Greg, who tells Jin Wang to leave her alone: "I want to make sure she makes good choices," he says. "We're almost in high school. She needs to start paying attention to who she hangs out with."[8] The thinly veiled implication of racism stings all the more since readers have come to trust Greg, who defended Jin Wang from bullies in the past.[9] Lacking the courage to confront Greg, Jin Wang backs down. Later, out of frustration at his own weakness, he makes an ill-guided pass at Wei-Chen's girlfriend, who hits him in the face—as does Wei-Chen when he finds out. In their final confrontation, Jin Wang lashes out at Wei-Chen, telling him "we are nothing alike." That night, Jin Wang dreams of a Chinese herbalist he had met in Chinatown years before, an elderly Chinese woman who told him his childhood wish of becoming a "Transformer" could come true if he was willing to "lose his soul."

The third narrative is framed as a television sitcom titled "Everyone Ruvs Chin-Kee," replete with audience applause and a laugh track (represented visually by the words "HAHAHAHAHA running along the bottom of several key panels). Danny, a Caucasian high school student, is studying with his classmate Melanie when they are interrupted by a visit from Danny's cousin. The cousin, Chin-Kee (see Figure 11.1), is not himself Caucasian—in fact, he is a gross exaggeration of every imaginable aspect of negative Chinese stereotypes, from slit eyes and buck teeth to grotesquely accented English. Danny is horribly embarrassed by Chin-Kee's appearance and behavior, a situation made exponentially worse when Chin-Kee accompanies Danny to school the next day. Danny's frustration finally spills out after Chin-Kee performs the hit pop song "She Bangs" while dancing atop

Figure 11.1 First appearance of Danny's "cousin," Chin-Kee. Gene Luen Yang (w, a). *American Born Chinese* (NY and London: First Second Books, 2006), 48. © Gene Luen Yang; used with permission.

a table at a local library. Danny hits Chin-Kee squarely in the jaw, knocking his head off—and revealing the Monkey King's form beneath. The Monkey King reveals that he is Chin-Kee, and that Sun Wei-Chen is actually his son. Chin-Kee's yearly visits to Danny, it turns out, were intended "to serve as your conscience—as a signpost to your soul."[10] Lesson learned, Danny magically reverts to his original identity of Jin Wang and seeks out his old friend to apologize. At the close of the novel, they renew their friendship.

Chinese immigration to the United States

Yang's exploration of Chinese-American identity in *American Born Chinese*—particularly, in the author's grotesque creation Chin-Kee—is so rich and complex that a grasp of the historical context is necessary in order to properly appreciate both the work and the character. Though the first Chinese came to the United States as early as the eighteenth century, immigration to the United States began in earnest after the discovery of gold in California in 1848. To be sure, there was no shortage of "push" factors on the Chinese side; increasing population, flooding, rebellion, and high taxes encouraged thousands of young males from the Pearl River delta to seek high wages in Gam Saan ("Gold Mountain," as the West Coast of the United States was known). Few made their fortunes, however, or anything close to it. When the gold was mined out a few years later, Chinese laborers moved on to the construction of Union-Pacific Railroad—one of the supreme technological achievements in the nineteenth century—and from there to agriculture, manual labor, and service industries. Between 1849 and 1930, over 380,000 Chinese immigrated to the mainland United States.[11]

Though initially there was some acceptance of the Chinese—they were often described as self-reliant and law-abiding—within a few years the trend reversed, due in part to fears that their large numbers were depressing wages and threatening the civic order. "Anti-coolie" clubs formed, anti-Chinese laws were passed, and the governor of California even described the Chinese as "a degraded and distinct people" whose immigration should be prohibited.[12] Ineligible to become citizens (post-Civil War law expanded naturalized citizenship to free blacks only), Chinese were limited in their pursuit of justice; rallies, demonstrations, roundups, and purges were all too familiar for much of the late nineteenth century.[13] Hostility toward Chinese as an alien Other was transmitted primarily through parodic verse and minstrel song, where we see the initial manifestations of what would eventually evolve into the "John Chinaman" stereotype—and into Chin-Kee himself. Verses from popular song such as "me likee bow wow, wellee goodee chow-chow" combined Canton English—a pidgin trade language dating back to the seventeenth century—with nonsense words to effectively reinforce the primacy of grammatical English and infantilize Chinese speakers.[14] Yellowface minstrel performances also introduced broader audiences to stereotypical Chinese traits such as eating cats and dogs, and the custom of wearing the hair in a braided plait.

This first chapter of Chinese immigration history to the United States came to an end in 1882, with the passage of the Immigrant Act, also known as the Chinese Exclusion Act—the first federal law to "proscribe entry of an ethnic working group on the premise that it endangered the good order of certain localities."[15] The Act expired in 1892, but was renewed for another 10 years and then made permanent in 1902. Even the repeal of the exclusion acts in 1943 did little to increase the ever-dwindling numbers of Chinese and Chinese-Americans. With the passage of the Immigration and Nationality Act in 1965, however, all racial discrimination in immigration law was abolished. This law had a tremendous impact on the Chinese population of the United States, which has doubled in size every decade since its passage.[16] Unlike the Chinese immigrants of the nineteenth century, who were primarily illiterate young males from the south, the new arrivals were marked by great heterogeneity in terms of gender, age, education, and social status. Many, like Jin Wang's parents, were middle-class college graduates who came to the United States to enroll in graduate school, clustering in urban populations on the West Coast. Jin Wang himself is a typical member of post-1965 "new second generation" of Chinese-Americans: he lives in a California suburb, attends public school, and his family appears to be comfortably middle-class. Also typical of his generation is his limited Chinese ability—in fact he seems to have lost his ability to read and speak the language sometime after third grade.[17] And like so many other twenty-first century Chinese-Americans, he faces a challenging path to social equality.

Deconstructing Chin-Kee

In his creator's words, Chin-Kee is the "ultimate Chinese stereotype."[18] On his stout frame, he bears the weight of nearly every racist trope of Chinese identity imaginable, inevitably raising the question of whether Yang ultimately undermines his own agenda by perpetuating negative stereotypes. I would argue that he does not—but we will need to peel back the dense layers of Chin-Kee's identity in order to make the case clear. Here I draw on the work of historian Lee, who in *Orientals* argues that a definable series of Chinese/Chinese-American stereotypes have marched across the stage since mid-nineteenth century: the "pollutant," the "coolie," the "deviant," the "Yellow Peril," the "model minority," and the "gook, in that order."[19] Chin-Kee, an overdetermined symbol of American-defined Chineseness, incorporates virtually every one of these stereotypical images.[20]

The idea of Chinese as a "polluting" influence in society, Lee says, stems from the first large-scale immigration of Chinese to California in the 1850s, when they "could no longer be imagined as simply foreign, made strange by their distance. Chinese in America were now alien and threatening through their very presence."[21] In *American Born Chinese*, Chin-Kee aggressively asserts his place in Danny's school as an antagonistic and unrepentant Other, from his clothing to his accent to his overbearing personality. Chin-Kee is not a pollutant simply because he is foreign; rather he contaminates because he "disrupts the narrative structure . . . he is out of place and creates a sense of disorder."[22] This is reinforced through associations with disease and disgust: Chin-Kee plays out the stereotype by bringing "clispy flied cat gizzards wiff noodle" to lunch—itself a nod to an overtly racist political cartoon by Pat Oliphant—and surreptitiously urinates in a soda can belonging to Danny's friend ("Me Chinese, Me Play Joke, Me go pee-pee in his Coke").[23] Even during Chin-Kee's impromptu singing performance at the local library (discussed below), Danny's classmates see Chin-Kee as a source of pollution—"his spit got on me!"; "Dude, you'd better go get checked out for SARS!" (202). The latter reference is to Severe Acute Respiratory Syndrome, a virus originating in south China in 2002. Despite the fact that there were no SARS-related deaths in the United States (and that all eight domestic cases were contracted abroad), rumors swirled of a Chinese-borne epidemic, virtually emptying Chinese restaurants across the United States for a time in 2003.

Another aspect of Chin-Kee's character that resonates strongly with Lee's categories of Chinese stereotypes is the "deviant," whose sexual mores contrast with Victorian ideas of purity and chastity. William F. Wu, in his survey of Chinese characters in American fiction, has similarly found widespread belief in the "alleged moral degeneracy of Asian people" and the concomitant threat of "genetic mixing of the Anglo-Saxon with Asians, who were considered a biologically inferior race."[24] The lecherous Chin-Kee makes his thoughts on such "genetic mixing" apparent immediately upon his first appearance in the novel. Just as Danny is about to reveal his feelings to his classmate Melanie, Chin-Kee bursts in: "Confucius say 'Hubba-hubba'! . . . Such pletty Amellican girl wiff bountiful Amellican bosom! [*sic*] Must bind feet and bear Chin-Kee's children!"[25] Wiping drool off his chin, Chin-Kee extends his claw-like hands toward Melanie—while Danny stands paralyzed with shame and horror. Chin-Kee continues this predatory behavior at Danny's school the next day, but has virtually no effect on anyone he meets—perhaps a nod to the related (but contradictory) trope of the emasculated Asian man.

Chin-Kee also exemplifies the classic "Yellow Peril" stereotype, a representation of Asians as an invading horde threatening to overrun and usurp—or "negatively Asianize," in Kent Ono and Vincent Pham's phrase—Anglo-Saxon hegemony.[26] The Yellow Peril was personified in popular culture in the form of Fu Manchu, the "archetypal Asian villain" created by British novelist Sax Rohmer.[27] Having appeared in diverse media including radio, film, television, and comic books, Fu Manchu's sinister mien, sallow skin, and trademark moustache have been familiar to Western audiences for nearly a century. While Chin-Kee, who is short and rotund in the 'Charlie Chan' mode, may not immediately call Fu Manchu to mind, he does manifest a "Fu-like" visage in two key instances. In the first, Chin-Kee relishes the prospect of attending school with Danny. Looking directly at the "camera," we see for the first time his orange, pupil-less eyes. Drooling onto his twisted, claw-like hands, Chin-Kee says, "Chin-Kee so ruv Amerillican school! Chin-Kee have such lorricking good time! [*sic*]"[28] In the second, his face twisted into a grotesque and threatening mask, Chin-Kee says not only that he "ruv Amellica," but that he "rive for Amellica" and planned to visit Danny "evely year forever [*sic*]."[29] In both examples, the emergence of Chin-Kee's Fu Manchu/Yellow Peril identity is linked directly with his "ruv" for the United States. A one-man "invading horde," Chin-Kee's very existence is predicated on the desire to disrupt, sow discord, and shame his cousin Danny.

The first truly *positive* stereotype of Asian identity in the United States was that of the "model minority," first appearing in the 1960s (before the immigrant influx made possible by the Immigration Act of 1965). News organizations such as the *New York Times* and *U.S. News and World Report* reported that Asian Americans—by dint of their educational achievements, low crime rates, work ethic, and ability to overcome discrimination—stood out as a "model" among non-white ethnic populations in the United States (mirrored in Jin Wang's parents, who arrive in the United States as graduate students). Implied, but not always stated, was a comparison to African-Americans, who had failed to reach similar levels of success in roughly comparable circumstances. Though the "model minority" thesis has long been rejected as an inadequate lens through which to view the relationship between race and socioeconomic success, the idea of the super-successful Asian student remains very much in the popular imagination. Chin-Kee reifies this stereotype when he attends class with Danny. In a series of panel sequences, the reader moves rapidly from American Government to History, Biology, Math, and Spanish; in every instance Chin-Kee has his hand raised, the answer to every question on the tip of his tongue. "L ≤ 0 or L ≥ 6!" Chin-Kee exclaims. "Branco Y Muy Grande!"[30] Danny is predictably embarrassed, though not by his own lack of knowledge (neither he or Jin Wang evince any desire to study or participate in class) but rather by the unselfconscious display of erudition, which marks Chin-Kee as even more "Chinese" than he already was.

Lee's final stereotype of Chinese-American identity is the "gook," defined in terms of Cold War foes such as the North Koreans and Viet Cong, and in popular culture as martial artists or violent gang members. The "gook" is stealthy and devious, a ninja or Shaolin warrior-monk, a fighter who by virtue of a mysterious, mystical, and deceptive combat style is able to defeat the Caucasian enemy—who is committed to "fighting fair." Sheng-Mei Ma, writing in *The Deathly Embrace: Orientalism and Asian American Identity*, identifies Bruce Lee in particular as archetypal "stereotype of the barbaric Oriental" who crystallizes this phenomenon of the martial Asian.[31] The image of the Asian martial arts expert—and the belief that "all Chinese know kung fu"—has persisted to the present day, in video games and the popular films of Jet Li and Jackie Chan. To no surprise, Chin-Kee also evinces his own kung fu mastery in a final confrontation with Danny/Jin Wang at the end of the novel. As the laugh track "plays" on-panel, Chin-Kee unleashes a series of "kung fu" moves—though they are all based on items from a Chinese restaurant menu: "Mooshu Fist!," "Hot and Sour Wet Willy!," "Kung Pao Attack!"[32]

To Lee's list of stereotypes, I would add another trope of Asian Americans embedded in contemporary media: the "geek." In contemporary parlance, the term refers almost endearingly to one who is at the opposite spectrum from "cool" in terms of clothing, social skills, and overall demeanor.[33] Though clearly related to the "model minority" stereotype in terms of academic achievement, the geek is primarily characterized by the lack of self-awareness and social grace. The apotheosis of this stereotype is seen in the hapless exchange student Long Duk Dong in John Hughes' 1984 teen comedy *Sixteen Candles*, who spoke broken English, wore unfashionable clothes, and used a fork and spoon as chopsticks. Chin-Kee marks himself as a member of this category during his impromptu concert in the library. His choice of song—"She Bangs"—is an obvious reference to a Chinese-American college student named William Hung, who performed a similarly off-key rendition on *American Idol* in 2004. Though Hung's performance was poor, he briefly enjoyed something of a cult following, appearing on several television programs, releasing music albums, and even starring in a low-budget film. For many in the Asian-American community, however, Hung reduced Asian identity to a group of undesirably nerdy characteristics; as documentary filmmaker James Hou said, "As Asian Americans, we look through this racial lens, and we see this guy who embodies all the stereotypes we're trying to escape from."[34] Through their clothing, hairstyle choices, and distinctive facial features—to say nothing of their lack of singing and dancing talent—Hung and Chin-Kee are undeniably geeks of the highest variety.

When one considers all the diverse aspects of the character, the fact that Chin-Kee drew some public criticism comes as no surprise. For example, in 2007, the then-popular website MySpace featured *American Born Chinese* in its book section. Understandably, many (especially those who had not actually read the book) found the accompanying promotional blurb offensive: "Chink-kee [*sic*] has buckteeth, packs dead cats for lunch, goes pee-pee in Cokes, excels at school, and lusts after a 'pletty Amellican girl wif bountiful Amellican bosom.'"[35] This summary of Chin-Kee's character, though accurate, demonstrates the fine line that Yang and his readers are forced to walk. Is the creator of such a grossly racist character perpetuating a stereotype, or undermining it? In response to complaints from the MySpace incident, Yang wrote: "Chin-Kee isn't meant to be funny. He's meant to come off the page and slap you in the face. If you're laughing at him, I want you to do so with a knot in your stomach and a dry throat." If the character comes across as offensive, that is the point. "The fact of the matter is, sometimes you have to exaggerate to get your point across. Sometimes a stereotype needs to be dressed up in bright yellow skin and a queue in order for folks to recognize its severity." That Chin-Kee embraces all of his disparate and self-contradictory aspects and still hangs together as a credible character is a testament to Yang's writing. Ultimately, he says, if he had not written the character of Chin-Kee into his novel, "I would not have been able to behead him."[36]

More than meets the eye

The theme of transformation is at the heart of *American Born Chinese*, just as it is at the heart of the American immigrant experience. As long as there have been new arrivals at Ellis Island and Angel Island, there has existed the belief that one should shed the customs of the old country and embrace the "melting pot" of the new world. For some, this meant speaking English at home, and adopting American dress, customs, and culture. For others it meant casting off that core marker of human identity—the name—and adopting a new one. What could be a greater transformation than the shedding of Angelo Siciliano or Moses Teichman in favor of all-American Charles Atlas and Arthur Murray, for example? In one respect, Asian Americans are similar to other immigrant communities in that they are the product of suffering, hardship, and exclusion. However, no matter how assiduously they have tried, Asians have had no such ability to "abandon their ethnic identities." The shape of their eyes, the color of their hair, and the complexion of their skin have marked them as "forever foreigners," or in Ronald Takaki's phrase, "strangers" to the United States with no organic roots to American society.[37]

Jin Wang, born in America to Chinese parents, spends the first several years of his life in San Francisco's Chinatown, with no apparent awareness of his identity as "stranger" or as a child of immigrants—his friends are all Chinese, as is their language of preference. The day his family moves to the suburbs, however, Jin Wang begins life as a negatively racialized "stranger," an Other whose goal of assimilation can never be completely realized . . . at least not without magical intervention from a Chinese herbalist. Jin Wang begins his transformation in the seventh grade, when he perms his hair in order to impress his classmate Amelia—a change she notes, ironically, without compliment ("Jin? That Asian boy with the afro?"[38]). As one of only three Asians in his school, Jin Wang considers his own hair to be just as "Chinese" as a braided queue would have been.

Jin Wang's American-style hairdo has an added benefit: the lighting-like jolts that emanate at key moments to enable him to act with a courage he was previously lacking. With his perm's "help," he successfully asks out Amelia and puts his arm around her at the movies. Ultimately, however, Jin Wang's hair becomes his undoing. His perm-jolt of confidence fails him when the time comes to stand up to Greg, and reappears in an ill-advised attempt to kiss Wei-Chen's girlfriend. The resulting conflict with Wei-Chen causes him to reject his best (and only) friend, and signals Jin Wang's final rejection of his Chinese identity, prompting the herbalist to appear in his dream and tell him that he had "finally done it"—that is, lost his soul. His appearance as Danny the next morning is the ultimate reversal of circumstances—rather than the typical scenario of Caucasian playing an Asian character in "yellowface" makeup, Jin Wang plays his life out in "whiteface" and is finally able to assimilate into the Caucasian community. In the end, however, Chin-Kee—who as the Monkey King serves as the "signpost" to Jin Wang's soul—convinces Danny of the error of his ways. "You know, Jin, I would have saved myself from five hundred years' imprisonment beneath a mountain of rock had I only realized how good it is to be a monkey."[39] Just as the Monkey King has come to accept "the smell of his fur," Jin Wang comes to terms with his own identity. At the novel's close, this message is brought home: their meeting at a Chinese-American café, and effortlessly communicating in both English (Jin Wang) and Chinese (Wei Chen), confirms the novel's message that Jin Wang does not have to choose between being "American-born" or "Chinese," but rather can negotiate an identity that harmonizes both cultures.

Conclusion

Sucheng Chan, writing in *Asian Americans: An Interpretive History*, notes that the history of Asian immigration to the United States can best be understood if we see Asians "as both immigrants and members of nonwhite minority groups." As immigrants, she says "many of their struggles resemble those that European immigrants have faced," but "as people of nonwhite origins bearing distinct physical differences, they have been perceived as 'perpetual foreigners' who can never be completely absorbed into American society and its body politic. . . . Even as they acquired the values and behavior of Euro-Americans, they simultaneously had to learn to accept their standing as racial minorities."[40] In *American Born Chinese*, Chin-Kee symbolizes Jin Wang's inability to fully accept his standing as a Chinese-American. Satisfyingly, though, it is precisely the same character who spurs Danny/Jin Wang to finally come to terms with his own identity at the close of the novel.

Kent A. Ono and Vincent N. Pham have written that, in contemporary America, "racism has not gone away, and that there is no progression, not even a slow one, toward a better representation of Asians and Asian Americans in the mainstream media."[41] One hopes this pessimism has been somewhat tempered by the success of *American Born Chinese*, which was one of five finalists for the National Book Award for excellence in Young People's Literature in 2006, and the first graphic novel ever to be nominated in any category in the award's 57-year history. The book was also the recipient of Michael L. Printz Award for excellence in young adult literature—again, the first graphic novel to be so honored. *American Born Chinese* has clearly shifted the negative embedded discourse on Asian Americans in a new direction, using the popular format of comics to achieve a high degree of critical visibility. By self-consciously appropriating racist stereotypes, Yang deftly and subversively robbed them of their marginalizing power—leaving readers instead with a final image of Jin Wang and Wei Chen renewing their friendship over bubble tea, a small glimpse of the optimism and promise of post-racial American society.

Notes

1 Robert G. Lee, *Orientals: Asian Americans in Popular Culture* (Philadelphia: Temple University Press, 1999), 4.

2 Min Zhou and Jennifer Lee, "Introduction: The Making of Culture, Identity, and Ethnicity among Asian American Youth," in idem, ed., *Asian American Youth: Culture, Identity, and Ethnicity* (Routledge, 2004), 22.

3 Jonathan Baylis, "Interview: Gene Yang: Writer/Creator of "American Born Chinese," *The Trades*, December 13, 2006, http://www.the-trades.com/article. php?id=5053 (accessed November 21, 2011).

4 Gene Yang, "Origins of American Born Chinese—Part 1," *First Second Books—Doodles and Dailies*, August 8, 2006, http://www.firstsecondbooks. com/authors/geneYangBlogMain.html (accessed November 21, 2011).

5 Gene Luen Yang, *American Born Chinese* (New York and London: First Second, 2006), 15.

6 Ibid., 26.

7 Ibid., 31.

8 Ibid., 179.

9 Yang has said that he does not see Greg as racist, but that "he just cares more about his popularity than anything else." See Kristy Valenti, "The Gene Yang Interview," *The Comics Journal* #284 (July 2007), Fantagraphics Books, 129.

10 Yang, *American Born Chinese*, 221.

11 Ronald Takaki, *Strangers from a Different Shore: A History of Asian Americans* (Back Bay Books/Little, Brown, and Company, 1998 updated and revised edition), 31.

12 Roger Daniels, *Asian America: Chinese and Japanese in the United States since 1850* (University of Washington Press, 1995), 36.

13 See Jean Pfaelzer, *Driven Out: The Forgotten War Against Chinese Americans* (University of California Press, 2008).

14 Lee, *Orientals*, 37.

15 "Chinese Exclusion Act (1882)," *Our Documents: A National Initiative on American History, Civics, and Service*, http://www.ourdocuments.gov/doc. php?flash=true&doc=47 (accessed November 21, 2011).

16 Iris Chang, *The Chinese in America: A Narrative History* (Penguin Books, 2004), 265.

17 Min Zhou, "Coming of Age at the Turn of the Twenty-First Century: A Demographic Profile of Asian American Youth," in *Asian American Youth*, 41.

18 Baylis, "Interview: Gene Yang."

19 Lee, *Orientals*, 8.

20 Yang does not draw on the paradigm of the Chinese "coolie" (or indentured laborer) in his creation of Chin-Kee, perhaps because it has the least valence in contemporary American society.

21 Lee, *Orientals*, 28.

22 Ibid., 3.

23 The April 9, 2001 cartoon features a Chinese character accidentally dumping a plate of "crispy fried cat gizzards and noodles" all over Uncle Sam.

24 William F. Wu, *The Yellow Peril: Chinese Americans in American Fiction, 1850–1940* (Hamden, CT: Archon Books, 1982), 1.

25 Yang, *American Born Chinese*, 50.

26 Kent A. Ono and Vincent N. Pham, *Asian Americans and the Media* (Malden, MA: Polity Press, 2009), 25.

27 Wu, *The Yellow Peril*, 164.

28 Yang, *American Born Chinese*, 120.

29 Ibid., 211.

30 Ibid., 111–113, 119.

31 Sheng-Mei Ma, *The Deathly Embrace: Orientalism and Asian American Identity* (Minneapolis: University of Minnesota Press, 2000), 53.

32 Yang, *American Born Chinese*, 207–211.

33 Closely related is the Japanese stereotype of the obsessive fan, or *otaku*.

34 Emil Guillermo, "William Hung: Racism, or Magic?" *SF Gate*, April 6, 2004, http://www.sfgate.com/cgi-bin/article.cgi?file=/gate/archive/2004/04/06/eguillermo.DTL (accessed November 21, 2011).

35 J. K. Parkin, "*MySpace members cry foul on American Born Chinese*," *Newsarama*, May 2, 2007, http://blog.newsarama.com/2007/05/02/myspace-members-cry-foul-on-american-born-chinese/ (accessed November 21, 2011).

36 Gene Yang, "Gene Yang on Stereotypes." First Second blog, May 1, 2007, http://firstsecondbooks.typepad.com/mainblog/2007/05/gene_yang_on_st.html (accessed November 21, 2011).

37 Takaki, *Strangers from a Different Shore*, passim.

38 Yang, *American Born Chinese*, 101.

39 Ibid., 223.

40 Sucheng Chan, *Asian Americans: An Interpretive History* (New York: Twayne, 1991), 187.

41 Ono and Pham, *Asian Americans*, 84.

CHAPTER TWELVE

Agent of Change

The Evolution and Enculturation
of Nick Fury

Phillip G. Payne and Paul J. Spaeth

In 1963, Jack Kirby and Stan Lee launched the comic book *Sgt. Fury and His Howling Commandos*. The two men, veterans of the comic book industry and World War II, are best known for their role in the Silver Age renaissance of Marvel super hero comics, but here they explored another popular genre of the day, war stories. The creative team brought their wartime experiences into the new book, creating a celebration of the "Good War" for the 1960s generation.[1] The Fury character started as a tough-as-nails leader of an ethnically diverse special assignment squad, a heroic everyman and citizen soldier. During the Cold War, Fury transitions into a super-agent who eventually becomes a cynical, post-patriotic presence that appears throughout the Marvel Universe, acting as a kind of deus ex machina. By the early twenty-first century, Nick Fury had shifted from being a symbol of paranoia to his contemporary status as a reflection of the darker mood of a complacent nation.[2]

From the outset, the Nick Fury character has been a part of the process of war commemoration in popular culture. Public memory and commemoration reduces a complex historical event into a much simpler tale that can be celebrated, and that can teach a moral lesson. Comic books often have black and white narratives pitting heroes against villains. These narratives, combined with the melodramatic stories, unapologetic patriotic symbolism, and an intended audience of boys and young men, make comic books an excellent venue for conveying public memory. Lee, Kirby, and other creators did not hesitate to use the Sgt. Fury title to teach the "historical" lessons of World War II. For example, Lee and Kirby include catalogs of the weapons, vehicles, aircraft, and uniforms used during the war in the back pages of early issues. All of this death-dealing equipment becomes as harmless as collecting baseball cards, becoming "historical" without dealing with the moral ambiguity the real war might have produced.

Readers in the 1960s who picked up *Sgt. Fury and His Howling Commandos* would have found themselves in familiar territory. As with other popular culture treatments of World War II, Lee and Kirby used familiar tropes of the Good War: rugged individualism and democracy versus Nazi conformity and brutality. In the process, they ignored historical realities that as veterans they would have known. The fictional Howling Commandos is an integrated unit in an Army that would have been segregated in reality. However, depicting a segregated United States Army would have undermined the story of American forces fighting for freedom and tolerance. In addition, depictions of the enemy were caricatures borrowed from public stereotypes. Hitler is shown in *Sgt. Fury* #1 (May 1963) as a madman Queen of Hearts calling for the execution of those not listening to him. The fictional character that became Fury's arch-enemy, Baron Strucker, is modeled after the Prussian looks of silent film star Erich von Stroheim. On the other hand, Field Marshal Erwin Rommel is treated with some dignity as a German worthy of praise, appearing in person but only as a distant enemy. For the most part, Fury and his Commandos confront nameless German soldiers commanded by fictional, sometimes farcical, officers.

A key to the unfolding historical and commemorative aspects of the Fury character is his relationship to Captain America, another character co-created by Jack Kirby. Nick Fury and Captain America became symbolic of contrasting versions of American exceptionalism. Fury represented rugged individualism, while Captain America represented a kind of nationalistic collective identity. Fury symbolized the individualistic American grunt chafing under the conformity required by the Army. In contrast, Captain America's identity was lost in his patriotism; he was literally wrapped in the flag. Lee and Kirby link the 1940s-created character of Captain America to the 1960s-created Sgt. Fury in *Sgt. Fury and his Howling Commandos* #13 (Dec. 1964) where the two are shown as part of a newsreel. The Howlers are unappreciated by the English audience viewing the film, while Captain America is cheered. This issue is part of the introduction of the 1940s-created Captain America into the Silver Age Marvel Universe. Linking Captain America to Sgt. Fury brings a nationalistic symbol of the Good War to a 60s youth culture that would soon be rejecting any and all patriotic symbols.

Comic book continuity and history making

Comic book fans are notorious for their concern with continuity. Fans ask if an event in one issue corresponds with developments in previous issues. They need to see that the fictional universe is coherent within itself. Such concern with continuity, that is consistency and reasonable explanations for change, lends itself to historical thinking. As the Fury character evolved over the decades, he became a central feature in the continuity of the Marvel Universe. When Lee, Kirby, and others were creating the Silver Age Marvel Universe, they had to create continuity in their fictional historical narrative spanning from the 1940s to the 1960s.[3]

Comic book depictions of World War II actually predate Pearl Harbor. Rather famously, Joe Simon and Jack Kirby's first issue of *Captain America Comics*—cover dated March 1941—featured Captain America punching Adolf Hitler. Stan Lee reflected that when he entered the comic book business "it was just before World War II and many of our super heroes, especially Captain America, the Human Torch, and the Sub-Mariner were already fighting Hitler and the Nazis. So, years later, when Jack and I had a chance to do stories about those epic battles, but this time do them in a more realistic way, you can imagine what a kick that was for the two of us." Lee made a direct connection between his and Kirby's service in World War II and their passion for working on the Sgt. Fury book.[4]

In creating this comic book continuity, Lee and Kirby participated in a commemorative process that taught a younger generation the values of what would become known as the "Greatest Generation."[5] This is the generation that grew up during the Great Depression, fought World War II, and became the parents of the Baby Boomers. Through the character of Nick Fury, Lee, Kirby and others not only commemorated the Good War but they also established a historical narrative for the developing Marvel Universe that served as an important link to the lessons of "real" history.

Lee, Kirby, and later colleagues used the *Sgt. Fury* book to create back story for the Silver Age characters. For example, Reed Richards (Mr. Fantastic from the Fantastic Four) appeared as an OSS agent in *Sgt. Fury* #3 (Sept. 1963). As a kind of preface to his transition into a secret agent, Nick Fury appears as a CIA agent in *Fantastic Four* #21 (Dec. 1963) and then, starting in August of 1965 in *Strange Tales* #135, Fury appears as an agent of a secret spy organization called S.H.I.E.L.D. that combats super villains and evil secret societies on a global scale. The character of Fury himself links the era of the Good War to that of the Cold War and beyond, changing with the times in a way that Captain America could not.

Sgt. Fury and His Howling Commandos: Publication history and backgrounds

Sgt. Fury and His Howling Commandos originated from a dare from publisher Martin Goodman. Lee was given the worst possible title for a new book, and it was his job to make it a success.[6] Despite the clunky title, Lee and Kirby, joined by artist Dick Ayers and writers Roy Thomas and Gary Friedrich, turned *Sgt. Fury and His Howling Commandos* into a popular book.

That first series featuring the Fury character ran from 1963 until 1981. This included over 100 original stories out of the 167 issues published, not counting the annuals and specials. Over 60 of the later issues were reprints. Jack Kirby did the artwork on the first 7 issues and issue 13. Stan Lee wrote the first 28 issues and then only one more issue. But it seems reasonable to say that those earlier issues were collaborative, as seen in the attribution of issue 13, stating that the book was "written and drawn by the titanic duo" of Lee and Kirby. Following Kirby, Dick Ayers takes up the artwork, having previously inked Kirby's pencils. The writing is handled by Roy Thomas for a time, but later Gary Friedrich becomes the primary writer.

As Stan Lee points out, it says something about the popularity of the series that despite the lack of new content the book continued with reprints, the comic book equivalent of a television show going into reruns. As Lee notes, whenever he thought about canceling the book, fans demanded that it continue.[7] Partly, the book's popularity can be explained by the familiarity of the postwar generation with World War II combat movies and television shows. Some of the most popular television series of the mid to late 1960s revolved around the war, such as *Twelve O'Clock High* about an American bomber squadron stationed in England, *The Rat Patrol* about an American combat group in the deserts of North Africa, and *Combat!* about an American infantry squad fighting its way through Italy. Then there were popular comedies, *McHale's Navy* set in the Pacific theater and *Hogan's Heroes* about American POWs in a German camp.

Before these television series, there were, of course, popular war comic books. *Blackhawk* was one of the few series that started during the war and continued on into the 1980s (with some breaks), running to over 250 issues. Most World War II books stopped when the war ended, but the 1950s saw the emergence of new titles such as *Star Spangled War Stories*, *G. I. Combat*, *Fightin' Marines*, and *Fightin' Army*. Perhaps the most popular series were two DC titles *Our Army at War* (301 issues from 1952 to 1977) and *Our Fighting Forces* (181 issues from 1954 to 1978). The main character of *Our Army at War* was Sgt. Rock, and his namesake book would continue its numbering, finally ending its run in 1988 with issue 422.

Sgt. Fury and His Howling Commandos: The story

Given the popularity of the war genre, it seems unlikely that either the title or the Marvel method accounted for the success of *Sgt. Fury*. Still, efforts were made to embed Fury in the Marvel Universe, to such an extent that the first 12 issues of *Sgt. Fury* seem to build to issue #13 with a story entitled "Fighting Side-By-Side with . . . Captain America and Bucky!" (December 1964). This issue closely followed the introduction of Captain America into the Silver Age in *Avengers* #4 (March 1964). The buildup to the appearance of Captain America in *Sgt. Fury* includes a series of standard war stories, but also the introduction of Baron Strucker and Dr. Zemo, both of whom go from being Nazi-era bad guys to Silver Age supervillains, fighting against Captain America, Nick Fury, and the Avengers.

At its base, *Sgt. Fury and His Howling Commandos* is the story of an army platoon that takes on high-stakes missions. Despite Lee's protestations that he wanted the stories to be more realistic, Fury and his Commandos take on the Desert Fox, attempt to capture Adolf Hitler, get involved in the battle of Okinawa (traveling from the European to the Pacific Theater to do so), and save a French resistance fighter before he can turn over the plans for the D-Day invasion. Clearly, the stories found in the book were outside the experiences of the average combat soldier. Compared to DC's Sgt. Rock, the adventures of Sgt. Fury were over-the-top fantasy. Perhaps the characters were meant to be realistic in contrast to Lee and Kirby's superhero stories and in this way it can be said that *Sgt. Fury* was a "realistic" portrayal of America at war. Lee writes: "This was probably the first series to feature an Irishman, a Southerner, a Jew, an Italian and a Black, not to mention, later on, a newcomer who might have been gay."[8]

These characters, despite Lee's retroactive insistence of authenticity, were stereotypes. Nick Fury fits the stereotype of the hard-as-nails-heart-of-gold noncommissioned officer (see Figure 12.1). On the first issue's splash page we read that Fury is a six foot two, steel-muscled, iron-nerved fighting man! The rest of the platoon would be familiar types to any viewer of World War II films or television shows: an ex-jockey from the blue grass country of Kentucky, an Irish one-time circus strongman, an African-American trumpet player, a Jew with family ties to Eastern Europe, a college-educated ivy-leaguer, and an Italian-American who gave up a promising career as an actor to serve in the army. In an unusual plot development for a comic book of the period, the college kid dies and is replaced by an Englishman named Percy "Pinky" Pinkerton, the character who Lee said was gay.

The first issue serves as a good example of the series' standard story as Fury and his commandos are dispatched to rescue a captured French resistance leader. For some undisclosed reason, this resistance leader knows the plans for D-Day and Fury and his crew have to rescue him before he "spills the beans."[9] As usual, American innovation and individualism are able to triumph over German regimentation. Fury and his Commandos perform superhuman feats and each has a trademark visual gimmick. Fury has his

Figure 12.1 Nick Fury as hard-as-nails, heart-of-gold World War II noncommissioned officer. Jack Kirby (p) and Chic Stone (i). *Sgt. Fury* #12 (November 1964), Marvel Comics, cover. Marvel, Nick Fury, and all related characters © and ™ Marvel Entertainment, LLC. All rights reserved and used with permission.

cigar, Dum Dum his hat and strength, Gabe his horn, and so forth. The Germans are all callous fools, the French all belong to the freedom-fighting underground, and the backdrop is the most important campaign of the war. Public memory is kept intact as the commemoration of wartime events is kept within simplistic lines and remain consistent with commonly held notions about World War II.

While German soldiers tended to be stereotypes that followed orders, the German Nazi leaders in some ways have the characteristics of supervillains. Fury and the primary German leaders enter into personal vendettas having the quality of a superhero/supervillain fight. In *Sgt Fury #5* (January 1964), Baron Strucker is introduced. Lee and Kirby use the issue to contrast the virtues of the self-made American against those of the European aristocrat. After seeing the hard-driving Fury pushing his men in the field, we transition to Baron Strucker's castle in Bavaria where he is practicing his skills at swordplay. A General brings orders directly from Hitler that Strucker is to eliminate Fury. The Baron initially rejects the orders, declaring that Fury "is not worthy of my skills! He is neither an officer, nor a fellow aristocrat!" He eventually accepts the mission as an opportunity to "toy" with the "brash commoner."[10]

Fury's individualism, evidenced by his frequent inability to follow orders, has kept him at the rank of sergeant. The characteristic that makes him a successful fighter makes him a poor soldier. In defiance of orders, Fury clandestinely accepts a personal challenge from Strucker. Here we see contrasting portrayals of masculinity between the formality of Strucker and Fury's brawling style. Strucker summarizes the contrast: "We Junkers are a proud breed! We are gentlemen! Something a savage like you would never understand!"[11] But we see the falseness of the Baron when he secretly drugs Fury before the match and then uses Fury's defeat for propaganda purposes. In the end, rough-edged American virtue prevails when Fury raids a German base where Strucker is located and beats him in an unrigged fight. Notions of American fair play and working class ethics win out over European formalism and trickery.

Following two other traditional war stories, the team of "ex-sergeant" Lee and "ex-corporal" Ayers have Fury and his Commandos take on a Nazi with a high-tech weapon in a story more fitting for a superhero book than a war comic (*Sgt. Fury #8*, July 1964). Fury and the Commandos have a mission to go deep into Germany and capture the Nazi scientist Dr. Zemo before his death ray leads to the Allies' defeat. But Zemo, like other Nazis, fails to live up to his boasting about being a member of a master race.

With this issue, we see the introduction of a new Howler, Percival Pinkerton, the character Lee in later years identified as probably being homosexual. However, it is hard to see the text as a clear-cut call for tolerance. Pinkerton is presented as an over-refined, almost effeminate character wearing glasses, a beret, an ascot, and carrying an umbrella. When introduced, one Howler proclaims, "Ain't that about the cutest lookin' soldier ya ever did see?" Another replies, "Don't let 'im hear ya . . . Some of those British guys are tougher than they look!"[12] Pinkerton is an interesting case of contrasting American roughness with European cultivation, providing a different side of this refinement from what has been presented by the Germans. Pinkerton proves his mettle and gains acceptance by defeating the Howlers using his umbrella while lecturing the "riff raff" on the need for manners. Perhaps more interesting, and a better argument for tolerance,

Figure 12.2 Sgt. Fury meets Captain America. Jack Kirby (p) and Chic Stone (i). *Sgt. Fury* #13 (December 1964), Marvel Comics, cover. Marvel, Nick Fury, and all related characters © and ™ Marvel Entertainment, LLC. All rights reserved and used with permission.

is the character of Gabe Jones, the African-American Howler who emerges as the hero of the story by nearly sacrificing his life to save the company from a German tank. Gabe's heroism and self-sacrifice is seen in contrast to the false bravado of the Germans.

Sgt. Fury #13 (December 1964) features the return of Jack Kirby to the book and the appearance of perhaps his most famous creation, Captain America (see Figure 12.2). As mentioned earlier, Fury's relationship with Captain America is central to incorporating the commemoration of World War II and the Golden Age of comics into the emerging Silver Age. The issue opens with Fury and his girlfriend watching a news reel. In another opportunity to explore American rugged individualism as contrasted with European manners, Fury is irritated that the British audience is not cheering the exploits of the Howlers. His date explains that "we British think just as highly of Nicholas! But you know how reserved we are!" However, the audience wildly cheers the exploits of Captain America and Bucky, leaving Fury jealous. "Mebbe I oughtta wear a nutty mask with two cornball wings on it too! PHOOEY!"[13]

The contrast here is between the common man Fury created for a 1960s audience and the masked hero originally created during the 1940s. Sgt. Fury is the work-a-day soldier on the frontlines, while Captain America is a symbol of the nation. In a scene set in a pub where Fury has taken his date (interestingly they are drinking tea and she is praising him for behaving like a "perfect gentleman"), his rival Sgt. Bull McGiveney enters like the proverbial bull in a china shop. Fury ends up brawling with McGiveney when he picks on a rookie private named Steve Rogers, who is later revealed to be Captain America in his regular army uniform.

In a somewhat bland plot, Captain America and Bucky go on a secret mission to the European mainland. Although Fury has earlier been dismissive of Captain America, Cap is shown to have respect for Fury and his Howlers by sending for them when help is needed. Fury initially resists the call for help but his commander explains that the publicity the Howlers would get for helping out "that masked glory-hound" will get them all promotions. Fury follows up with, "and I'll be able to prove we're more soldier than he could ever be!"[14] But the story goes on to have Fury and Captain America fighting side by side, as it says in the title of the issue, on a mission to stop the Nazis from tunneling under the English Channel in order to invade the island nation. The team successfully destroys the tunnel and, of course, Fury discovers that he was wrong about Captain America.

The story has many interesting implications for both the continuity of the Marvel Universe and for viewing Fury as commemoration. Captain America's secret identity, Private Steve Rogers, is almost inconsequential, and Nick Fury's rank and title are almost unimportant to him. Fury rejects the rank and adulation that Captain America embodies for the purpose of wartime propaganda. Captain America serves in a patriotic, symbolic role that links the character to the Golden Age of comics and to the time being commemorated in the *Sgt. Fury* book. Also, Captain America provides legitimacy and continuity to the new Marvel superheroes with his reintroduction in *Avengers* #4 (1964). His appearance in the *Sgt. Fury* book serves to give credence to the idea that Captain America, like Fury, was a representative of the Greatest Generation and was a true super-soldier. Later, the image of Fury fighting side-by-side with Captain America during the war years will give credibility to his incarnation as an agent of S.H.I.E.L.D.

"Nick Fury, Agent of S.H.I.E.L.D.": Publication history and background

Just as Lee and Kirby took advantage of the popularity of combat stories, so also they turned to the spy genre. The early Cold War saw the rise of the spy and espionage genre in both novels and television. Certainly Ian Fleming (1908–1964) had much to do with this, thanks to his immensely popular series of 14 James Bond novels running from 1952 to posthumous publications in 1966. And starting in the 1960s, they became the basis of one of the most popular film series of all time. Although Agent Fury was not as cultured as Bond, they both were technologically equipped super-spies fighting organized criminal agencies bent on world domination. Television series dealing with spies were also hugely popular. Shows like *The Saint* and *Danger Man* in England drew large viewing audiences, as did the U.S. productions *I Spy* and *Mission Impossible*, and the comedy *Get Smart*. Perhaps the greatest direct influence on Agent Fury was *The Man from U.N.C.L.E.* whose agents fought against the villainous organization THRUSH.

The transition from Sgt. Fury to Agent Fury would seem to be a natural one, moving from traditional soldier to cold-warrior. Lee and Kirby were looking to develop a spy character to take advantage of the genre's popularity; it was a natural evolution to make Nick Fury that spy.[15] "Nick Fury: Agent of S.H.I.E.L.D." was first introduced in *Strange Tales* #135 (August 1965) and the character continued in that book, sharing it with Dr. Strange, until its end with issue 168 (May 1968) when both received their own titles. Surprisingly, the Fury title lasted only 18 issues. Agent Fury, now a colonel, had a much shorter run (52 issues from 1965 to 1971) than did his army counterpart.

As John Morrow lays out the chronology, CIA Agent Fury first appeared in *Fantastic Four* #21 (December 1963), 7 months after the debut of *Sgt. Fury and His Howling Commandos*.[16] This set the stage for the creation of S.H.I.E.L.D.[17] The revamping of Nick Fury followed a familiar creative pattern. Stan Lee and Jack Kirby created the initial stories. They then transitioned the title to another artist who worked with Kirby for a period of time before taking over the title.

As Morrow explains:

> While Stan scripted most of the issues presented [in *Marvel Masterworks: Agent Fury*, Volume 1], Kirby was undoubtedly the guiding creative force. This was the era of the Marvel Method, where the artist broke down the story following a basic plot discussion, adding huge amounts of creative input to the story before turning in the pages, leaving margin notes to explain it all to the scripter. This process allowed Kirby to cut loose with

some of the most way-out and far-fetched technological gadgets ever seen in comics, which was right up his alley, being a lifelong sci-fi fan.[18]

The creative talent that was tutored by Kirby in the Marvel Method on this title makes an impressive list, many of whom would go on to be prominent names in the industry.[19]

With *Strange Tales* #151 (December 1966), Jim Steranko was brought in as one of Kirby's assistants. Steranko had only one comic book credit to his name before he started this assignment. But within 2 issues, he not only had taken over the artwork as a whole but became the writer through nearly 20 issues, taking the character into the early issues of his own self-titled book.

After this first series of "Nick Fury, Agent of S.H.I.E.L.D., the character appeared, and continues to appear through the present day, in a number of mini-series and has come to be an ever-present figure throughout the Marvel Universe. Perhaps his grimmest later appearance has been in volume 1 of the *Secret Warriors* series (2009), entitled *Nick Fury: Agent of Nothing*.

Nick Fury: Agent of change

For Lee and Kirby, the Fury character served as a bridge linking the time of the Golden Age to that of the Silver Age, giving their new fictional universe a sense of historical and internal continuity. Sgt. Fury stood at one end of the bridge, while at the other end stood Agent Fury. The S.H.I.E.L.D. stories helped to embed the emerging Marvel Universe within a collective origin story, a key element to the creation of social memory. The emergence of Fury in the Cold War continued the Good War themes while allowing the Marvel creative staff to avoid the actual politics of the Cold War. Good and evil were self-apparent, with Lee, Kirby, and other Marvel creators sometimes not bothering to explain the villain's motives other than world conquest and a link to Nazi Germany. The villains were evil because their antecedents were Nazis. The good guys were heroic because they fought the Nazis in the Good War.[20]

Nick Fury, Agent of S.H.I.E.L.D. followed the familiar themes established in *Sgt. Fury*. Like the World War II stories, the plot here generally involved Fury leading a band of brothers against evil villains. Two Howling Commando characters followed Fury into the new stories, Dum Dum Dugan and Gabriel Jones. Captain America, as a recurring guest, also connected the 1940s to the 1960s. The S.H.I.E.L.D. cast is later joined by Jasper Stillwell, an Ivy League educated rookie who is like the earlier character from *Sgt. Fury*. The early stories contained a great deal of nostalgic references to the World War II adventures of the Howling Commandos.

There was a kind of dichotomy in the book between the nostalgic characters that highlighted the values of the Greatest Generation and the Cold War context. Lee and Kirby's treatment of the Commandos as unchanged from the 1940s highlighted this duality. They placed characters that were relics of World War II in charge of a contemporary high-tech counter-terrorism organization. Although never mentioning communism or any communist country, the stories also contained strong Cold War themes.[21]

During the actual Cold War, the United States government created new national security agencies, including the C.I.A., and joined international agencies, such as N.A.T.O., to combat communism. S.H.I.E.L.D. is a fictional variation of those agencies. The stories contain typical Cold War plots, utilizing such themes as brain washing (with the subsequent loss of free will), infiltration (with the inability to trust friends and comrades), and super science (with the concern that humanity could lose control of its own technology).

Not surprisingly given the variety of writers and artists working on the title, there is an uneven quality in the creative work, resulting in plot ambiguities. For example the actual status of S.H.I.E.L.D. is not clear. Is it an international agency or an agency of the United States government? Its title identifies it as "International," but Fury and his agents seem to be associated with the United States government. Fury has the military rank of colonel, but seems to be the only S.H.I.E.L.D. agent that has such a rank. It is not clear if S.H.I.E.L.D. is meant to be a clandestine spy organization, a branch of the military, or an overt law enforcement agency that publicly slugs it out with the bad guys.

The first story arc, with Lee, Kirby, and Ayers (all from the *Sgt. Fury* book) listed as the creative team, opens with the S.H.I.E.L.D. technicians making an android duplicate of Fury. These duplicates become a standard feature of S.H.I.E.L.D. stories, suggesting a theme of loss of identity and humanity amid technology. The highly individualistic Fury is technologically cloned, and the duplicate becomes another faceless cog in the machine, fodder to be sacrificed in the fight against global domination. Loss of identity and shifting identities become major themes. In later stories, Fury is controlled by villains who place a blank mask over his face that robs him of his free will. The returning villain Baron Strucker threatens to use Fury as a model for an army of androids that will take over the world. A.I.M., a criminal organization, attempts to create an army of nondescript humanoids, again faceless, for world conquest. Later, S.H.I.E.L.D. is infiltrated by the leader of HYDRA, another criminal group, who transforms Fury's appearance using super science.

"The Man for the Job" (*Strange* Tales #135, August 1965) introduces readers to Agent Fury and to S.H.I.E.L.D. Much of the issue is devoted to showing off various gadgets, such as the android duplicates, flying cars, and the S.H.I.E.L.D. "helicarrier" mobile headquarters. In some ways, the high-tech gadgetry replaces the historic cataloging of weapons from the *Sgt. Fury* book, and in other ways it echoes James Bond's outfitting at the beginning of his movies.

The character of Tony Stark, "the playboy arms inventor," who is also in "charge of the special weaponry section," recruits Fury to lead the newly formed S.H.I.E.L.D. Stark's appearance raises some interesting questions. He would seem to be a logical character to appear since as both Stark and Iron Man he is one of the few Marvel characters at the time to directly confront the communists.[22] In the context of this book, though, Stark will confront global domination as a businessman, not a superhero.

Despite the changed context, Fury remains a representative of the everyman, a kind of citizen soldier. As Fury is about to be interviewed by Stark aboard S.H.I.E.L.D.'s mobile command headquarters, he thinks to himself, "Some of the most famous Joes from every nation in the world are sitting around that circle! But I still don't get it!! Where does a clown like me fit in?" Fury initially refuses the job, explaining, "You've got a million scientific gimmicks—rays—rockets—things I can't even pronounce. I'm outta my league!" However, Fury's discovery of a bomb planted at the meeting convinces him to take the job because "That means it's them—or us—right?"[23] Fury is selected to lead S.H.I.E.L.D. not because of his tactical or technical skill, but because he is a man of action.

The next several issues feature Fury leading S.H.I.E.L.D. against a HYDRA plan to extort money from the world using the threat of a space-based missile, mirroring another Cold War concern that the space race would become part of the arms race. HYDRA is a vaguely fascist secret society bent on world domination.[24] The image of HYDRA's tentacles encircling a globe is an echo of the common Cold War image of the global reach of communism. HYDRA works collectively, much like Cold Warriors of the period imagined the Communists doing. Its slogan was "Cut off a limb, and two more shall take its place."

The leader of HYDRA, like Stark, is also the head of a major corporation. Ironically, the HYDRA leader is killed by his followers who do not recognize him without his padded robes and hood (*Strange Tales* #141, February 1966). The story's ending is ambiguous. It may be seen to emphasize the stature of the American businessman Tony Stark in the world of technology against that of a corrupt business leader who falls prey to his own devices.

There was a distinct decline in the quality of work on Agent Fury as Jack Kirby took less of a role in the creative process. The stories became disjointed and lackluster. Even when Kirby comes back to work on the Fury crossover team-up with Captain America in *Tales of Suspense* #78 (June 1966), there is not much improvement. What the issue does do is to echo the commemorative themes found in Sgt. Fury's earlier meeting with Captain America. Like issue 13 of *Sgt. Fury* (December 1964), the significance of the story is the interaction between Nick Fury and Captain America as purveyors of public memory of the Good War. While the action was at best formulaic, Kirby and Lee clearly bring more creative energy to the nostalgic memory of World War II than to the standard superhero team-up plot.

That issue also serves as a transition. Lee and Kirby will gradually leave the book to be replaced by Jim Steranko. Steranko's work on Nick Fury would be short-lived. However, it is often cited as ground breaking work that stretched the limits of what was permissible under the Comic Code Authority. Steranko's work is significant in that it drops most of the commemorative autobiography brought into the Sgt. Fury and early Agent Fury stories by Lee, Kirby, and other World War II veterans in favor of a more modern style. Steranko guides Fury fully into the fantastic Marvel Universe of superheroes. While Steranko will deemphasize Fury's Howling Commando background, he will take note that the Fury character should have aged 20-plus years and will resurrect the Nazi character of Baron Strucker as the new leader of HYDRA.

As was the pattern, Steranko began his work on Agent Fury by penciling over Kirby's layouts and working with Lee's script. However, Steranko found his apprenticeship frustrating. Within 3 months, Steranko assumed creative control over the character and the new title, *Nick Fury: Agent of S.H.I.E.L.D.* According to him, Kirby's S.H.I.E.L.D. issues had started out with a bang, but the book had since stagnated, in part because Fury remained the same character as he had in the *Sgt. Fury* book.

Steranko's artistic innovations, which he called "Zap Art," made it difficult for him to continue treating the book in the same way Kirby had done.[25] Under Steranko's guidance, the Fury stories seemed less of a war comic set in a spy context and became more modern and complex both in plot and in visuals. Steranko notes in his introduction that he used his life for story ideas just as Lee and Kirby relied on their wartime experiences. He also aged Fury slightly, with a touch of white at the temples, and dropped the trade-mark five o'clock shadow. He increased the emphasis on super science. Fury now spoke and dressed like the head of an international espionage unit, not as a gruff army sergeant. He also began to fit in with the costumed superheroes, adopting at times a black leather jump suit with utility belts (see Figure 12.3). Under Steranko's guidance, Fury became the more cynical, world-weary character that we know today.

Steranko's deemphasizing of the public memory of World War II can perhaps best be seen in his treatment of Captain America and Dum Dum Dugan, Fury's second-in-command in both the Howling Commandos and S.H.I.E.L.D. Following a team-up covering 3 issues (*Strange Tales* #159–161), Captain American eventually disappears from Steranko's work. When he does appear in these issues, Captain America is more of a costumed adventurer and less of a patriotic symbol of the Good War. Similarly, Dum Dum and Gabe Jones, Fury's fellow Howling Commandos,

Figure 12.3 Sterakno's Fury is a super-spy with fewer connections to World War II. Jim Steranko (a). *Strange Tales* #167 (April 1968), Marvel Comics, cover. Marvel, Nick Fury, and all related characters © and ™ Marvel Entertainment, LLC. All rights reserved and used with permission.

assume a much smaller role as Steranko introduces new characters, such as Contessa Valentina Allegro de Fontaine, a female agent and Fury's romantic interest.

Conclusion

Nick Fury and S.H.I.E.L.D. have come to play a role in most of the major events in the Marvel Universe, helping writers create a sense of cohesion in the increasingly frequent cross-over story arcs. In Marvel's Ultimate

Universe, for example, General Fury (who is African-American and modeled after the actor Samuel L. Jackson) is a catalyst for the creation and recruitment of superheroes. In some of the recent Marvel movies, the Fury character (played by Jackson) fulfills the same role.

Clearly, for Sgt. Lee, Infantryman Kirby, and Corp. Ayers, the Fury character provided an opportunity to inject an autobiographical element into the Marvel Universe by commemorating the Good War. Later creators would put this commemorative element into the service of fighting the Cold War. And Fury emerges at the turn of the twenty-first century as something of a timeless character, becoming more cynical to serve as a counter-point to the politics of this new era.

But through these changes, the commemorative aspects of the original Lee and Kirby stories still remain in the background. Despite being nearly a century old, Fury remains an active hero, allowing him to dispense wisdom inherent in the historical lessons from the Greatest Generation. Although Fury continues to serve as an exemplar of older values and masculinity, in the new century he appears alienated and, more often than not, unsure who is the villain and who is the ally. In post 9/11 America, Fury finds S.H.I.E.L.D. to be ineffective as the super villain Norman Osborn (a.k.a. the Green Goblin) takes over the agency, transforming it into H.A.M.M.E.R. The new agency represents the corrupted power that Fury had long fought as both a sergeant and an agent.

Nick Fury and his old Howling Commandos find that their values put them at odds with the nation. The moral certainties of the G.I. Generation that fought the Good War became grayer in the Cold War. Ironically, during the War on Terrorism, the moral certainty that characterized Nick Fury transformed him into an "agent of nothing" just as the nation fought real versions of secret societies that had been such a staple in his fictional world.[26] In one of his most recent appearances, Nick Fury leads his men on the "Last Ride of the Howling Commandos" in an effort to restore the values of the Greatest Generation to the nation as a restored new creative team looks to restore Nick Fury's commemorative power.[27]

Notes

1 Calling World War II the "Good War" seems to have first been widely popularized by Studs Terkel's *The Good War: An Oral History of World War Two* (NY: Pantheon, 1984).
2 For this essay we have primarily used the collected *Marvel Masterworks* editions dealing with the Fury character. *Marvel Masterworks: Sgt. Fury vol. 1* (2006) reprints *Sgt. Fury and His Howling Commandos* 1–13 (1963–1964) and *Marvel Masterworks: Sgt. Fury vol. 2* (2008) reprints 14–23 and Annual no. 1 (1965). *Marvel Masterworks: Nick Fury: Agent of S.H.I.E.L.D. vol. 1*

reprints *Strange Tales* 135–153 and *Tales to Astonish* 78 (1965–1967). *Marvel Masterworks: Nick Fury: Agent of S.H.I.E.L.D. vol. 2* reprints *Strange Tales* 154–168 and *Nick Fury: Agent of S.H.I.E.L.D.* 1–3 (1967–1968).

3 Matthew J. Costello, *Secret Identity Crisis: Comic Books and the Unmasking of Cold War America* (New York: Continuum, 2009), 12. Costello uses Richard Reynolds' work to suggest that "structural continuity lends a mythopoetic power to the narratives."

4 Stan Lee, "Introduction," *Marvel Masterworks: Sgt. Fury vol. 1.*

5 The term "The Greatest Generation" has been given prominence through its use as the title of a book by Tom Brokaw (*The Greatest Generation*. NY: Random House, 1998). The year of its publication saw the release of both *Saving Private Ryan* and *The Thin Red Line* in movie theatres. An earlier, perhaps better treatment was done by Studs Terkel ("*The Good War": An Oral History of World War Two*. NY: Pantheon, 1984). Also see, *Generations: The History of the America's Future, 1584 to 2069* by W. Strauss & N. Howe (NY: Morrow, 1991) for a sociological treatment. For an academic treatment of the memory of World War II, see John Bodnar, *The "Good War" in American Memory* (Baltimore: Johns Hopkins University Press, 2010).

6 Stan Lee has told this story at many places. For one example, see his interview on the National Public Radio series *Fresh Air* (October 27, 2010).

7 Lee, "Introduction." *Marvel Masterworks: Sgt. Fury vol. 1.*

8 Ibid. Lee also makes this point in his *Fresh Air* interview of October 27, 2010.

9 *Marvel Masterworks: Sgt. Fury vol. 1*, 6.

10 Ibid., 106. Fury's class identity is also emphasized by his English girlfriend who frequently attempts to teach him some gentlemanly manners throughout the series.

11 Ibid., 113.

12 Ibid., 176–77.

13 Ibid., 288.

14 Ibid., 299.

15 Jim Steranko recalled that Stan Lee gave him a "sample sequence for a super spy" developed by Jack Kirby when he first went to work for Marvel. The two-page treatment featured a mystery spy with an eye patch who was the "Director of External Atomic Threat Headquarters." This super-spy was revised to become Agent Nick Fury (Steranko, "Introduction," *Marvel Masterworks: Agent Fury*, vol. 2).

16 Stan Lee (w), Jack Kirby (p), and George Roussos (i). "The Hate-Monger!" *Fantastic Four* #21 (December 1963), Marvel Comics. Nick Fury is even announced on the cover as being "more exciting than ever!"

17 S.H.I.E.L.D. stood for Supreme Headquarters International Espionage Law-enforcement Division.

18 John Morrow, "Introduction." *Marvel Masterworks: Agent Fury*, vol. 1.

19 They are Dennis O'Neil, Roy Thomas, John Severin, Joe Sinnott, Don Heck, John Buscema, Jim Steranko, and others.

20 Costello, *Secret Identity Crisis*, 68–71.

21 Ibid., 8.

22 Ibid., 63.

23 *Marvel Masterworks: Agent* Fury, vol.1, 10–12.
24 In the 2011 film *Captain America: The First Avenger*, there are explicit connections made between HYDRA and the Nazis.
25 Steranko, "Introduction." *Marvel Masterworks: Agent Fury*, vol.2.
26 "Nick Fury: Agent of Nothing" is the title of a story arc in *Secret Warriors* #1–6 (April–September 2009).
27 Jonathan Hickman (w) and Alessandro Vitti (a). "The Last Ride of the Howling Commandos." *Secret Warriors* #17 (August 2010).

CHAPTER THIRTEEN

The U.S. HIV/AIDS Crisis

and the Negotiation of Queer Identity in Superhero Comics, or, Is Northstar Still a Fairy?

Ben Bolling

A 2003 Henry J. Kaiser Family Foundation study notes that during the period from 1981 to 2002, American news media coverage of the HIV/AIDS pandemic peaked in 1987 with over 5,000 stories appearing that year among the print and broadcast news outlets followed in the study.[1] Since 1987, news coverage of HIV/AIDS among these same media outlets dwindled steadily to fewer than 1,000 stories in 2002.[2] This "AIDS fatigue" is certainly a matter deserving of further inquiry, especially given the media's lackluster performance in addressing the emergence of AIDS in the early 1980s, as depicted in Randy Shilts's *And the Band Played On* (1987). But beyond the confines of the newsroom, its effects may also be observed across the spectrum of American cultural production. The "AIDS-arts timeline" and "AIDS-Arts Bibliography," hosted by Artery: The AIDS-Arts Forum and edited by activist and art historian Robert Atkins, demonstrate that the responses to AIDS in cultural texts have also been insufficient, particularly since the mid-1990s.[3] Part of the reason for this paucity of representations is the unwieldiness of emplotting the virus itself and the failure of the HIV/AIDS crisis to conform to entrenched narrative structures that govern responses to contagious diseases.

A key reason why many AIDS narratives that *have* garnered popular attention struggle in their representation of the pandemic is due in large part to the failure of HIV/AIDS to conform to what Pricilla Wald, in *Contagious: Cultures, Carriers, and the Outbreak Narrative* (2008), defines as "the outbreak narrative." In Wald's configuration, "[t]he outbreak narrative—in its scientific, journalistic, and fictional incarnations—follows a formulaic plot that begins with the identification of an emerging infection, includes discussion of the global networks through which it travels, and chronicles the epidemiological work that ends with its containment." While infections such as Severe Acute Respiratory Syndrome (SARS) and the H1N1 "swine flu" may conform more productively to the narrative constraints outlined above, Wald notes that "HIV/AIDS is not well suited to the formula of an outbreak narrative."[4] As a result, AIDS stories frequently take on alternative plots. For instance, many AIDS narratives emphasize "the heroism of afflicted individuals in the face of adversity and the communities that form around them, as in Jonathan Demme's 1993 *Philadelphia*" or the disease may be mobilized "in the service of broader social commentary, increasingly with a global focus" as in Tony Kushner's 1993–1994 *Angels in America* or Darrell Roodt's 2004 film *Yesterday*.[5]

But there are some texts that depict viral agency—a key element of the outbreak narrative—while sidestepping the elusive "plot point" of containment. By "viral agency," I refer broadly to the rhetorical act of personifying the virus or imbuing it with qualities such as wiliness, stealth, or maliciousness that inflect its biological imperative to reproduce. Perhaps most famously, the aforementioned *And the Band Played On* chronicles political, scientific, and community in-fighting in the early years of the American AIDS crisis, ultimately using these conflicts as a backdrop for a medical detective thriller in which intrepid researchers doggedly search for the evasive cause or causes of the emerging epidemic. Though Wald contends that "[t]he legacy of Shilts's depiction of viral agency has not been evident in the considerable artistic output generated by the HIV/AIDS epidemic,"[6] there are AIDS stories that divorce the issue of viral agency from the epistemology of outbreak in an effort to address social and political concerns obscured by the scientific focus of the outbreak narrative. Two types of these stories are the "Patient Zero containment fantasy" and the "gay redeemer narrative." In the "Patient Zero containment fantasy," the viral host—the virus embodied—is primarily represented not as a harbinger of contagion, but as a member of a risk group predisposed to viral infection who may be contained and dispatched *before* he becomes what Wald terms a "superspreader" of disease.[7] In the "gay redeemer narrative," a member of America's most prominent risk group is dogged by the specter of HIV, but remains resistant to infection in an effort to sever the ideological link that first characterized AIDS as a "gay plague," particularly in the United States.

The primary object of my analysis in examining both of these AIDS narratives is not a text, but a character enmeshed in a matrix of texts.

Jean-Paul Beaubier, Marvel Comics's mutant speedster known as Northstar, is widely considered to be one of the earliest, if not the first, openly gay superheroes in mainstream comics.[8] Because the character's publication history spans over 30 years (from 1979 to the present)—almost perfectly shadowing the emergence of AIDS in American cultural history—Northstar provides an excellent site for analyzing the evolving depiction and understanding of queerness in post-1980 popular culture, particularly the imbrication of gay male identity politics and HIV/AIDS. The relatively long duration of Northstar's ongoing development is significant because the mainstream comics medium, through serialized publication, gives rise to a unique rhetorical situation that I have elsewhere described as "serial historiography."[9] Serialized publication and the comics marketplace encourage unprecedented interchange among comics producers and readers in the ongoing, open-ended adjudication of narrative truth claims in comics' fictional universes. In this case, the "truth" about Northstar—who he is, whom he loves, whether he lives or dies—provides insight into the negotiation of ideas about both homosexuality and HIV/AIDS in broader American culture.

Northstar first appeared in April of 1979 in *Uncanny X-men* #120. As a member of Alpha Flight, the premier Canadian superhero team, Northstar was among the agents charged with reclaiming their government's humanized weapon, the popular X-Man Wolverine. Originally conceived simply as an element of Wolverine's back-story, artist and writer John Byrne created Alpha Flight to be nothing "more than a bunch of superheroes who could survive a fight with the X-men."[10] But as is sometimes the case when the market and reader input are able to affect a text's development, Alpha Flight garnered so much popularity among comics fans that it was granted its own ongoing series in 1983.

In his first appearances in *Uncanny X-men*, Northstar is established as Jean-Paul Beaubier—a French Canadian, a famous Olympic ski champion, and an arrogant and impetuous mutant gifted with the powers of super-human speed, flight, and the ability to generate blinding flashes of light when in physical contact with his teammate and twin sister, Aurora. But as early as *Alpha Flight* #1 in 1983, Northstar's sexuality became central to his characterization. In this story, a severe nun accosts Aurora when she catches the dowdy young woman returning to her room in the Catholic school where she lives and works with an unfamiliar man in tow. Aurora responds to Sister Anne's accusations of impropriety by saying, "But this is not a man—I mean, of course he's a man, but he is also my brother."[11] This momentary gender ambiguity is not a lone marker of queerness, however. When we first see Northstar in his civilian identity of Jean-Paul Beaubier, he is fey and lithe, surrounded by swooning schoolgirls who are enchanted by his boyish good looks, style, and celebrity—but whom Northstar seems all too eager to escape.[12] A few issues later, in *Alpha Flight* #7, readers are introduced to Raymonde Belmonde, a cravated dandy who is "more than a father, much more than a friend, he had found Jean-Paul, scarcely more than a boy, alone and frightened. Frightened of what he thought he was, and what he feared he might become."[13]

These are just a few examples of the "clues" to Northstar's sexual orientation scattered throughout creator John Byrne's 28-issue run on *Alpha Flight*. In a 2004 interview, Byrne reveals the politics behind his characterization of Northstar in a passage worth quoting at length:

> Unfortunately [Alpha Flight] proved enormously popular, and so Marvel began pushing me to do an *Alpha Flight* book. . . . I had recently read an article in *Scientific American* on what was then (the early 80s) fairly radical new thinking on just what processes caused a person to be homosexual, and the evidence was pointing increasingly to it being genetic and not environmental factors. So, I thought, it seemed like it was time for a gay superhero, and since I was being "forced" to make *Alpha Flight* a real series, I might as well make one of *them* gay. . . . Of course, the temper of the times, the Powers That Were and, naturally, the Comics Code[14] would not let me come right out and state that Jean-Paul was homosexual, but I managed to "get the word out" even with those barriers.[15]

Byrne suggests that his decision to make Northstar gay was influenced by shifting cultural ideas about homosexuality in the late 1970s and early 1980s, explicitly linking the unfolding history of the fictional Marvel universe to real world historical events—particularly the strides being made for LGBT civil rights in parts of the United States.

More important, the effort to "get the word out" about Northstar's queerness instructed consumers in a way of reading the character for decades—a hermeneutics of suspicion that often relied upon pervasive clichés concerning gay men to signal the "unspeakable" depths of the character. Initially these clues were innocuous enough, if stereotypical. There was the hot pool boy who answered Jean-Paul's phone,[16] the oft-alluded to secrets that made Northstar feel isolated,[17] mention of "special friends,"[18] and a ubiquitous incredulity regarding Jean-Paul's interest in reciprocating the romantic advances of women.[19] Fan letters published in the pages of *Alpha Flight* illustrate that not only did fans perceive these "hints" as markers of Jean-Paul's queerness, but some readers wanted creators to dispense with the insinuations and have Northstar "come out" as early as 1986; in a letter published in *Alpha Flight* #39, reader Brian Nelson writes bluntly: "Admit that Northstar is gay."

But Northstar's sexual orientation, like that of a number of high-profile celebrities, remained a public secret in the late 80s until John Byrne's successor, writer Bill Mantlo, employed a "gay trope" with the potential of outing Jean-Paul in the same manner as Rock Hudson. In January 1987's *Alpha Flight* #42, Northstar is afflicted with a racking cough that quickly progresses to wounds that will not heal[20] and an increasingly fragile immune system.[21] When Alpha Flight faced the villain Pestilence in the March 1987 issue, the supernatural/biological terrorist seemed to elucidate the cause of Northstar's illness in the following exchange:

Northstar: "What are you—?"
Pestilence: "Doing? Why, merely feeding on the decay I sensed within you to make myself stronger!"
Northstar: "What do you *koff! koff!* mean—'decay within me?!!'"
Pestilence: "That you are dying, speedster! Haven't you sensed it? And my kiss has accelerated the slow disease spreading like a cancer through your cells!"[22] (see Figure 13.1)

Though remaining somewhat oblique, Pestilence nonetheless describes symptoms commonly associated with AIDS and Northstar's previous prodromes align to support such a diagnosis: he has an infection that has remained dormant or undetected for some time, a pathogen that preys upon the body's

Figure 13.1 Pestilence accelerates the disease that is slowly killing Northstar. Bill Mantlo (w) and David Ross (a). "Plague!" *Alpha Flight* v1 #44 (March 1987), Marvel Comics, 16. Northstar and all related characters © and ™ Marvel Entertainment, LLC. All rights reserved and used with permission.

cells, a disease that spreads like and sometimes manifests as cancer (e.g. the common opportunistic Kaposi sarcoma that was common among early people with AIDS in the United States), and a debilitating respiratory illness not unlike *Pneumocystis carinii* pneumonia (PCP), another opportunistic infection that was a common cause of death among people with AIDS in the 1980s. And perhaps most significantly, Pestilence—the very manifestation of contagion—senses Northstar's infection when he kisses the young hero on the forehead in a suggestive display of homoeroticism. This image, in which one man shows twisted affection to another, recalibrates the clues that signify Northstar's queerness with the symptoms of the disease often still characterized in the late 1980s as "the gay plague." The reading skills the text once fostered so the reader might recognize the cues of Northstar's sexual orientation are repurposed for epidemiological detective work. Additionally, this act of suspicious reading reverberates with Shilts's description of scowering obituaries in the early 1980s for "symptoms" of AIDS-related deaths, "the vague long illness or the odd reference to a pneumonia or skin cancer striking down someone in, say, their mid-thirties."[23]

And so the emergence of Northstar's mystery illness marks the beginning of the first AIDS narrative of viral agency that I want to examine more closely. The "Patient Zero containment fantasy" relies upon the general structure of the outbreak narrative—identification, detection, and containment—but in this fantasy the viral agent that would cause a pandemic is diagnosed and quarantined *before* an outbreak may occur. This fantasy of containment develops in response to the jarring reality that U.S. public health protocol failed to isolate the cause of AIDS or take bold actions to arrest the spread of HIV before thousands of Americans were infected and/or dead. Furthermore, HIV/AIDS emerged at a time when the global North had—with the signing of the World Health Organization and UNICEF sponsored *Declaration of Alma-Ata* on September 12, 1978—forecast the virtual eradication of communicable disease by the year 2000.[24] Modern science's inability to contain HIV/AIDS constituted a serious threat to the outbreak narrative (which depends on "containment" as a narrative end point), and as Priscilla Wald argues, the creation of "Patient Zero" was central to the resuscitation of a narrative capable of making meaning of the AIDS epidemic.[25]

"Patient Zero" refers to Gaetan Dugas, a French-Canadian flight attendant who was identified in journalistic reports, scientific literature, and popular media as one of the first people to be infected with HIV in North America and the "superspreader" responsible for widely disseminating the virus across the continent (if not the world) through intercontinental air travel. In *And the Band Played On*, Dugas evolves over the course of the text from a beautiful, charismatic libertine whose promiscuity celebrates the sexual liberation of metropolitan queer communities of the 1970s to a harbinger of a "gay epidemic" to a human-virus hybrid who stalks the San

Francisco bathhouses monstrously intent upon spreading the infection that marred his own vanity. The science necessary to make Dugas into the AIDS "superspreader" is suspect at best, but as Wald persuasively argues, "Patient Zero" is first and foremost a construction—a narrative device animated by Shilts's poetic license that takes us inside the thoughts of this viral-human hybrid to make sense of "the recalcitrant disseminator who embodies the public-health dilemma and the malevolence of the virus itself."[26]

The impact of Shilts's book—and particularly the attention given to "Patient Zero" in his account—on public discourse surrounding AIDS cannot be understated. In the October 1988 issue of *Scientific American*, William Blattner, chief of viral epidemiology at the National Cancer Institute, called *And the Band Played On*—somewhat pejoratively—"*the* AIDS book [that] has been a potent factor in the public perception of the AIDS problem."[27] Blattner's critique of the book hinges largely on Shilts's sensational treatment of Dugas, but "Patient Zero" was undoubtedly one of the elements that gained *And the Band Played On* attention in the first place. A cursory overview of previews and reviews of the book illustrates the prevalence of the "Patient Zero" narrative—a comparatively small component of the 600-plus page text—in the excerpts, essays, and head-lines used to promote the work. But as a narrative device, Patient Zero is attractive. In his human-virus form, the cause of AIDS is isolated, the networks through which it travels are illuminated, and with his death on March 30, 1984, an illusory sense of containment is achieved.[28] But when *And the Band Played On* was published in 1987, HIV/AIDS had not been contained and though the "Patient Zero narrative" helped make sense of the outbreak, it could not prevent it.

It was also in 1987 that Northstar was afflicted with a mysterious degen-erative illness. And though the similarities are undoubtedly coincidental given that Jean-Paul Beaubier first appeared in print in 1979, the similar-ities between Northstar and Gaetan Dugas are striking. Both are not just Canadian, but French Canadian and thus susceptible to emplotment as "foreign," a characteristic common to the carrier of the outbreak narra-tive.[29] In Shilts's characterization of Dugas and in all writers' portrayals of Northstar, both men are vain, charming, petulant, brash, and terminally self-important. But perhaps most foreboding, Dugas and Northstar each possess an ability to travel the world with alarming speed.

But whereas Dugas is consistently characterized as sexually vor-acious, Northstar is effectively virginal. With the exception of Raymonde Belmonde—who is killed by a supervillain four pages after his introduc-tion—the "clues" to Northstar's homosexuality are outward trappings of stereotypical gayness such as flamboyant aestheticism, a distaste for the romantic advances of women, and physical effeminacy, but never the sug-gestion of romantic or sexual relationships with other men. If Northstar was infected with HIV, then certainly it had been transmitted to him by someone, somehow, but as with Gaetan Dugas, the "Patient Zero" device supports if not encourages an idea of immaculate conception of the virus. To be "Patient Zero" is to be the first viral carrier. And so by imagining the sex out of Northstar's sexuality, Mantlo and others created a "Patient Zero" analogue whose viral provenance need not be contemplated and who may be contained *before* inciting an outbreak.

But Northstar's illness was not caused by HIV/AIDS. In September 1987's *Alpha Flight* #50, Loki, Thor's villainous step-brother and the Asgardian god of mischief, reveals that Northstar and Aurora are not human-mutants, but half-elves from the faerie realm of Alfheim.[30] Jean-Paul's degenerative disease (and Aurora's paranoid schizophrenia) is caused by living on Midgard (i.e. Earth) rather than within the pure light of Alfheim.[31] Aurora decides to share her "inner light" with Northstar, an act that heals Jean-Paul completely but leaves his sister vulnerable and she is pulled into the dark recesses of Svartalfheim (yet another Asgardian world) by its demonic inhabitants.[32] At issue's end, with Aurora missing, Northstar soars into the sky where a heavenly gate to Alfheim opens to "welcome him home."[33]

Though unsubstantiated, lore among comics readers and Alpha Flight fans commonly holds that Mantlo intended for Northstar to be diagnosed with AIDS and die from the syndrome, but was directed toward the elven alternative by Marvel editors.[34] The bizarre plot turn led writer Peter David to quip, "Yes, that's right . . . [Northstar] wasn't gay. He was just a fairy."[35] Regardless, the "fairy story" is a clear AIDS analogue and provides the resolution of the "Patient Zero containment fantasy." The disease "spreading like a cancer through [Northstar's] cells" is revealed to be truly *foreign* and the product of deadly miscegenation. Northstar's human father and elven mother are both killed by elves who refuse to let their "bloodline be polluted."[36] The racialization of Northstar's origin and his illness parallels the "Africanization" of AIDS. The "African origin thesis" of AIDS popularized by Shilts and scientific literature of the late 1980s casts the image of a diseased continent populated by an infectious race that announces, in Wald's terms, a "Third World present and a First World future."[37] But in the "Patient Zero containment fantasy," the Africanization of the world is averted when the carrier with the power to initiate an outbreak is contained before he disseminates the contagion. In the Northstar fantasy, the mixed-race carrier is returned to the site of his illness's origin—a death-like place that locates the healthy world beyond his infectious reach.

Ultimately, the idea of containing the HIV pandemic proved to be a fantasy, much like the "Patient Zero" narrative itself. The beginning of the 1990s saw the number of people living with HIV in the United States alone increase to nearly 800,000.[38] The precipitous increase in people with HIV throughout the 1980s brought new issues into public discourse about the virus. The "gay redeemer narrative" appeared during this moment when commentators from across the political, scientific, and public health spectrum sought to extricate gay male identity politics from its place of centrality in HIV/AIDS discourse. Some queer activists and scientific researchers had long disdained monikers like "the gay plague," "gay cancer," and Gay-Related Immune Deficiency or GRID (a proposed diagnostic term that was supplanted by the more scientifically accurate Acquired Immunodeficiency Syndrome in 1982) on the grounds that such terms suggested that infectious agents recognized nonphysiological differences among humans.[39] These misleading terms also effaced other "risk groups" (such as hemophiliacs and intravenous drug users in the early 1980s) and individuals who did not identify as gay, but were nonetheless living with AIDS. And in the hands of moralists and bigots like Jerry Falwell and Pat Buchanan, the rhetoric of AIDS as a gay plague could be mobilized to justify the suffering exacted by the syndrome as "natural" or even "supernatural" retribution; in a widely-published newspaper editorial in May of 1983, Buchanan wrote, "The poor homosexuals—they have declared war upon nature, and now nature is exacting an awful retribution."[40]

As James W. Jones argues, "the view of homosexuality as an illness has a long history, reaching back at least to the Middle Ages" but AIDS "moved the focus from the psychological to the physical."[41] As a result, the "gay redeemer narrative" operates not only to depathologize, but also to decontaminate gay male identity from its associations with HIV infection. To do so, the narrative stages a confrontation between the gay man and the viral agent in which the redeemer establishes himself as a psychologically "normal" (or at least acceptable) component of a heteronormative society and thus imbued with an ability to avoid infection—an ability not shared by those "other gays" who insist upon keeping sex at the forefront of their sexual orientation. The serialized text provides an ideal site for observing the "gay redeemer narrative" because it allows the reader to track the changing parameters of affect and behavior delineated as culturally acceptable for the redeemer—as well as those that are not acceptable.

In the pages of *Alpha Flight*, Northstar remained in Alfheim until 1990 when in issue #81, new writer James D. Hudnall revealed that the whole elf origin story had been a huge goof perpetrated by Loki.[42] Aurora rescues Northstar from the elven land and readers learn that the twins are, in fact, human-mutants, but Northstar's mysterious illness is never quite parsed out.[43] This sort of willful forgetfulness on the part of readers and creators represents one of the more dangerous aspects of serial historiography. Commonly referred to as a "retcon" or "retroactive continuity," the effacement of an event or narrative meme from a character's past signifies a willingness among both consumers and producers of a text to deliberately change the historical record. In this instance, disillusionment with the failed rhetorical promises of the "Patient Zero containment fantasy" necessitated the erasure of the "fairy story" in order to resuscitate Northstar as both a hero and a gay man. If Northstar could not effectively contain the contagion, then in order to salvage his superheroic prowess, he must never have been infected. And not coincidentally, Northstar's return to health and superheroics coincided with his transformation from fairy to gay redeemer par excellence.

In March 1992's *Alpha Flight* #106, Northstar came out as gay—but the story had very little—if anything—to do with the character's sexuality.[44] During a high-octane superhero battle, Northstar discovers an abandoned infant in a trashcan and after rescuing her he learns that the child is dying of AIDS.[45] Jean-Paul adopts the hospitalized infant and uses his considerable celebrity as a superhero and "Montreal's Most Eligible Bachelor" to call for increased AIDS awareness and prevention programs in public schools.[46] The media frenzy surrounding the incident incenses World War II-era Canadian superhero Major Mapleleaf, who lashes out at Northstar saying, "My son, Michael, was a victim of AIDS as well! But he was gay—so people didn't afford him the luxury of being 'innocent.' . . . He was just one of thousands who died of AIDS last year! His whole life, reduced to a statistic!"[47] It is in the context of a physical confrontation with Mapleleaf that Northstar announces his sexual orientation while winding up for a punch, no less (see Figure 13.2) and then comforts the grieving father, saying, "It is past time that people started talking about AIDS. About its victims. Those who die . . . and those of us left behind."[48] Soon after Northstar's adopted daughter dies of AIDS-related complications as Jean-Paul whispers a prayer to her and Major Mapleleaf assures the mourning superhero that "they're together. Michael is watching over her."[49]

Figure 13.2 Northstar announces his sexual orientation in battle. Scott Lobdell (w) and Mark Pacella (a). "The Walking Wounded." *Alpha Flight* v1 #106 (March 1992), Marvel Comics, 20. Northstar and all related characters © and ™ Marvel Entertainment, LLC. All rights reserved and used with permission.

The story told in *Alpha Flight* #106 was (and sadly still is) progressive in its call to destigmatize AIDS, its indictment of "homophobic politicians who refuse to address the AIDS crisis,"[50] and its disavowal of the culture of silence that frustrates public discourse about AIDS prevention, treatment, and advocacy. And though the story directly complicates the dichotomy between "innocent" people with AIDS (e.g. infants, consumers of blood products, and medical professionals) from "regular" people with AIDS (e.g. gay men, ethnic minorities, and drug users), it is significant that Northstar—a character whose publication history so problematically imbricates sexual orientation and HIV status—emerges from the narrative as a gay man who is not HIV positive, but who has immense compassion for those who are. Northstar is a "good gay." But his negative HIV serostatus is not the only factor that makes him acceptable. We are reminded that Northstar is a former Olympic athlete and artist Mark Pacella's pencils render Jean-Paul a virile powerhouse with impossibly huge musculature—a far cry from the lithe dandy portrayed by John Byrne. Furthermore, a bonus pin-up at the end of *Alpha Flight* #106 depicts Northstar amiably chugging beers with Wolverine and Puck, icons of straightness and Hemingway-esque masculinity in the Marvel Universe.[51] And not to be ignored, Northstar—the most arrogant, charmingly snotty, and cynical hero in the Marvel pantheon—is revealed to be a man of faith who whispers a Judeo-Christian blessing over his departed ward. In this historical moment, the gay redeemer—the good gay— is figured as a "straight-acting," (implicitly virginal) bachelor who fights as a national champion to protect the heterosexually hegemonic world; he is not the type of gay man who would have AIDS.

But viewed over time, the gay redeemer must prove *consistently* resistant to infection and capable of adapting to the shifting parameters of gayness acceptable to mainstream heterosexual culture. Northstar's outing garnered international media attention and *Alpha Flight* #106 sold out within a week of its publication, eventually selling 120,000 copies after a second printing.[52] Writer Scott Lobdell reflects that "the media reaction was awe-inspiring and to the best of my recollection it was 98% positive."[53] But despite the narrative's popularity, Marvel quickly grew mum on the subject of Northstar's sexuality; the topic was not substantially broached again in the pages of *Alpha Flight* before the series' cancellation in 1994. Northstar's silence regarding his sexual orientation following *Alpha Flight* #106 indicates one of the key values of the mid-90s' good gay: don't ask, don't tell. Like the vernacular title of the December 1993 U.S. Department of Defense Directive suggests, it is fine for a hero to be gay as long as he does not "flaunt" his sexual orientation.[54]

Immediately following *Alpha Flight*'s cancellation in March of 1994, Northstar appeared in his own four-issue limited series. The primary villain of the series, an aging aristocrat named Carl Kerridge manipulates assassins to push Northstar to the limits of his endurance so that the old patrician may kill the impudent hero.[55] Keeping to the "don't ask, don't tell" code of the good gay, the *Northstar* series never explicitly mentions Northstar's sexual orientation; the words "gay" or "homosexual" never appear in the text. But before the garrulous Kerridge finishes off Jean-Paul, the villain explains his disdain for the hero, saying, "What are you to me? You are change. You are disorder. Your and your kind typify the malaise that infects the modern world . . . the insidious progression towards a society lacking the most basic grasp of morality or responsibility."[56] Given the larger context of the story, it is hard to identify if Kerridge's "your kind" refers to superhuman mutants, queers, or arrogant French Canadians, but the distinction hardly matters as all of the categories of difference are effectively compressed into one due to the writer's and editors' linguistic gymnastics to avoid using the "g" word. Nevertheless, Northstar handily dispatches Kerridge, sending the clear message that he will not permit homophobia, even if the villain cannot speak the word "gay."

But perhaps the most rhetorically significant aspect of the *Northstar* series is that it provides the site for the hero's renewed conflict with the specter of HIV/AIDS. The thrust of Carl Kerridge's strange vendetta is to exceed the limits of Northstar's superhuman powers so that the hero may be killed by the feeble, *opportunistic* attack of an old man. Jean-Paul's body becomes the focus of a bevy of villains' assaults leading the hero to lament that "[l]imits I thought nonexistent have been reached . . . and exceeded! . . . Even my metabolism is slowing down, refusing to heal wounds that otherwise would be a memory!"[57] The deterioration of Northstar's body continues graphically as "muscles start to scream for relief, lungs wheeze wretchedly for air through raw throat tissue."[58] Finally, just before Kerridge deals the death stroke to Jean-Paul's enfeebled body, he says, "Your death will serve as a rallying cry, to all those who want to hold on to the hope, the dream, that this is and will be in the future, a sane habitable world."[59] But before Kerridge can strike, Northstar summons up the last of his heroic chutzpah and knocks out his adversary and then thinks, "Every bit of me . . . hurts! Good! I deserve it! Perhaps the pain will serve to remind me just how close my arrogance brought me to the edge!"[60] Northstar savors the horrific toll the confrontation exacts on his body because the hero's final triumph signals that he is ultimately immune to the corporeal corruption the aristocrat would have used to kill him. In defeating the old bigot, Northstar is brought to the edge of total bodily decay but rallies via hypermasculine physical exertion. And so the arc of the "gay redeemer narrative" is renewed and moralized; the force of corruption and decay reveals its homophobic agenda and the good gay triumphs and resists debasement by virtue of his masculine prowess.

The recurring conflict between homophobic forces of defilement and the virtuous good gay would constitute most of Northstar's comic book appearances throughout the 1990s and early 2000s as the hero faced off against a revolving spate of homophobes while barely escaping from a series of corrupting forces. In 2001, Northstar foils an attempt on his life while promoting his memoir, *Born Normal*.[61] Later in the same story, Jean-Paul throttles Paulie Provenzano, his teammate on an ad hoc X-men squad, when the young man attacks Northstar with anti-gay slurs.[62] This scene testifies to the weakening code of silence that once governed the actions of the good gay; after Jean Grey scolds Northstar for pummeling his less worldly teammate, Jean-Paul laments, "The homophobe gets to spout off and I get in trouble for defending myself. Typical."[63] In 2002, the "don't ask, don't tell" rule is again questioned when Northstar becomes a full-fledged X-man and instructor at Xavier's Institute after he fails to save a young man from the explosive first manifestations of his mutant powers.[64] As the young mutant's abilities punish Northstar's body with a series of uncontrolled explosions, Jean-Paul educates the boy in the religion of acceptance, saying, "You are what you are, my friend. There's no changing sides once God places you."[65]

But just as the gay redeemer faces an ongoing battle with homophobia from the moral high ground of the good gay, he must also continue to confront the specter of bodily corruption. In early 2005, Northstar was killed not once but three times in a matter of weeks: by a brainwashed Wolverine in the main Marvel continuity,[66] by Wolverine again in the alternate universe known as the Age of Apocalypse,[67] and by an explosion in Chris Claremont's imagining of the "final" X-men story, *X-men: The End*.[68] Northstar's systematic erasure and the response that it provoked from readers and queer media advocates is an issue deserving of its own study,[69] but for the purposes of my argument, I will linger on how this death figures into Northstar's narrative of gay redemption. In the primary Marvel continuity, Jean-Paul is raised from the dead, brainwashed, and weaponized by a group of ninja assassins.[70] He survives this brush with death and corruption, but is quarantined for "deprogramming" by the government agency known as S.H.I.E.L.D.[71] only to be repeatedly repurposed as a weapon against the X-men first by the villainous Children of the Vault[72] and then by the fanatical Acolytes.[73] After each incidence of corruption, Northstar recovers and takes part in vanquishing those who would pollute his mind and body, but his ongoing susceptibility to contamination is necessary to the narrative of the gay redeemer. Only after facing the possibility of his body being weaponized—like the body of Patient Zero—may the gay redeemer assert the control that differentiates him as a good gay.

Gay redeemers like Northstar pepper the post-AIDS cultural landscape. Belize in Kushner's *Angels in America* is a black, gay drag queen whose steady "man uptown" and role as the moral compass of the play's gay community insulate him from the threat of infection, though his job as a nurse to a number of people with AIDS keeps him in close proximity to HIV.[74] In Armistead Maupin's *Tales of the City* series, Michael Tolliver is infected with HIV—presumably by his longtime boyfriend John Fielding—but lives into the twenty-first century (supported by a series of monogamous partners) as the ethical heart of the novels who bears witness to the pain wrought by AIDS on the San Francisco gay community.[75] Ultimately, the gay redeemer narrative is a rhetorical act of scapegoating. By delineating what makes a good gay who is resistant to or capable of recovering from infection, the narrative also gestures to the space occupied by those "other" gays. For instance, in his study of "barebacking," or unprotected anal intercourse, Tim Dean illustrates how, in a post-AIDS context, sexual practices may be pathologized as the exclusive behavior of self-destructive, irresponsible, or deviant gay men.[76] The logic of the gay redeemer narrative is at work here: good gays use condoms and do not receive or transmit HIV, those other gays do not. Though I find Dean's argument problematic from a public health standpoint, I do agree that condemning sexual behaviors as pathological when practiced by some people, but not all people (e.g. heterosexual partners who engage in unprotected anal intercourse), smacks of sexual fascism.

Dean's study and other texts I have engaged above underscore the fact that narratives of disease, including the outbreak narrative, the "Patient Zero containment fantasy," and the "gay redeemer narrative," shape cultural responses to illness. Sometimes narratives scapegoat a figure like Gaetan Dugas in an effort to imagine the containment or prevention of outbreak while some narratives seek to recover an individual or a minority population from association with disease only to delineate subcategories of good and bad as a means of capitulating to the hegemony of the dominant cultural paradigm.

In the case of Northstar, recent publications indicate that the guidelines for being a good gay and stalwart gay redeemer continue to evolve. In 2009's *Uncanny X-men* #508, Jean-Paul is once again recruited into active service with the X-Men. But Northstar is now a successful celebrity athlete, gay advocate, businessman, and boyfriend.[77] In Tim Fish's 2010 story, "LDR," we see Northstar and his love interest/publicist, Kyle, navigating the pitfalls of their long-distance relationship—and perhaps even having sex off panel.[78] And most recently, in Greg Pak and Fred Van Lente's 2011 relaunch of *Alpha Flight*, Northstar and Kyle kiss, breaking Jean-Paul's 32-year dry spell.[79] These plot developments are certainly progressive strides in the movement to normalize the depiction of queer characters in mainstream superhero comics. But one must also consider Northstar's romance as the behavior of a gay redeemer. In his relationship with Kyle, Northstar sublimates his characteristic impetuousness, conforming to the hegemony of a committed, monogamous partnership—just like a good gay should.

Notes

1 Brodie, Hamel, Brady, Kates, and Altman, "AIDS at 21: Medical Coverage of the HIV Epidemic 1981–2002," *Columbia Journalism Review* (March/April 2004) supplement: 1–2.

2 Ibid., 2.

3 Artery: The AIDS-arts forum, http://www.artistswithaids.org/artery/index1. html (accessed November 21, 2011).

4 Priscilla Wald, *Contagious: Cultures, Carriers, and the Outbreak Narrative* (Durham, NC: Duke University Press, 2008), 2, 217.

5 Ibid., 217.

6 Ibid., 217.

7 Ibid., 3–9.

8 Northstar's sexual orientation was implied years before he officially "came out" by stating, "I am gay!" in *Alpha Flight* #106 in 1992. The ambiguity of the character's sexual orientation in early appearances has lead some readers and critics to suggest that the distinction of "first openly gay superhero" belongs to other characters, most consistently the DC Comics character Extraño who first appeared in 1988 (Steve Englehart (w), Joe Staton (p), and Ian Gibson (i), "The Summoning," *Millenium* #2 (January 1988), DC Comics). Regardless of when he was officially labeled as "gay," Northstar's queerness was an integral part of the character's mystique from the early 1980s.

9 Ben Bolling, "Serials, Trauma, and Representations of the Ineffable," *ImageTexT* (Fall 2011).

10 "How Does JB Feel About His Work on *Alpha Flight*?" Byrne Robotics: FAQ, last modified March 4, 1998, http://www.byrnerobotics.com/FAQ/listing.asp? ID=2&T1=Questions+about+Comic+Book+Projects#10 (accessed November 21, 2011).

11 John Byrne (w, a). "Tundra!" *Alpha Flight* v1 #1 (August 1983), Marvel Comics.

12 Ibid.

13 John Byrne (w, a). "The Importance of Being Deadly." *Alpha Flight* v1 #7 (February 1984), Marvel Comics, 13.

14 The "Comics Code" refers to the "Comics Code Authority," a body created by the Comics Magazine Association of America to self-regulate the content of American comic books. The Code was at least partially created to address the concerns of American parents alarmed by claims made in Frederick Werthem's *Seduction of the Innocent*. The 1954 book—which fueled hearings on comic books conducted by the U.S. Senate Subcommittee on Juvenile Delinquency—claimed that comics exposed impressionable young readers to violence, deviant sexuality, and other behaviors that would encourage delinquency. For more see David Hajdu, *The Ten Cent Plague* (New York: Picador, 2009).

15 "Was It Your Intent When You Created Northstar That He Would Be a Gay Man?" Byrne Robotics: FAQ, last modified August 24, 2004, www. byrnerobotics.com/FAQ/listing.asp?ID=2&T1=Questions+about+Comic+Book +Projects#10 (accessed November 21, 2011).

16 John Byrne (w, a). "How Long Will a Man Lie in the Earth 'Ere He Rot?'"
    Alpha Flight v1 #18 (January 1985), Marvel Comics.

17 Chris Claremont (w), Paul Smith (p), and Bob Wiacek (i). *X-Men: The
    Asgardian Wars* (New York: Marvel, 2009), 24, 33.

18 Bill Mantlo (w) and Terry Shoemaker (a). "Madness." *Alpha Flight* v1 #48
    (July 1987), Marvel Comics, 15.

19 John Byrne (w, a). "Rub-Out." *Alpha Flight* v1 #22 (May 1985), Marvel
    Comics, 17; Bill Mantlo (w) and David Ross (a). "It's Not Easy Being Purple."
    Alpha Flight v1 #41 (December 1986), Marvel Comics, 21; Bill Mantlo (w)
    and David Ross (a). "Auction." *Alpha Flight* v1 #42 (January 1987), 4.

20 Bill Mantlo (w) and David Ross (a). "Plague!" *Alpha Flight* v1 #44 (March
    1987), Marvel Comics, 15.

21 Bill Mantlo (w) and June Brigman (a). "Resurrection." *Alpha Flight* v1 #45
    (April 1987), Marvel Comics, 4.

22 Mantlo (w) and Ross (a). *Alpha Flight* #44, 16.

23 Randy Shilts, *And the Band Played On: Politics, People, and the AIDS
    Epidemic,* 20th Anniversary Edition (New York: St. Martin's Griffin, 2007),
    178.

24 Wald, *Contagious,* 266.

25 Ibid., 216.

26 Ibid., 233.

27 Qtd. in Wald, *Contagious,* 242.

28 Shilts, *And the Band Played On,* 438–439.

29 Wald, *Contagious,* 234–239.

30 Bill Mantlo (w), June Brigman (p), and Whilce Portacio (i). "This Mortal
    Coil!" *Alpha Flight* v1 #50 (September 1987), Marvel Comics, 23–26.

31 Ibid., 26.

32 Ibid., 28–29.

33 Ibid., 34.

34 Peter David, "When You Wish Upon Northstar," PeterDavid.net, last modified
    February 14, 1992, http://www.peterdavid.net/index.php/2004/11/23/when-
    you-wish-upon-northstar/ (accessed November 21, 2011).

35 Ibid.

36 Mantlo (w), Brigman (p), and Portacio (i). *Alpha Flight* v1 #50, 25.

37 Wald, *Contagious,* 237.

38 "HIV Incidence and Prevalence, US, 1977–2006," Centers for Disease Control
    and Prevention, last modified July 2010, http://www.cdc.gov/hiv/resources/
    factsheets/us.htm (accessed November 21, 2011).

39 Shilts, *And the Band Played On,* 121.

40 Ibid., 311.

41 James W. Jones, "The Sick Homosexual: AIDS and Gays on the American
    Stage and Screen," in Judith Laurence Pastore, ed., *Confronting AIDS through
    Literature: The Responsibilities of Representation* (Urbana: University of
    Chicago Press, 1993), 103.

42 James D. Hudnall (w) and John Calimee (a). "Prisoners." *Alpha Flight* v1 #81
    (February 1990), Marvel Comics, 11.

43 James D. Hudnall (w) and John Calimee (a). "The Under Kingdom." *Alpha
    Flight* v1 #82 (March 1990), Marvel Comics.

44 Scott Lobdell (w) and Mark Pacella (a). "The Walking Wounded." *Alpha Flight* v1 #106 (March 1992), Marvel Comics.

45 Ibid., 6.

46 Ibid., 11.

47 Ibid., 16.

48 Ibid., 22–23.

49 Ibid., 25–27.

50 Ibid., 22.

51 Ibid., 31.

52 Emmett Furey, "Homosexuality in Comics—Part II," Comic Book Resources, last modified July 17, 2007, http://www.comicbookresources.com/?page=article&id=10809 (accessed November 21, 2011).

53 Ibid.

54 Department of Defense Directive 1304.26, last modified March 4, 1994, http://biotech.law.lsu.edu/blaw/dodd/corres/html2/d130426x.htm (accessed November 21, 2011).

55 Simon Furman (w) and Dario Carrasco, Jr. (a). "Running on Empty." *Northstar* #4 (July 1994), Marvel Comics.

56 Ibid., 19.

57 Ibid., 6.

58 Ibid., 17.

59 Ibid., 22.

60 Ibid., 30.

61 Scott Lobdell (w) and Leinil Frances Yu (a). *X-Men: Eve of Destruction* (New York: Marvel Comics, 2005).

62 Ibid.

63 Ibid.

64 Chuck Austen (w) and Sean Phillips (a). "Fall Down." *Uncanny X-Men* #414 (December 2002), Marvel Comics.

65 Ibid., 26.

66 Mark Millar (w) and John Romita, Jr. (a). "Enemy of the State: Part 6 of 6." *Wolverine* v2 #25 (April 2005), Marvel Comics.

67 Akira Yoshida (w) and Chris Bachalo (a). *X-Men: The New Age of Apocalypse* (New York: Marvel Comics, 2005).

68 Chris Claremont (w) and Sean Chen (a). *X-Men: The End, Book 2: Heroes and Martyrs* (New York: Marvel, 2005).

69 Northstar's deaths and seeming dispensability did not escape the attention of readers or LGBT media critics. Writer and film producer Perry Moore published an online essay, "Who Cares About the Death of a Gay Superhero Anyway?" in which he catalogued mistreated gay comics characters in a form similar to writer Gail Simone's 1999 article, "Women in Refrigerators," which highlighted the violent objectification of women common in many superhero comics at the time. Some bloggers and media critics rallied around Moore primarily arguing that the systematic erasure of one of—if not the most—iconic representations of a minority was tantamount to denigrating that minority and it seemed for a moment that the discussion might provoke real change. But then in *Ultimate X-Men* #97 in August of 2008, Ultimate Northstar was the victim of a forced drug overdose that left him paralyzed

from the waist down while his boyfriend Colossus had his heart ripped out, once again by the iconic Wolverine, so that he was trapped in his steel form—thus rendering the couple sexually impotent.

70 Mark Millar (w) and John Romita, Jr. (a). "Agent of S.H.I.E.L.D." *Wolverine* v2 #26–32 (May–October 2005), Marvel Comics.

71 Ibid.

72 Mike Carey (w) and Chris Bachalo (a). "Supernovas: Part 2 of 6." *X-Men* v2 #189 (September 2006), Marvel Comics.

73 Mike Carey (w) and Mark Brooks (a). "Covenant." *X-Men Annual* v2 #1 (March 2007), Marvel Comics.

74 Tony Kushner, *Angels in America, Part Two: Perestroika* (New York: Theatre Communications Group, 1992), 96.

75 Armistead Maupin, *Michael Tolliver Lives* (New York: HarperCollins, 2007).

76 Tim Dean, *Unlimited Intimacy: Reflections on the Subculture of Barebacking* (Chicago: University of Chicago Press, 2009).

77 Matt Fraction (w) and Greg Land (a). *Uncanny X-Men* v1 #508 (June 2009), Marvel Comics.

78 Tim Fish (w, a). "LDR." *Nation X* #2 (March 2010), Marvel Comics.

79 Greg Pak (w), Fred Van Lente (w), Ben Oliver (p), and Dan Green (i). *Alpha Flight* v3 #0.1 (July 2011), Marvel Comics.

PART FOUR

Comic Books and Contemporary History

CHAPTER FOURTEEN

The Militarism of American Superheroes after 9/11[1]

A. David Lewis

"I want a new war."
Col. Nick Fury from *Fury* #1, on comic
stands September 10, 2001.[2]

First response

After a late resurgence in the 1970s, the only mainstream war comics on the stands by 1984 were DC's World War II-based *Sgt. Rock* and Marvel's *G.I. Joe*. Marvel would take a shot at the Vietnam War in 1986 with Doug Murray's *The 'Nam*, but that too would fold by 1993, alongside such series as *The Unknown Soldier*, *Fightin' Army*, *Fightin' Marines*, and *Weird War Tales*,—each having run well over 100 issues apiece. By and large, the war genre (which, along with horror, romance, crime, and western titles, had shared a major, mid-century portion of the medium's readership) had run its course, conceding defeat to the conquering superhero force. New stories in *Sgt. Rock* stopped in 1988 with a series of specials (i.e. reprints) running until 1992; Marvel's version of *G.I. Joe*, starring a government force organized to fight terrorism, was canceled in 1995.

Since the majority of comics' wartime characters had been mothballed—with primarily superheroic figures serving as the medium's most well-known faces—the for-charity works produced by Marvel, DC, Dark Horse Comics, et al. in the 4 months following September 11, 2001, utilized their respective stables of fantastic heroes to reflect on the real-life heroism of firemen and police. The loss experienced by imaginary characters was set against the genuine loss of life and loved ones. All of these messages echoed through a number of separate charitable publications, including Marvel's *Moment of Silence*, Dark Horse's *9-11, Volume One: Artists Respond*, and DC's *9-11, Volume Two: The World's Finest Comic Book Writers & Artists Tell Stories to Remember*. Further, characters like Superman, Spider-Man, and the Hulk became lenses through which their creators attempted to define the sense of loss but also unity that accompanied the national trauma. Known informally as "the Black Issue" for its all-black memorial cover, *Amazing Spider-Man* #36—with captions starting clearly in Spider-Man's voice but later shifting to a more universal narrator—declares: "In recent years we as a people have been tribalized and factionalized by a thousand casual unkindnesses. But in this we are one. Flags sprout in uncommon places, the ground made fertile by tears and shared resolve. We have become one in our grief. We are now one in our determination. One as we recover. One as we rebuild."[3] A similar unifying moment, though more mundane, takes place in Marvel's *Heroes* one-shot, where, in a Dearborn, Michigan, classroom, two students watch the World Trade Center towers crumble, with their "[h]ands held tight, Ellen McKenzie and Fatima Jaffal watched and cried . . . together."[4] Even supervillains like Doctor Doom and Magneto came to survey the damage, implying that the crime perpetrated here was worse than any villainy they could execute.

Yet for all of the brave sentiments these books eventually muster, meditations like the Black Issue contain stronger, more compelling questions. "Where were you?!" a fleeing couple asks their hero. "How could you let this happen?"[5] As he moves between the gurneys, Spider-Man (AKA native New Yorker Peter Parker) notes, "They ask the question. Why? Why? My God, why? I have seen other worlds. Other spaces. I have walked with gods and wept with angels. But to my shame I have no answers."[6]

Few pat answers—certainly, few *convincing* responses—could be given, save the idea that America would endure and, perhaps, that a sleeping giant had been awakened: "You wanted to send a message, and in so doing you awakened us from our self-involvement. Message received. Look for your reply in the thunder."[7] For all the egalitarian, nondenominational, and embracing messages of one anthology story, there would also be an accompanying sense of hostility and anger from another. For instance, there is artist Neal Adams' piece for DC's *9-11* volume; beneath a torn and soiled flag held by Superman and Uncle Sam reads a plaque, "First things first. Then we come for you."[8] Or, in keeping with the character, the massive, raging Hulk stands atop a pile of city rubble, his muscles tensed, and bearing the American flag—the sole accompanying caption reads: "Strongest one there is."[9]

That Hulk-like American strength of force was already being flexed in Afghanistan by the time the aforementioned books were each published. Some degree of false prescience leaked into the scripts, such as Beau Smith's story with Val Semeiks and Romeo Tanghal in DC's album: "On that day . . . we were all soldiers. 9-11-01. But in the days to come this country will call for a different kind of soldier. One who is trained to take the war to those that have attacked our own shores. . . . But this is not my grand-father's war. This is a war of rats. There's only one way to hunt rats that bite and then scurry off into dark holes. You send rat terriers into those holes after them. And they don't come out until all the rats are dead. We are those rat terriers . . . We're soldiers."[10]

Kabul had fallen in November, and the hills of Tora Bora were bombed and searched by American soldiers—by "rat terriers"—before the end of 2001. Constantly updated reports flooded 24-hour cable news channels and internet sites. The White House issued aggressive "dead or alive" state-ments on the overseas hunt for public enemy #1 Osama bin Laden, and, as talk of a new federal Cabinet department began, a Homeland Security Advisory System was fashioned to keep the populace ever-aware of the looming national threat.

It was in this developing wartime environment that a trend of increased militancy infiltrated mainstream comics. From 2002 to 2006, DC Comics and Marvel Comics released a succession of their customary crossover events—a major storytelling development spread across several different series—and new series now revolving around warfare.

By examining a particular strain of titles in relation to each other over the last 10 years—concurrent with the Global War on Terror at home and two wars abroad—a number of alarming themes emerge. A revised rela-tionship to authority becomes prominent as do aspects of the abuse of power. Further, the meaning of terrorism also morphs wildly, and a sense of historicity can be seen underpinning these endeavors—and perhaps serv-ing as their attempted justification.

The new resurgence of war

The antecedent for twenty-first-century superheroes as costumed soldiers came in 2001's *Our Worlds at War*, published by DC. This crossover chronicled a cosmic conflict between an alien entity named Imperiex com-ing to destroy Earth, extraterrestrial refugees, and the third-party planet Apokolips. To face these imminent threats, Earth's adopted son Superman must ally himself with his nemesis Lex Luthor who had been recently elected

President of the United States. Largely serving as a response to the misgivings about and literal vilifying of Bush, *Our Worlds at War* attempted to depict the realistic horrors of war albeit through fantastic characters. This event met with only moderate success and was widely panned, though its concluding issues coincidentally corresponded with the September 11, 2001 attacks.

Following both *Our Worlds at War* and the new national mood, the following catalog of superhero crossovers and series pursued this technique of spandex warfare and, particularly, commentary on Afghanistan and Iraq by proxy:

- *Captain America* v4 #1–3 (June–August 2002) from Marvel Comics by John Ney Rieber and John Cassaday. The World War II legend had his ongoing series revamped and restarted—"rebooted," as it were—with a psychological examination of national responsibility and violence.

- *JSA: Black Reign* (November 2003–January 2004) from DC Comics by Geoff Johns, Rags Morales, and Don Kramer. Former villain turned anti-hero Black Adam tests the ethics of his allies by leading a force into his native Middle East home of Kahndaq to liberate it and become its champion.

- *Secret War* (April 2004–December 2005) from Marvel by Brian Michael Bendis and Gabriele Dell'Otto. Without governmental permission, top spy Nick Fury enlists a number of superheroes to wage a stealth campaign against the Prime Minister of Latveria who has been illegally equipping American criminals with hi-tech weaponry.

- *We3* #1–3 (October 2004) from DC by Grant Morrison & Frank Quitely. An experimental trio of cyborg animals escapes their creators.

- *Ultimates 2* #1–12 (February–August 2005) from Marvel by Mark Millar and Bryan Hitch. Marvel's premier superteam, the Avengers, is reimagined for the twenty-first century; in the second volume, they are made to invade pre-war Iraq and then are betrayed from within, leaving America open to foreign assault.

- *Civil War* (August 2006–February 2007) from Marvel by Mark Millar and Steve McNiven. Hero fights hero as legislation passes to make the registration of identities and powers requisite.

- *World War III* (April 18, 2007) from DC by Keith Champagne, John Ostrander, Pat Oliffe, Drew Geraci, et al. Black Adam, now leader/dictator of Kahndaq, takes the rage over his slain family against the wider world.

- *World War Hulk* (May 2007) from Marvel by Peter David, Al Rio, Lee Weeks, et al. A savvy, enraged Hulk returns to Earth on a mission of vengeance after being cast into outer space—for the safety of the planet—by his former colleagues.

- *Secret Invasion* (April–December 2008) from Marvel by Brian Michael Bendis, Lenil Francis Yu, Mark Morales, and Laura Martin. The infiltration of world governments and superteams by shapeshifting extraterrestrial Skrulls is revealed, and hero and villain alike are forced to band together to push back the alien force.

- *Siege* (January 2010–May 2010) from Marvel by Brian Michael Bendis, Olivier Copiel, and Laura Martin. Megalomaniacal Norman Osborne, once the villainous Green Goblin, has been appointed America's top intelligence chief, and he uses his authority to order an attack on Thor's misplaced homeland Asgard precariously hovering over heartland Oklahoma.

- *War of the Supermen* (May 2010) from DC by James Robinson, Sterling Gates, Eddy Barrows, Jamal Igle, et al. A society of kidnapped Kryptonians is freed and establishes New Krypton on the opposite side of the Sun from Earth, only to have the planet sabotaged by humans against whom the survivors declare eradication.

None of these books addressed Iraq or Afghanistan directly. Unlike September 11th—which happened suddenly, could not be denied, and had already concluded—these wars appeared too unwieldy, too complex, or too uncertain to boil down into superhero plotlines. Rather, the aforementioned titles each presented an ersatz conflict, one that could parallel the issues raised by the real-life wars without directly engaging them. Metaphorically, they would paraphrase, not quote.

The Bush administration

Superheroes rarely age in "real time"; even those heroes who have lived through more than 40 years' worth of government administrations will be only held narratively to roughly the last 10 years' worth of history. For example, Iron Man's Vietnam War origins have been slid to the Gulf War, and Batman's parents were murdered in the late 70s rather than the roaring 20s. Rare exceptions, such as Nick Fury, Captain America, and the original Green Lantern, enjoy extended lifetimes, thereby maintaining their World War II roots but explaining their modern-day vitality by means of some extraordinary circumstances.

Therefore, while readers have a published record of them all, only certain characters actively recall their encounters with the multiple twentieth-century Presidents. To further complicate matters, as in the case of Lex Luthor, companies will, depending on the editorial policy in place at a given time, substitute a fictional president with whom they can take greater creative liberties for the real-life Commander-in-Chief.

Few presidents and administrations, though, have elicited such strong portrayals as George W. Bush. Although the president in *Secret War* remains hidden in carefully placed shadows by Dell'Otto, hints of the former Texas governor can be found in Fury's angry response to America's inaction against Latveria: "I've been through 12 presidents in my time, and all I can say I have learned from it . . . is that the American people will elect just about anybody. And yeah, my job gets pretty complicated . . . but I made a promise to myself years ago that if I had to choose between a publicly elected millionaire's back-hand oil and technology dealings . . . and the safety of innocent people . . . there's no choice at all."[11]

A more direct reference to George W. Bush, particularly as a wartime president, appears in Marvel's *Avengers: The Initiative*, in which budding heroes are taken to a superhuman boot camp in order to train them for service in a series of state-by-state superteams. When Texas is threatened near Crawford, the Initiative is called upon, and a ranch-dwelling President Bush is shown clearly standing his ground: "I'm not going anywhere. I made a promise to the American people—that during this time a' war, they'd be safe at home. So the last thing I'm gonna do—is cut n' run from mine."[12] On one hand, this is a noble portrait of Bush; on the other hand, his presence at the ranch—rather than in Washington DC—can be read as an inside joke, along with his use of the "cut 'n' run" language popularly utilized against his Democrat detractors. These same words were attributed to the president under similar circumstances in another series, *Ultimates 2*: A multinational team calling themselves the Liberators had attacked the United States for using the Ultimates force overseas. Aboard Air Force One, Bush wavered, "Is hiding absolutely necessary, Danny? I don't want to be seen like I'm cutting and running."[13]

The election of Lex Luthor was DC Comics' provocative attempt to capture the split sentiments over Bush's election; other critiques of his selection would be more coy. Before the Liberators' invasion, this public sentiment against Bush is initially aimed at Captain America: The superhero has drinks spilled over his head by people saying, "That's for working for the Thief-in-Chief!"[14] Putting this opinion in the mouths of rowdy club-goers allays the writers or publishing company of any direct responsibility. Further, as in Frank Miller's *The Dark Knight Strikes Again*, drawing unnamed, derided White House officials to look like Donald Rumsfeld or Dick Cheney still leaves creators inculpable since the representatives' identities are not ironclad.

In the *Shazam: The Monster Society of Evil* mini-series, creator Jeff Smith employs the reverse tactic—not of criticizing a person but, rather, a position. Here, the Attorney General of the United States is the villainous Dr. Sivana, eager to uncover the secrets of the massive, supposedly robotic creatures that have appeared in the city square. He says, "Robots are just machines— tools for powerful men. Tools of war. And war . . . is profitable."[15] Billy Batson, empowered with Captain Marvel's might, brings his concerns about Sivana to his vagrant friend Tawky Tawny, who replies, "War profiteering! That is immoral—and illegal. We can stop him, Billy!"[16]

In short, in these worlds of supermen and leagues of justice, governmental authority is not to be trusted absolutely. As Captain America says to Nick Fury's replacement, Commander Maria Hill, "Don't play politics with me, Hill. Super heroes need to stay above that stuff or Washington starts telling us who the supervillains are."[17]

Reflecting both the short-lived unity following September 11th and the political schism felt across the country, this distrust between elected officials and powerful, public avengers goes both ways. Naturally, that Superman feels ill-at-ease taking orders from his nemesis is an understatement, and he makes his feelings clear. "When this is over, there are those who will be held accountable for the choices they make under the guise of 'wartime necessity.' For your sake, I hope this choice was the right one."[18] However, it is the wise and war-tested Major Lane, father to Superman's mate Lois Lane, who expresses the alternate viewpoint: "If you had any inkling as to what may be coming, you'd get right in line behind your governing executive and pledge your support, as I have!"[19] As the death toll and apparent futility of war against Imperiex becomes more and more apparent, even the Man of Steel begins to buckle; being near-invincible and super-strong, he has never had to experience the horrors and cost of wartime. (Again, this is the 2001 Superman whose immediate history does not date back to World War II, Korea, or even, presumably, Vietnam.) Privately, Superman pleads, "I can't do this anymore . . . I can't . . . [. .] I'm so lost. Please, God . . . Tell me what to do. Tell me how to fight on."[20] Only upon hitting this state of desperation does he come to terms with falling in line behind President Luthor. As the orphan of a dead planet, he says to Luthor, "I know how to sacrifice. Believe me. Tell me what to do, Mister President. Whatever it takes to win this . . . I'm yours."[21] Superman's words to Luthor echo those that he directed to God; once he saw the true abomination faced, he recognized the necessity of his supporting the president.

Heroism redefined

This debate between Superman, Lane, and Luthor stems from the larger question: How do the heroes obtain *their* authority? And who grants it? In

Amazing Fantasy #15, Stan Lee famously wrote, "With great power comes great responsibility"—but it does not grant them the corresponding authority. Captain America's unwillingness to police the Superhuman Registration Act (SRA) leads Commander Hill to quip, "I thought supervillains were guys in masks who refused to obey the law."[22] The catastrophic explosion in Stamford, Connecticut—the Marvel universe's own mini-9/11—which brought about the SRA is viewed by Iron Man as having a secondary effect: "As far as I'm concerned, Stamford was our wake-up call. What alcoholics refer to as a moment of clarity. Becoming public employees makes perfect sense if it helps people sleep a little easier."[23] As Captain America predicted, not all of the masked adventurers agree with Iron Man, driving them to "war with one another," the germ of which can be espied from the following dialogue: Falcon says, "I can't believe I'm hearing this. The masks are a tradition. We can't just let them turn us into super-cops"; Yellowjacket replies, "Are you kidding? We're lucky people have tolerated this for as long as they have, Sam. Why should we be allowed to hide behind these things?"[24]

Unless they were to concede that might *does* make right in unabashed anti-Arthurian fashion, most of the superheroes seek their wartime license as agents of the state or dispel the indictment of illegal vigilantism—not to mention simple criminality in defying the SRA—by other means. Of course, there may be a third, more radical contingent, like Miller's Batman, who accepts and even revels in a borderline status. Green Lantern is chagrined by his old teammate's long-standing attitude: "Bruce, you were right. When you laughed in our faces, all those years ago—when you called the rest of us a pack of fools—you were right. Of course we're criminals. We've always been criminals. On this planet we have to be criminals."[25]

Heroism that flaunts the law, particularly idealized and pseudonymistic superheroism, is an endangered species during wartime when the chain-of-command principle is so vital. Whereas these superheroes frequently partake in life-and-death adventures, having them engage in them during a time of real-life war fatalities has the effect of foregrounding their fictionality. In confronting the Liberator leader, Captain America faces his Middle Eastern mirror image of himself minus the U.S. frills: "I am simply Abdul al-Rahman and I was a farmhand in the northwest province of Azerbaijan, Captain. I'm afraid I have no interest in these super hero codenames. Don't you think it's a little immature to indulge in such childish conventions?"[26] Further, Nick Fury uses precisely this distinction between himself as a soldier and his troops as gaudy superheroes to justify his unilateral decisions: "And I'm sorry I had to unplug you a little, but I just don't have the time or inclination to debate the finer points of wartime morality with a bunch of people who wear masks."[27]

A soldier's morality does not seem to match that of a superhero. In these series, the moral concerns of superheroes cannot compare to the needs of reality, as seen by soldiers and those who recognize the "real" threat.

Both *Secret War* and *Our Worlds at War* feel compelled to deliver similar speeches, both of which come from an authorized commander to a reluctant superheroic audience. As Fury says, "I'm a wartime general. I have weapons and I have soldiers and I have a job to do. Some of you understand this and some of you don't. And you'll have to forgive me, but it just doesn't matter to me either way. What happened here tonight: This is what I'm up against—this is what I was trying to avoid. I bought us a year, and tonight we bought another, maybe. They hate us. I didn't start this war, but damn it to hell, I'm not going to lose it."[28]

Compare this to President Luthor's own speech: "Reserve your judgments, if you don't mind. We're in a state of emergency here. This is, by far, the greatest threat we've ever faced. To combat this threat, desperate measure had to be taken, no matter what the cost. This is war. And you should consider yourself drafted, Superman."[29]

The war has priority, and it trumps heroism. His mission complete, Fury leaves a robot copy of himself behind to explain his actions. Malfunctioning, it stutters, "You are herrrroes. More than me. Maybe one day you'll lll-look around and you'll see the world like I have to, and you'll knowww I did the right thing. Or at least you'll underssssstand why I did it."[30] It is as if a dedication to the principles of heroism, however we might define them, blinds us to the reality Fury sees.

Fury and Luthor's criticisms can be applied to superheroism as a metaphor for the empowerment of the individual, yet, as with the examination of the Presidency, it can be reversed; superheroes stand opposed to what defines their supervillain counterparts, namely the abuse of power. Mark Millar and Bryan Hitch have Larry King report the following to playboy genius Tony Stark, alter ego of Iron Man, live on his show: "In fact, this morning Thor tendered his resignation from The Ultimates because he says that [abusing his power is] exactly what Cap was doing in Iraq. According to Thor, this whole Homeland Security thing was just one big scam to get public opinion on your side before launching preemptive strikes against anyone who ticks you off."[31]

Thor's protestations do little to sway his partners at first, particularly the loyal soldier Captain America—they believe their ethics can still line up with the government's orders. Eventually, though, they are told by Fury, "Something's come up in the Middle East,"[32] and they depart to forcibly disarm an unidentified Arab nation, perhaps Azerbaijan. In effect, they have "crippled a nation this morning."[33] Thor, now imprisoned, speaks to Iron Man about how far they have fallen from their ideals, all in the name of America's defense: "They've got you, haven't they? All they have to do now is say 'nuclear weapons' and Tony Stark falls into line like the rest of them. Do you think that's how they'll get you to invade all their other target countries? Supposing they decide China's a threat a few years down the line? . . . I used to think you were the smart one, Tony."[34]

Each of the Ultimates soon realizes the abuse of power that has taken place, and they rally to fight off the Liberators and restore pre-invasion normalcy. Yet, the lesson, as spelled out in *Dark Knight Strikes Again*, is just how easily personal reservations can be sidelined in the name of national emergency: "The way things were, our hold on power was more tenuous than it appeared. Now we've got all the excuse we need to do what we should've done at the get-go!"[35]

Terrorism and living in the now

When it comes to "the excuse we need," the word that has undergone the most development, perhaps *over*development, since the World Trade Center attacks is easily "terrorism;" combating this threat appears to act as an authority all its own. Thieves, murderers, and rapists aside—those who menace America and its stability now have greater import. For instance, Dr. Sivana explains to Billy what could motivate the man to interrogate the child: "Now, why would the Attorney General of the United States be standing in your filthy room while two alien monsters are threatening the American public? Because the entire city witnessed a flying man in red tights talking to the monsters—and I know that this flying Captain Marvel is actually a bad little boy! Are you plotting with the aliens to attack our country? Are you?!"[36]

Just as "Shazam!" is the magic word which transforms Billy into Captain Marvel, "terrorism" is the word that makes any situation instantly dire. In *Secret War*, for example, Fury hopes to urge the President and cabinet to take action by reframing his intelligence. Rather than seeing each armored villain as an isolated danger, he emphasizes their shared backing, thus "by definition, these are no longer crimes and these are no longer criminals . . . they're terrorists."[37] Largely, Fury seems to accept the veracity of terrorism's peril, especially when he addresses his own guilt in waging a Secret War: "[I]t was an act of war. Actually, without permission from the U.N. and the World Court, it was worse than that. An act of global treason—terrorism!"[38]

Rather than "falling in line like the rest of them," some of these tales also seek to deflate the terror in "terrorism." Frank Miller cannily reminds readers that among Batman's earliest credos and rationales for wearing the batsuit was "to strike terror in the hearts of criminals everywhere." In *Dark Knight Strikes Again*, a cocky, contented Batman quips, "Striking terror. Best part of the job,"[39] a line that has altogether different—though perhaps unworthy—meaning than its original 1930s use. Likewise, those labeled terrorists, such as Captain America's opponent Faysal Al-Tariq, can easily dismiss that tag and turn it upon the accusers: "I am not a terrorist. I am a messenger—here to show you the truth of war. You are the terrorists!"[40] Cap may not agree, but even he has to question the origin of Al-Tariq's animosity: "Are we only hated because we're free—Free and prosperous and good? Or does the light we see cast shadows that we don't—Where monsters like this al-Tariq can plant the seeds of hate?"[41] Do monsters grow in that blind spot? And is it a point of darkness similar to the superheroes' perception of war needs?

The actions—and the atrocities—undertaken in the present do not find their value now, no matter how they might be labeled. Perhaps only the future matters. "I have been through this before," says Black Adam, on the eve of retaking Kahndaq. "They are going to call us villains. They are going to call us mad. Let them. The present can never be agreed upon. But history will view us with veneration."[42] Or, conversely, only the past matters, according to Fury: "It's all happening again. They have the information, they have it! They know who and they—Irrefutable evidence in their hands as to who their enemy is . . . and they are going to sit on it and do nothing. They are going to blink and follow rules of diplomacy that no one else plays by . . . and people are going to die. Innocent people are going to die because of this right here. I can't—I can't go through it again. It's happening all over again."[43]

So, we find a revision here: The present matters *both* in terms of *future* judgment and *past* errors. Like Fury, Cap tells himself as he digs out possible World Trade Center survivors, "This time—This time—Let it not be . . . Too late."[44] The casualties of past wars make his actions now that much more essential. One can even hear, as he races to save civilians from Al-Tariq, a word missing from Cap's thoughts. "Today—It matters that you're here. It's going to make a difference. Today—there's hope. You're not too late" . . . again.[45] Saving these people matters all the more to Cap because of the victims of the past, particularly those dead in the recent past at Ground Zero. He does not focus on the future, because like Al-Tariq or Black Adam, Cap is certain that future parties will judge his actions correct . . .

. . . Unless there is, as noted above, a blind spot. The superheroes have already had to question whether there had long been a weak point in their agency as pseudo-vigilantes without being answerable to some consenting authority. Likewise, the very concept on which the wars both in Afghanistan and Iraq have been predicated, terrorism, has been scrutinized for its own frailties. Are there aspects to this storytelling, to these wars, that will later reveal themselves as defective, inconsequential, or—worst yet—damaging? Do comic book writers avoid setting their stories in Iraq and Afghanistan not because they may alienate readers or suddenly become out-of-date, but because history has not judged these wars yet? Luke Cage, one of Cap's SRA-opposing Avengers, senses something awry: "I'm steamin' because I think there's a lot more goin' on here. I feel manipulated. I feel someone pulling my strings. S.H.I.E.L.D., Hydra, our Secret War, the Civil War . . . I think they're connected. Do you? And does that idea scare the holy crap out of you?"[46]

Bendis and Marvel would satisfy Cage's anxiety with *Secret Invasion*, the mini-series revealing that both human and superhuman society had been infiltrated some time ago by shapeshifting alien Skrulls planning to conquer the Earth. To some degree, this explains a bit of the pall under which Cap and Cage's underground heroes found themselves operating: their circumstances were a result of outside forces, not their own authentic comrades. If they raise any army up to defy the aliens' invasion forces, then all could be set right again. That rationale, though, proves only so strong when, in the wake of the repulsed Skrull attack, the U.S. government names former supervillain Norman Osborn as the top intelligence officer of the country. Perhaps there had been corruption by outside forces, but the poison is now within American society—a homegrown malevolence that cannot be pinned to one President, to the shadow of terrorism, or to alien subversion. Though Osborn is thwarted by, again, an army of superheroes, Thor's home of Asgard is a casualty (as is Superman's revivified home of New Krypton at DC Comics). And Cage's suspicions remain unanswered on a scale far larger than he likely intended. Why have superheroes been made to go to war?

If he were aware of his own fictionality, Cage could neatly conclude that this manipulation comes at the hands of his writers, particularly Brian Michael Bendis or Mark Millar. But, more likely, neither could not have had this entirely roadmapped from the outset, especially across two publishing companies, having instead to improvise and build his stories upon the readership's tone. If the war in Iraq ended quickly, we would probably not have the continued variety of superhero war titles from which to choose. Therefore, is there manipulation here, or does an extended wartime, one about which storytellers are reticent to directly write, create these tales simply by its pervasive existence? In response to Cage, all his partner Iron Fist can say, all anyone can say, is that "I agree everything *is* upside down. I agree. But . . . What if there is no real bad guy? What if it's all just upside down?"[47]

Notes

1   An earlier version of this chapter appeared online at *Magazine Americana*.
2   Garth Ennis (w) and Darick Robertson (a). "Be Careful What You Wish For." *Fury* v2 #1 (November 2001), Marvel Comics, 26.
3   J. Michael Straczynski (w) and John Romita, Jr. (a). "Stand Tall." *Amazing Spider-Man* v2 #36 (December 2001), Marvel Comics, 20.
4   Fabien Nicieza (w), Patrick Kircher (p), and Derek Fridolfs (i). "12." *Heroes* #1 (December 2001), Marvel Comics, 12.

5 Straczynski and Romita, "Stand Tall." 4.

6 Ibid., 15.

7 Ibid., 20.

8 Neal Adams (w, a). Untitled, in *9-11: The World's Finest Comic Book Writers and Artists Tell Stories to Remember* (New York: DC Comics, 2002), 176.

9 Dale Keown (w, a). "58." *Heroes* #1 (December 2001), Marvel Comics, 58.

10 Beau Smith (w), Val Semeiks (p), and Romeo Tanghal (i). "Soldiers." in *9-11: The World's Finest Comic Book Writers and Artists Tell Stories to Remember* (New York: DC Comics, 2002), 94.

11 Brian Michael Bendis (w) and Gabriele Dell'Otto (a). *Secret War* (New York: Marvel Comics, 2009), 116.

12 Dan Slott (w) and Stefano Caselli (a). *Avengers: The Initiative* (New York: Marvel Comics, 2007), 38.

13 Mark Millar (w) and Bryan Hitch (a). *The Ultimates 2 [Vol. 2]: Grand Theft America* (New York: Marvel Comics, 2007), 117.

14 Mark Millar (w) and Bryan Hitch (a). *The Ultimates 2 [Vol. 1]: Gods & Monsters* (New York: Marvel Comics, 2005), 39.

15 Jeff Smith (w, a). *Shazam!: The Monster Society of Evil* (New York: DC Comics, 2007), 123.

16 Ibid., 137.

17 Mark Millar (w) and Steve McNiven (a). *Civil War* (New York: Marvel Comics, 2007), 23.

18 Jeph Loeb (w), Mike Wieringo (p), and José Marzán (i). *Superman: Our Worlds at War: Book One* (New York: DC Comics, 2002), 191.

19 Joe Kelly (w), Kano (p), and Marlo Alquiza (i). "The End of the Beginning," *Action Comics* #780 (August 2001), DC Comics, 14.

20 Jeph Loeb (w), Phil Jimenez (i), and Marlo Alquiza (i). *Superman: Our Worlds at War: Book Two* (New York: DC Comics, 2002), 25–26.

21 Loeb, Wieringo, and Marzán, *War: Book One*, 250.

22 Millar and McNiven, *Civil War*, 23.

23 Ibid., 19.

24 Ibid., 19.

25 Frank Miller (w, a) and Lynn Varley (c). *The Dark Knight Strikes Again* (New York: DC Comics, 2004), 229.

26 Millar and Hitch, *Ultimates 2 [Vol. 2]*, 141.

27 Bendis and Dell'Otto, *Secret War*, 124.

28 Ibid., 125.

29 Loeb, Wieringo, and Marzán, *War: Book One*, 186

30 Bendis and Dell'Otto, *Secret War*, 128.

31 Millar and Hitch, *Ultimates 2 [Vol. 1]*, 9.

32 Ibid., 120.

33 Ibid., 144.

34 Millar and Hitch, *Ultimates 2 [Vol. 2]*, 13.

35 Miller and Varley, *Dark Knight*, 216.

36 Smith, *Shazam*, 121.

37 Bendis and Dell'Otto, *Secret War*, 18.

38 Ibid., 117.

39 Miller and Varley, *Dark Knight*, 110.

40 John Rey Nieber (w) and John Cassaday (a). "Soft Targets." *Captain America* v4 #3 (August 2002), Marvel Comics, 18.
41 Ibid., 20.
42 Geoff Johns (w) and Rags Morales (a). *JSA: Black Reign* (New York: DC Comics, 2005), 2.
43 Bendis and Dell'Otto, *Secret War*, 23.
44 John Rey Nieber (w) and John Cassaday (a). "Dust." *Captain America* v4 #1 (June 2002), Marvel Comics, 8.
45 Ibid., 36.
46 Brian Michael Bendis (w), Alexander Maleev (a), and Leinil Francis Yu (a). *The New Avengers: Revolution* (New York: Marvel Comics, 2007), 103.
47 Ibid., 104.

CHAPTER FIFTEEN

September 11, 2001

Witnessing History, Demythifying the Story in *American Widow*

Yves Davo

"We've gotta get out of here!" Alissa Torres thinks to herself as she walks by preparations for the first anniversary of the September 11th terrorist attacks.[1] Even 21 days before the commemoration, she knows perfectly well that she will not have the strength to attend this event of shared grief and national sorrow that will be broadcast worldwide. Bringing along her young son, she decides to fly to Hawaii to be far from the political and media manipulation of a catastrophe she has experienced in the flesh. Alissa Torres is indeed one of the collateral victims of these terrorist attacks: Eddie, her husband and father of the child she was then carrying, disappeared in the collapse of the north tower of the World Trade Center. *American Widow*, created in collaboration with illustrator Sungyoon Choi, is the graphic memoir on her experience as a pregnant widow of the September 11, 2001 attacks. This 2008 non-fiction narrative is a testimony that alternates between describing the traumatic experiences of widowhood, pregnancy, media attention, and bureaucratic challenges and relating her memories of the love story she shared with her late husband. In the end, she focuses on the isolating nature of grief and the difficulties of life as an alienated widow and mother-to-be. Throughout this graphic narrative, illustrated in simple black, white, and light blue, Alissa Torres sheds an intimate light on this event as she deliberately and inexorably disposes of any attempt to take 9/11 away from her. *American Widow* works best as a reminder that this horrific event is, at its core, personal, arguing that making 9/11 into myth took away some of its power as history.

9/11 as history

According to a 2006 survey, 30 percent of Americans have forgotten the very year of the terrorist attacks, but 95 percent of them remember that they took place on September 11th.[2] These two percentages show how the expression "9/11" has been sanctioned by common usage to name the event. The syntagmatic unit "9/11" has been nominalized and even used as an adjective in the immediate aftermath of the catastrophe, coming to designate a unique referent which corresponds to the pragmatic function of the proper noun. From a historical fact, determined and intimately felt, the date of the attacks becomes a paradigmatic fact, like some blind spot in the media discourse, circulating from article to article without anybody ever questioning either its interpretation or its alleged reality. This metonymical drift—the idea that the terrorist attacks are not called that but rather go by the name of something intimately associated with them (i.e. the date)—has altered the semantic status of "9/11."

This enunciative process appropriates the symbolic space of September 11th and therefore takes away any significant affect from those few hours. Its interpretation is set rigidly in a unique and arbitrary reading, that of the critical point between two periods. Jacques Derrida and Jürgen Habermas have defined the events of September 11, 2001, as a "concept" and a phenomenon of language that says something more than the mere experience of a victim, which shifts the concrete of an intimate trauma to its collective abstraction: "I always believe in the need to first be attentive to the phenomenon of language, of naming, of dating. To what it means, signifies, or betrays. Not to be caught in the language, but instead to try to understand what precisely happens *beyond* the language, where the language and the concept find their limits."[3] Therefore, the event raised up to be a symbol still bears the mark of some betrayal, as far as the victims and their relatives are concerned, because, as one transforms on it, one makes all real suffering immaterial: "the fact of designating an event by a date gives it a historical status in the first place, transfixes it [le statufie]."[4] The choice of the term "9/11" names the event in its relation to history, and makes a mythological tale of modern times out of it.

The mechanism of myth

"The myth tells a sacred history; it recounts an event which took place in the primordial times, the fabulous times of 'beginnings.' . . . It is therefore always the story of a creation: what is reported is how something was produced, has begun to be. . . . The myths describe the various, and sometimes dramatic, emergences of the sacred into the world," explains Mircea Eliade.[5] The combined effect of the naming of the terrorists attacks by the date, of the ad nauseam repetition of the images of those planes as they crash into the towers, of the staggering effect it had on witnesses and TV viewers, and of the short-lived inability of the media to provide any analysis of what was happening gave birth to these new "fabulous times of beginnings" and immediately started the process of sacralization in which human beings (for example, the firemen) become almost supernatural beings and the event acquires a magical aspect as if it is being set into fiction. Eliade does not tell us anything else because, according to him, "*Mythos* indicates all that cannot really exist."[6] 9/11, as a myth, is a construction of the real which heralds a collective sense of grief but obliterates the personal one. This swing from reality to myth refers obviously to the semiotics of Roland Barthes: "The function of the myth is to evacuate reality: it is, literally, a ceaseless flow, a drain, or, if one prefers, an evaporation, in short a significant absence." The evaporation of reality by appropriation, by "theft of language" reflects this process of mythification of the event by its excessive media coverage, its politicization, its commemoration, its fictionalization.[7]

The mechanism of appropriation

From the first establishing shot onwards, and in opposition to the pale blue calm of the opposite page, the first image of *American Widow* overflows with dialogue balloons evoking the force of television and the first interventions of the journalists. The multiplication of the languages, the shapes of the balloons, and the different typographic elements accentuate even more the universal and striking characteristic of the images broadcast on the screen. Moreover, the representation of this TV set, placed in full center of the page, symbolizes the appropriation of the event by world media. The six boxes on page 8, giving the same point of view from six different countries, testify to this media overkill reporting live, since the participation of the TV viewer is today a sine qua non condition of the event, already theorized by French historian Pierre Nora in 1974:

> By abolishing the deadlines, by unrolling the dubious action under our eyes, by miniaturizing real-life experience, live broadcasting definitely bowdlerizes the event from its historical characteristics to project it in the life experience of the masses. . . . The characteristic of the modern event is to be seen, and this "voyeurism" gives to current affairs both their specificity towards History and their already historical perfume.[8]

The prevalence of the images of reality over reality itself places the "specta-tor-voyeur" in a fallacious role of victim, giving to the whole western world the feeling of being a victim of 9/11:

> Reality has always been interpreted through the reports given by images. . . . In the preface to the second edition (1843) of *The Essence of Christianity*, Feuerbach observes about our "era" that it "prefers the image to the thing, the copy to the original, the representation to the reality, appearance to being."[9]

And beyond this representation of reality, because "myth . . . is a commu-nication system, it is a message,"[10] the media behave as "mythographs," according to Alissa Torres, since they transform the event into symbol, a totemic icon, that the "falling men" photographs endlessly re-present. She as well will indeed imagine her husband Eddie as a falling man, but from a very far, discreet angle, and not in a spectacular way anymore.[11] If the media interpreted the attacks of September 11, 2001, as an original and foundational event, they also exploited its spectacular nature.

The critical eye which Alissa Torres casts on this media deviancy is irrev-ocable: the sequence in which she describes her experience as a young mother and the media morbidly involved in this thirst for testimony proves it.[12] The use of her child's picture and the cynical takeover of her traumatic experi-ence are systematically refused: "Stay the hell away from him. . . . We're getting out of here," she announces to the media.[13] Through this expres-sion, chanted like a mantra throughout the narrative, Torres thus denies this characteristic of the modern event: the prevalence of emotion and the veiled appeal to affects, what Nora names the "emotional virtualities."[14]

The media, by hijacking the attacks of September 11, 2001, have openly taken on the mourning process of the nation. They have built the "script" of the new (super) hero through the use of the figure of the firemen and the other rescuers at Ground Zero. Many graphic, literary, and cinematic works have also contributed to this script, such as the 2006 film *World Trade Center*, by Oliver Stone, or the cover of the graphic collection *9-11 Emergency Relief* that shows a firefighter in a particularly heroic pose.[15] In doing so, the narrativization of the event into a simplified dramaturgy sets up its own commemoration; as an event in the process of being car-ried out and already commemorated, "September 11, 2001, shows to the extreme the logic of the contemporary event which, being given to see as it actually happens, becomes historic at once, and is already for itself its own commemoration."[16] Once again, according to Alissa Torres, the commemoration of the attacks is hijacked by the media and the American administration. The final chapter of her narrative clarifies this misappro-priation, this cynical abuse of memory which has already been questioned by Tzvetan Todorov:

The ritual commemoration is not only of poor effect for the education of the population when one just confirms in the past the negative image of the others or one's own positive image; it also contributes to divert our attention from the present urgencies, while cheaply salving our conscience.[17]

This salving of conscience, built by the media, will develop a new script, that of good against evil, and will facilitate the security plans created by the U.S. government. Torres, in the span of a panel and its accompanying caption, does not forget that the administration did not take long before providing legislative and military answers to this collective "trauma" and in using her own personal trauma to justify warlike revenge.[18] Todorov again develops the idea of the memory "put into service" by the politicians in order to "achieve new goals."[19]

Television is a recurring image in *American Widow* because it serves as a mediation of national mourning by absorbing the intimate tragedies, becoming thus the privileged vector of the moral responsibility for all.[20] It creates a morbid feeling of proximity, along with a feeling of pity, which enervates all the narration, creating what French sociologist Luc Boltanski has called "the policy of pity," which is a product of sorrow and biblical pity, in the American evangelic context.[21] This feeling of pity is made clear throughout the graphic novel, through the various experiences at the American Red Cross, the Salvation Army, the discussion groups set up by official therapists, and the Federal 9/11 Victim Compensation Fund. This unexpected confrontation between compassion and charity becomes dramatically vivid in the full-page panels on utterly black background, where Torres, lying on her back, her eyes closed, is assailed by erratic balloons proposing some help,[22] until their tails end like snakes seizing their prey.[23] This visual effect demonstrates very effectively how Alissa Torres, as a victim, is deprived of her grief and is alienated from this event immediately because of its transformation into myth: "The myth distorts but does not abolish the meaning, it alienates it."[24] While choosing to witness history, she endeavors to take over her story back.

9/11 as her story

"Memory is always and only individual; the collective memory is not a memory but a speech evolving in public space," Todorov writes.[25] As a counterpoint to the public discussion of 9/11, which is thus not memory, Alissa Torres confronts the official images of that day with her own, swapping her memories with the constructions of a collective imagination. In this graphic narrative, she creates a work of memory rather than a duty of remembrance: "Yes, I understood you died here, although this reality would continue to escape me. This visit did nothing to change that. It just made me remember."[26] She fights against the programmed reifying of all those victims and against the *com*-memorizing which evacuates any true *re*-memorizing. The outstanding place taken in her narrative by her memories about her intimate relation with Eddie underscores her inflexible will to give a name to the anonymous victims, to tell a story behind History. Chapters 2 and 3 are entirely devoted to these recollections, while the many pages on black background stand for accounts within the account, like a *mise en abyme* of a certainly digressive, yet still (re)constructive, memory.[27]

> Memory plays the key role. One is freed from the work of Time by remembrance, by *anâmnèsis*. This technique goes thus with the archaic design to know the origin and the history of a thing, in order to be able to control it.[28]

The mechanism of testimony

Using her own point of view, Alissa Torres always places her narrative under the seal of intimacy, even and especially when she deals with government aid and struggles against all the speeches of victimization, be they fictional or not, which try to make use of the event: "As words to articulate what happened stayed lodged in my throat, authors were busy creating their Great Works of Art. It makes me sick just to see the book covers or movie posters."[29] She has decided to speak through this graphic novel so as to make us hear her voice as a victim. The reader can indeed hear it in each page, in each panel, all of which demonstrate her grief, her anger, her failure to understand, her fears as a widowed young mother; this voice and this critical analysis show the difficulty of giving a shape, and thus a meaning, to the unspeakable. Alissa Torres makes a constant use of this witness status in order to incorporate her own memories of being a victim into the public sphere, in an autobiography of trauma; bearing witness, according to Todorov, "competes with the historical discourse, in the opinion of the general public in particular."[30]

In her article published in the 2006 edition of *Modern Fiction Studies*, Gillian Whitlock defines the graphic autobiography as *autographics*, so as to distinguish it from the mere textual autobiography which lacks images.[31] According to her, this very difference, far from directing and thus limiting the reader's imagination, offers to the author of *autographics* a procedural deepening and thus a better investigation within the intimate psyche. The reader, by swinging between images and text, becomes a real spectator and discovers the words as matter and the drawings as narration.[32] In addition, by interweaving of these two elements, Edward Said argues in his foreword to the graphic documentary *Palestine*, by Joe Sacco:

> Comics seemed to say what couldn't otherwise be said, perhaps what wasn't permitted to be said or imagined, defying the ordinary processes of thought. I felt that comics freed me to think and imagine and see differently.[33]

Each page of *American Widow* is filled with the force and sincerity of her graphic testimony, creating what Damien Zanone calls "truth": "the asserted truth refers to the inner feeling of the author, we should name it sincerity."[34] Alissa Torres' sincerity can be found in her account of her love affair with Eddie, told without leniency or embellishment. The very morning of September 11, 2001, she remembers that she is terribly angry at him, that she may even split up with him, before she hears about the first plane crash into the north tower of the World Trade Center.[35] Throughout her autobiographical testimony, or *autographics*, she makes her past resurface in order to shed light on her present: "There is no such thing as a present speaking *about* the past but a past speaking *in* the present."[36]

The mechanism of images

American Widow, as a narrative of reappropriation, or "counternarrative,"[37] is not comics by chance. It should not be forgotten that the heroic characters of mainstream American comics represent the modern version of the mythological heroes (Superman, Iron Man, Thor, etc.[38]). The use of this particular medium, which thus echoes ancient myths in the collective imagination, gives its author the opportunity to deconstruct these modern myths of the hero by drawing the outlines of her late husband Eddie, a hero, or anti-hero, of her everyday life. The ordeal has been, without any doubt, a test of acknowledgment for Alissa Torres's work, and her choice of graphic narration recalls the decision of Art Spiegelman in his own account of September 11, 2001, to remain as close as possible to the images he still had in his mind: "My strips are now a slow-motion diary of what I experienced."[39] Torres's political struggle might have been less visible than that of Spiegelman,[40] but her opinions resonate throughout, for example, when she criticizes someone opposed to spending money to help people via the compensation funds given to the families of the victims of the attacks.[41] Like Spiegelman, but in a more oblique way, Alissa Torres rises up against what Joan Didion has called the "infantilization of citizens"[42] and thus gives to her admittedly more personal story more political overtones.

The various comics techniques that her illustrator uses offer a new relationship between visuality and the transmission of personal and cultural trauma. The faithful drawing of the main protagonists of her story (the CEO of Cantor Fitzgerald Howard Lutnick, the administrator of the federal 9/11 victim compensation fund Kenneth Feinberg, etc.) gives a proper face, a concern for authenticity, to her testimony. Yet, this authenticity becomes obvious to the reader as soon as these drawings, as realistic as they can be, are overshadowed by photographs which plunge the narration into the crudest reality: "Photographed images do not seem to be statements about the world so much as pieces of it, miniatures of reality."[43] Indeed, Alissa Torres's narration is literally pierced twice by the insertion of photographs of the husband, on page 113 and again on pages 198–199.

This choice of "transparency," as Sontag would say, suddenly makes reality arise beyond the already "sincere" drawn pictures.[44] A second level of authenticity is reached here, in which the ordinary reader of comics also becomes a voyeur, since he/she enters the deepest intimacy of the author, who has surprisingly given up any decency in her struggle against the misuse of her personal trauma. The double-page spread on pages 198–199, with its set of photographs forming a multiple photo frame about Eddie's life, ultimately announces him as the sacrificial victim of the September 11, 2001, attacks. The reader, inevitably overwhelmed by its pathos, is caught in a double bind:

> As the fascination that photographs exercise is a reminder of death, it is also an invitation to sentimentality. Photographs turn the past into an object of tender regard, scrambling moral distinctions and disarming historical judgments by the generalized pathos of looking at time past.[45]

As for the very last picture of the book, it is a holiday photograph of Alissa Torres and her young boy, both smiling in the turquoise blue water of Hawaii.[46] This depiction of blunt reality, by its very presence, gives her testimony its memorializing characteristic, but at the same time it emphasizes the tragic and commemorative aspect of the event, inexorably reincorporating it into History.

9/11 as tragedy

In her narrative of mourning, Alissa Torres enumerates each psychic stage which the survivor must undergo, from the silence of the ineffable to despair, from the denial of reality to depressive anger, from the yielding of absence to possible resiliency. Sigmund Freud theorized this work of mourning, or *Trauerarbeit*, and made a vital distinction between melancholia and

mourning.[47] While the latter represents an active working-through of a traumatic loss, the former is characterized by inertia and isolation. *American
Widow* reproduces this state of apathy, this complex of melancholia "like
an open wound [which] empties out the 'I' until total depletion."[48] This
exclusive relinquishment to mourning and absence is perfectly illustrated
by the silences of the first pages of the graphic novel.

The mechanism of absence

In *American Widow*, in the minutes which precede the collapsing of the
towers as well as in the collapse itself, and the sudden tragedy that it signifies for her, the complete absence of any narration is obvious.[49] Wordlessness
resonates in every panel. Alissa Torres and Sungyoon Choi have decided to
let the images "speak" for themselves. This void, or rather, this lack of
language, because it refers to the unspeakable, proves the inadequacy of
words, the powerlessness of the linguistic means, all inoperative to Torres.
Neither balloon nor caption could render the "visual truth" of the images
drawn in her autobiography, which becomes this "non-speaking speech"
(*parole non parlante*) as Maurice Blanchot put it.[50] It is also possible to
argue that no sound could compete with the instantaneous mark on the
memory which the images of the planes crashing into the towers conferred,
of the jumpers, of the collapse, of Manhattan buried under the debris. This,
the most documented event in history, is remembered through a sequence
of images rather than by a soundtrack.

As a medium combining text and images, comics provides a large
number of formal strategies in order to represent sound in its pages.
However, *American Widow* rejects all these strategies to strengthen the
significance of the drawings: "with silence, the truth does not have to
suffer any more from the impurities and the fragmentation necessarily
involved in discourse."[51] This textual silence obviously underscores the
tragic absence, beyond suffering and distress. The full panel on page 87
is emblematic of this irrevocable absence, the impossibility of good—
despite the birth of the child—which alienates any possible regeneration
and displays the narrative in a tragic mode. Alissa Torres' story goes thus
beyond the bounds of a mere "autographics" to present a shared experience of mourning. She registers her intimate and personal story into a
common cultural history through which each one can expurgate his/her
own fear. She writes,

> As a sun of reality peered in, shining strong on the fact that you were
> dead and I was still alive and this being [the baby] bearing the name of
> tragedy would never know you except as I built you in his memory.[52]

The mechanism of catharsis

Aristotle in the first place sets out to account for the undeniable, though remarkable, fact that many tragic representations of suffering and defeat leave an audience feeling not depressed, but relieved. In the second place, Aristotle uses this distinctive effect on the reader, "the pleasure of pity and fear," as the basic way to define tragedy.[53]

Aristotle's *catharsis*, which in Greek means "purgation" or "purification," is a concept turned toward the reception of a piece of work. Through the various processes analyzed here, the reader of Alissa Torres's work is indeed trapped in this mixing up of pity and fear. The cathartic effect of the traumatic account fully succeeds since it makes it possible to tame the past, for want of a distressing present: "One can't possess reality, one can possess (and be possessed by) images, as one can't possess the present but one can possess the past."[54] Just like the author, the reader clings to the singularity of the past, by transforming it into an adjustable key that is supposed to clarify the present. The magnifying glass effect, which allowed Torres to take her story back, also functions in the opposite direction; the very title of the work, *American Widow*, by its syntactic indetermination, may give the story its mythological function, in the Barthian sense of the term. The American widow who takes off her veil under the eyes of her reader suddenly speaks for all the other American widows.

Likewise, by including the "real" figure of her husband through photographs, the author shifts the emphasis of the comics toward a magic use of the image, which then remythologizes all her narration. As Sontag suggests, "A photograph is pseudo-presence and a token of absence. . . . All talismanic uses of photographs express a feeling both sentimental and implicitly magical."[55] Alissa Torres herself understands the magic effect of her desperate attempt to recreate her own story: "I now suspect there was a part of me that believed the truth might have some magic in it: the power to roll back time, the power to fix it. To bring Eddie back."[56] The cathartic effect of her testimony is very similar to the work of psychological resiliency, theorized by French ethologist Boris Cyrulnik who explained that any victim can use it to overcome a traumatic experience. Torres's narrated tragedy enters the category of works which, by their exemplary nature, give the reader a possibility of interpreting their distress:

> The work of resiliency consisted in remembering the shocks to turn them into a representation of images, actions and words, in order to interpret the wrench.[57]

Following this notion of resiliency, the reader-voyeur will find, in the very last page, a final photograph, figuring that the trauma had been resolved, which could embody the eschatological myth of the end of a world which ultimately starts over again: "I knew so fiercely that I was alive, together with my son, and that it was a beautiful day."[58]

We have analyzed the various processes which Alissa Torres used in her account of the catastrophe to make it leave its mythological ground, to try to reappropriate the pain, so intimate and personal, of mourning, specifically of September 11, 2001. The author, by refusing the immediacy of solely textual language, by fighting against the excessive media coverage as well as the victimization, by choosing graphic testimony, or "autographics," without indulgence, gave to her account its political impact, against all the administrative, media, or fictional attempts to hijack the event. The tragic impossibility to fill the gap of the very last minutes lived by her husband entrapped in the north tower of the WTC forced Alissa Torres to tell her story, to "re-memorate" it compulsively. After all these years of painful blank spaces—government mishandling, grievous disappointment, useless commissions, and assorted fictions—she realizes that she must recreate her own myth: "Myth (*mythos*) tells indirectly what the *logos* cannot tell."[59] By witnessing history and testifying about her own open wounds, Alissa Torres knows too well that she is reduced to invent some parts of it so as to fill in the blanks: "In the absence of concrete facts about how my husband died, I created my own story."[60] However, by using the inherent pathos of the photographic images, she gave the tragic vision of her own story cathartic lineaments which unavoidably set the catastrophe back to its highly mythological aspect. The power of her testimony about U.S. contemporary history, enhanced by the use of comics, seems thus outstripped by that of the photographic compact, which, through its paradoxical immediacy, recalls this Edenic, mythological past, underscored by Sontag: "those ghostly traces, photographs, supply the token presence of the dispersed relatives."[61]

Notes

1 Alissa Torres, *American Widow* (New York: Villard Books, 2008).
2 *The Washington Post*, August 9, 2006.
3 Jacques Derrida and Jürgen Habermas, *Le "Concept" du 11 septembre, dialogues à New York* (Paris: Galilée, 2004), 136; all translations in this essay are my own.
4 Ibid., 211.
5 Mircea Eliade, *Aspects du Mythe* (Paris: Gallimard, 1963), 16.
6 Ibid., 12.
7 Roland Barthes, *Mythologies* (Paris: Éditions du Seuil, 1957), 230, 217.
8 Pierre Nora, "Le Retour de l'Événement," in *Faire de l'Histoire* (Paris: Folio, 1974), 295.
9 Susan Sontag, *On Photography* (New York: Farrar, Straus & Giroux, 1977), 153.

10 Barthes, *Mythologies*, 193.
11 Torres, *American Widow*, 197.
12 Ibid., 191–202.
13 Ibid., 201.
14 Nora, "Le Retour," 293.
15 See also in this volume the story "Letters from a Broken Apple" for the grave portrait of a fireman with the caption, "Where are our super-heroes when we need them? And then it hits me. They're right there." Neil Kleid (w), Mark Hempel (a), John Staton (a), Harry Roland (a), Mark Wheatley (a), and Gray Marrow (a). "Letters From a Broken Apple," in Jeff Mason, ed., *9/11 Emergency Relief* (Gainesville, FL: Alternative Comics, 2002), 127.
16 François Hartog, *Régimes d'Historicité: Présentisme et Expérience du Temps* (Paris: Éditions du Seuil, 2003), 116.
17 Tzvetan Todorov, *Mémoire du Mal, Tentation du Bien. Enquête sur le Siècle* (Paris: Robert Laffont, 2000), 251–252.
18 Torres, *American Widow*, 127.
19 Todorov, *Mémoire du Mal*, 185.
20 Torres, *American Widow*, 192.
21 Luc Boltanski, *Le Nouvel Esprit du Capitalisme* (Paris: Gallimard, 1999), 6–24.
22 Torres, *American Widow*, 43, 50, 106.
23 Ibid., 109.
24 Barthes, *Mythologies*, 208.
25 Todorov, *Mémoire du Mal*, 191.
26 Torres, *American Widow*, 118–119.
27 Ibid., 95–98; 110–111; 141–142; 159–162; 179–183.
28 Eliade, *Aspects du Mythe*, 115.
29 Alissa Torres, "9/11 Widow: Do I really Want the Truth ?" http://www.salon.com/life/feature/2009/09/11/911_widow (accessed May 7, 2011).
30 Todorov, *Mémoire du Mal*, 189.
31 She explains, "By coining the term 'autographics' for graphic memoir I mean to draw attention to the specific conjunctions of visual and verbal text in this genre of autobiography." Gillian Whitlock, "Autographics: The Seeing 'I' of the Comics," *Modern Fiction Studies*, 52, no. 4 (Winter 2006): 965–978.
32 In *American Widow*, see for instance page 45 and the choice of child's drawing to depict the towers in flame or page 85 whose text serves as drawing, like an illusory announcement of birth.
33 Edward Said, "Introduction," to *Palestine: The Collection* (Seattle: Fantasgraphics Books, 2001), ii.
34 Damien Zanone, *L'Autobiographie* (Paris: Ellipses, 1996), 27.
35 Torres, *American Widow*, 28–32.
36 Philippe Le Jeune, *Le Pacte Autobiographique* (Paris: Éditions du Seuil, 1975), 53.
37 See Don De Lillo, "In the Ruins of the Future," Harper's, December 2001.
38 See Alex Nikolavitch, *Mythe et Super-héros* (Lyon: Moutons Électriques, 2011).
39 Art Spiegelman, "Foreword," in *In the Shadow of No Towers* (New York: Pantheon Books, 2004).

40 Spiegelman wrote, "When the government began to move into full dystopian Big Brother mode, all the rage I'd suppressed after the 2000 election, all the paranoia I'd barely managed to squeltch immediately after 9/11, returned with a vengeance. New traumas began competing with still-fresh wounds and the nature of my project began to mutate." (Ibid., "Preface.")

41 Torres, *American Widow*, 136.

42 Joan Didion, *Fixed Ideas: America since 9/11* (New York: New York Review of Books, 2003), 13–14.

43 Sontag, *On Photography*, 4.

44 "A photograph, any photograph, seems to have a more innocent, and therefore more accurate, relation to visible reality than do other mimetic objects. . . . It's transparency." (Sontag, *On Photography*, 6).

45 Ibid., 71.

46 Torres, *American Widow*, 210.

47 Sigmund Freud, *On Murder, Mourning, and Melancholia* (London and New York: Penguin Books, 2005), 206.

48 Sigmund Freud, *Oeuvres Complètes*, Vol. XIII (Paris: PUF, 1988), 272.

49 Torres, *American Widow*, 38–41.

50 Maurice Blanchot, *L'Entretien Infini* (Paris: Gallimard, 1969), 358.

51 George Steiner, *Langage et Silence* (Paris: Éditions du Seuil, 1969), 31.

52 Torres, *American Widow*, 83.

53 M. H. Abrams, *A Glossary of Literary Terms*, 7th edition (Fort Worth, TX: Harcourt Brace College Publishers, 1999), 212.

54 Sontag, *On Photography*, 162.

55 Ibid., 16.

56 Torres, "9/11 Widow."

57 Boris Cyrulnik, *Le Murmure des Fantômes* (Paris: Odile Jacob, 2003), 64.

58 Torres, *American Widow*, 210.

59 Pierre Van Den Heuvel, *Parole, Mot, Silence: Pour une Poétique de l'Énonciation* (Paris: Librairie José Corti, 1985), 278.

60 Torres, "9/11 Widow."

61 Sontag, *On Photography*, 9.

CHAPTER SIXTEEN

"The Great Machine Doesn't Wear a Cape!"

American Cultural Anxiety and the Post-9/11 Superhero

Jeff Geers

Within a week of the terrorist attacks of September 11, 2001, the following joke was circulated on the internet:

> Q: Why didn't Superman stop the planes from hitting the Twin Towers?
> A: Because he's a quadriplegic.[1]

While incredibly crass, this joke reveals a crucial perspective on the events of 9/11. Over the last half-century, comic book readers have seen Superman stop crashing jets, falling satellites, and even comets and meteors. Yet, on the morning of September 11th, no red-caped hero stood between the Towers; no webbing held back the planes. On September 11th, the American superhero failed. Not only did the destruction of the World Trade Center represent the collapse of one of the most dominant symbols of American and Western culture, but it also reminded Americans of the vulnerability of their cultural worldview and identity. If Superman, the paradigmatic representation of "Truth, Justice, and the American Way" could not promise security, what could? Writing only months after the attacks, Bradford Wright noted that

> Superheroes had responded to national calamities before, from the Great Depression to the threat of nuclear war. . . . But could superheroes who

had so deftly blurred fantasy and reality in the past handle the challenge this time?[2]

The usual comic books stories with Lex Luthor or Doctor Doom threatening American citizens took on new meaning; even the classic phrase "Up in the sky! It's a bird. . . . It's a plane . . ." could not be said without alluding to the tragedy. As such, one of the lasting cultural effects of 9/11 was the insufficiency of the American superhero and the subsequent creation of a new post-disaster superhero mythos.

Comic book superheroes, traditionally symbolic of the strength and invulnerability of American culture, struggled to find a way to respond to the September 11th attacks, which represented not only physical destruction, but identified weaknesses and vulnerabilities in American collective identity and culture. Where the traditional hero failed, new, post-disaster superheroes emerged in direct response to cultural anxieties. This essay examines The Great Machine, the superhero protagonist of Brian K. Vaughan's series *Ex Machina*. Vaughan's series consciously creates a new mythic superhero that responds to the cultural anxieties of post-9/11 America. *Ex Machina* manipulates the familiar aspects of the comic-book superhero: locating the heroic origin within a traumatic experience, the opposition of supervillains, distinctive costuming, and superhuman powers and abilities. However, as this essay will demonstrate, these familiar elements are inverted in Vaughan's series, representing a significant shift in both superheroes and American culture after 9/11.

Disaster and cultural identity

In this sense, we are not examining disaster in regards to physical destruction or loss of life. Rather, "disaster" is considered, in the words of rhetorician Robert Wade Kenny, utter destruction and loss of a socially and rhetorically constructed "dwelling place."[3] In experiencing a disaster, we are forced to witness the death of our fragile identities, the impossible made actual. From an existentialist or phenomenological point of view, disaster is defined by the individual experiencing the phenomenon; disaster occurs when an event actually intrudes and assaults the individual's own being. Every person organizes his or her life and experiences into a meaningful structure, a "home" of sorts which serves as his or her reality. Disaster intrudes upon this reality by shaking the very foundations of our worldview; according to Kenny, it is the "collapse of a planned life."[4]

Such an existential focus would normally concern itself with the individual experience and response to a disaster. However, contemporary media systems have created a construct which allows for a shared experience of the disaster. Thanks to live news footage, viewers across the country experienced the immediate occurrence of September 11th in real time, witnessing the Towers collapse and then reviewing the moment in slow-motion replays. Such an event has a widespread effect on the entire culture, transforming it into cultural trauma. The sociologist Neil Smelser defines cultural traumas as "social dislocations and catastrophes [that] massively disrupt organized social life."[5] Just as individual trauma destroys the victim's worldview, cultural trauma manages to "undermine or overwhelm one or several essential ingredients of a culture"[6] such as economic or political structures. As a cultural trauma, the September 11th terrorist attacks had the greatest impact on American ideological systems; the failure of superheroes was symptomatic of a failure of an American mythos.

Traditional superheroes on September 11

Just as the American public was forced to deal with the grim realities of 9/11, comic book heroes (some of whom were not only explicitly American, but were additionally New Yorkers) addressed the disaster on their own terms. Within the pages of popular comic series, superheroes addressed the destruction and loss of life in terms of their own fictional limitations. Spider-Man and Captain America worked alongside police and firefighters to clear the wreckage and look for survivors. "We could not see it coming. We could not be here before it happened. We could not stop it," the narrator of *Amazing Spider-Man* tells us, "But we are here now."[7] Other popular heroes admitted their own limitations. In *9/11*, a collection of stories whose proceeds went to various September 11th charities, Superman, perhaps the most powerful hero in the DC comics universe, lamented:

> I can defy the laws of gravity. I can ignore the principles of physics. . . . But unfortunately . . . the one thing I can not do . . . is break free from the fictional pages where I live and breathe . . . become real during times of crisis . . . and right the wrongs of an unjust world.[8]

As the established myths prove insufficient in light of 9/11, new myths have emerged as a newly constructed worldview. Perhaps the most definitive example of this post-9/11 hero myth is presented in Brian K. Vaughan's series *Ex Machina*.

Brian K. Vaughan's *Ex Machina*

While he has since written many notable stories for several superhero series at both DC and Marvel (as well as being a principal writer for the television program *Lost*), Brian K. Vaughan's reputation was definitively established by three series he created: *Y: The Last Man, Runaways*, and *Ex Machina*. *Y: The Last Man*, published by DC/Vertigo, tells the story of a mysterious plague that instantly kills every male on the planet except for a failed escape artist and his pet monkey, who are forced to survive in a radically different and dangerous world. *Runaways*, published by Marvel, features a group of children who learn that their parents are actually a sinister sect of supervillains. Both titles explicitly incorporate themes of trauma, most significantly in the loss of worldview, as Yorick, the last man, witnesses the collapse of established society and the six runaways are confronted with the unacceptable knowledge that their parents are murderers and terrorists, part of a supernatural plot to destroy/conquer the world. The protagonists in each series struggle to make meaning in a post-trauma world, and these texts provide insightful glimpses of post-9/11 culture. However, while the runaway children are super-powered and interact with standard Marvel continuity, *Runaways* is more of a story of teen and young adult coping rather than a traditional superhero story; similarly, while *Y: The Last Man* is riddled with allusions to comic book superheroes (as the sole surviving male, Yorick Brown is literally "the strongest man on Earth"), the series is best classified as science-fiction.

It is within his third original series, *Ex Machina*, that Vaughan creates the first superhero to emerge as an explicit response to the cultural trauma of the September 11th terrorist attacks. *Ex Machina* was published by Wildstorm (a DC comics imprint) initially in August of 2004 and it ended its 50-issue run in 2010. The main character in the series is Mitchell Hundred, a retired superhero who has been elected mayor of New York City after his heroic actions on September 11th. The series is set during Hundred's term in office, but the narrative is interspersed with flashbacks to Hundred's earlier days as the costumed superhero, The Great Machine. While *Ex Machina* exists outside of any superhero continuity, dominant heroic narratives play a crucial part in its cultural significance; the series recognizes the failure of traditional superheroes and re-envisions the narrative tropes and constructs of classical superhero myths in order to construct a new worldview.

Several prominent contemporary comic series focus on allegories of classic superheroes, as seen in the way the characters of Kurt Busiek's *Astro City* and Warren Ellis and Mike Millar's *The Authority* deconstruct the dominant superhero myths. Vaughan's heroes, on the other hand, are subtly shown to be inversions of the classic elements of the dominant genre conventions. Instead of Clark Kent's farmer parents in Smallville, Mitchell Hundred is raised by a political activist single mother, and his only father figure is a Soviet expatriate nicknamed "Kremlin," who learned English from reading comic books and tends to quote both Silver-Age comics and Marx's *Das Kapital*. Gary Engle notes that Superman is "the consummate and totally uncompromised alien, an immigrant whose visible difference from the norm is underscored by his decision to wear a costume of bold primary colors."[9] Kal-El was not only born on another planet, but is often derided as an "alien" by villains and his detractors. This divide between Superman and the American public he protects is a common theme in the various incarnations of the Superman narrative. *Ex Machina*'s Mitchell Hundred, by contrast, emphasizes his American origins. When a reporter accuses him of being an alien (a frequent slur used by Superman's enemies), questioning the normalcy of his last name, Hundred notes that he is "a thirteenth-generation American," whose ancestors renamed themselves after the Brandywine Hundred in Delaware.[10] Whereas Superman validates the immigrant experience and the role of the immigrant within popular culture, Mitchell Hundred is presented as an everyman, an American. While his circumstances as mayor and his powers of communication may distinguish Hundred from the rest of the populace, he nevertheless shares the firsthand experience of trauma in a way that Superman cannot. This suggests that the mythic response to trauma can come from within the affected culture, rather than from an outside source.

One common element in the classic superhero myth was the presence of trauma in the birth or creation of the superhero. Superman is "born" out of the destruction of his home planet; Batman is defined by the cold-blooded murder of his parents; Spider-Man chose to become a hero after the murder of his surrogate father. However, the classic hero experiences trauma as an individual. Bruce Wayne and Peter Parker are the only individuals explicitly traumatized by the murders of their loved ones; to the rest of the community, the deaths are only the unfortunate result of crime. Even though the entire planet of Krypton is destroyed, only Kal-El is traumatized, as he is the only survivor left to experience it. Yet, since September 11th was a disaster experienced at once by an entire culture who viewed the events as they occurred on television, the superhero myths that emerge after 9/11 address mass trauma. *Ex Machina* includes individual trauma, as Mitchell Hundred gains his powers in an explosive exposure to an unknown object; yet, Hundred's role as mayor is defined by the shared experience of September 11th. *Ex Machina* is actually the story of two heroes: the "traditional" hero, The Great Machine, borne out of individual trauma, and the collective hero, Mayor Mitchell Hundred, that emerges from the cultural trauma of 9/11.

Like the classic hero myths, the post-9/11 heroes are defined, in part, by the villains who oppose them. In Vaughan's text, the villains are those who cannot respond to the disaster event, who lack the imaginative vision to create a new worldview. In fact, the villains of *Ex Machina* are people who have been driven hopelessly mad by a disaster event. While, the hero, Mitchell Hundred, uses his exposure to the artifact, which throughout the series symbolizes the unimaginable and incomprehensible disaster event, to become a hero and ideally improve the world, every other figure in the story who is exposed to the artifact is destroyed by the experience. They are driven mad, killing their loved ones and themselves. One character equates seeing the artifact with "looking into hell,"[11] while another brutally murders her husband, child, and the family dog in an attempt to "fix what was broken."[12]

Perhaps the character most illustrative of this point is The Great Machine's "archenemy" Jack Pherson, who is hinted at throughout the regular series, but did not appear until the *Ex Machina Special*, a 2-part miniseries that was released in Summer 2006 that consisted of a single flashback to 6 months before the 9/11 attacks. Whereas Hundred and the other villains experienced trauma first-hand in their direct exposure to the artifact (and later in his participation in the September 11th event), Pherson experiences trauma indirectly; his traumatic exposure comes when a parrot mimics a recording of The Great Machine's "command voice." As expected, Pherson's trauma forms him into the antithesis of Hundred, able to communicate with animals just as Hundred talks with machines. Pherson decries The Great Machine's heroics: "You were given the ability to end so much suffering on this planet, and yet you do nothing with it. . . . You claim to speak for the helpless, but you've squandered your voice."[13] Unlike most villains, whose existence only justifies the actions of the corresponding superhero, Pherson's role is to show Hundred the meaninglessness of his superheroics. It is only after Pherson is killed (the only death Hundred has been directly responsible for in the series) that Hundred "retires" his alter ego and decides to run for mayor of New York City.

The outfit worn by The Great Machine is a marked contrast from the traditional superhero cape and tights. When Hundred first meets with his NSA handler Jackson Georges, the agent notes: "You looked a lot less . . . dorky on CNN," to which the hero replies, "Yeah, well, everyone looks cool when they're flying 150 mph above Manhattan."[14] In a 2006 interview, Vaughan credited series artist Tony Harris with the design:

> I told Tony it was a story of this mayor who was a retired superhero and I said, "He can talk to machines but I picture him as an archetypal iconic superhero with a cape and a mask." Tony was the one who was like, "Well look, if he can talk to technology his appearance should reflect that and if we're going to be so grounded in the real world it should have this clunky aesthetic to it." It was a brilliant, obvious observation and it made the book 100 times better.[15]

Instead of the usual sleek, form-fitting unitard worn by most superheroes, Harris' illustrations of The Great Machine show mismatched zippers, buttons, and buckles, and protective padding disrupts any smooth lines or rippling musculature; the design of The Great Machine much more closely resembles a biker's leather riding outfit than any comic book superhero.

In several flashbacks, Hundred and his "team" are shown developing his equipment piecemeal, building The Great Machine through trial-and-error. The outfit is primarily functional: Hundred's distinctive pilot's helmet is worn not to protect his secret identity or strike fear into his enemies, but to protect his skull in the case of an accidental crash (while the helmet protects his skull, its attached faceplate consistently shatters, disabling The Great Machine before he ever throws a punch). The only visual icon of The Great Machine's superhero status is a simple, but subdued, design of a cog nearly hidden on the front of his chest piece; the only visible evidence of Hundred's superhuman abilities, green "circuitry" etched into the side of his face, is completely hidden underneath his helmet. It comes as no surprise that The Great Machine, prior to his widely televised actions during the World Trade Center attacks, is rarely recognized as a superhero; witnesses assume he is a performance artist, political activist, or simply a fireman or police officer in special gear. Whereas traditional superheroes have long been identified by their colorful costumes, Vaughan distinctly sets up his character as being inspired by this tradition, but nonetheless functioning as a completely different type of hero.

In defining the mythic superhero character, Richard Reynolds notes that "the extraordinary nature of the superhero [is] contrasted with the ordinariness of his surroundings."[16] Where a classic comic book superhero's powers are established through physical supremacy or unnatural feats of strength, Hundred's supernatural abilities are comparatively mundane and underwhelming to a typical comics audience. As told in the first flashbacks of the series, a mysterious explosion and exposure to an unknown "artifact" left Mitchell Hundred with circuit-like scarring on his face and neck, giving him the ability to communicate with both simple and complex machines. When The Great Machine uses his ability, his eyes glow green and his voice itself changes, represented by a distinctive green block font designed specifically for the series by artist Tony Harris. The bounds of Hundred's powers are unclear, as he has been shown to accidentally shut down all machine activity for several blocks[17] and, with concentration, he can communicate without using speech, although this causes nosebleeds.[18] Additionally, advanced technology, such as his jetpack and "stun-gun," appear to Hundred in his dreams, although he usually relies on others to actually build the devices.[19] The "ordinariness" of Hundred's surroundings is amplified by *Ex Machina*'s realistic setting: the series is set in a universe where, before The Great Machine, superheroes were limited to the pages of comic books. The realistic nature of this world only enhances the impact of a disaster event, even if it is a "fictional" terrorist attack—the familiar superheroes will not appear to prevent the 9/11 disaster. The Great Machine is the sole superpowered individual in this reality; the series is set in a universe where familiar Marvel and DC superheroes are the subjects of conversation—not as diegetic characters, but as elements of popular culture. Several of the main characters in the series, including Mitchell Hundred, are lifelong superhero comic book readers and consciously model their behaviors and moral codes after heroes like DC's Superman.

As a result, The Great Machine is continually compared to the pantheon of fictional comic book superheroes. However, Hundred's superhuman abilities are clearly of a different sort than those seen in traditional superhero narratives. He does not possess the mythic strength, speed, or invulnerability of a "godlike" hero, such as Superman. In fact, The Great Machine can only fly with the mechanical assistance of his often-faulty jetpack. Nor has he attained near-superhuman capabilities through study and training, the typical path of "exceptional human" heroes like Batman; Hundred mentions that he "took some [boxing] lessons,"[20] but beyond that he has no specific training in fighting injustice, crime, and evil. While the character of The Great Machine is certainly presented against these traditional superhero archetypes, Hundred's powers more closely parallel a third type of hero, the "cyborg hero" described by Mark Oehlert as "subtle man-machine integration."[21] Oehlert's archetype is typified by heroes such as Captain America and Wolverine, whose human bodies were merged with artificial systems that grant the cyborg hero superhuman abilities. The Great Machine is a cyborg not only in nature, but his power is essentially an ability to interface directly with technology, without the "ordinariness" of mediated technological interfacing.

Yet, the hero of *Ex Machina* is also not a typical comic book cyborg. Oehlert notes that cyborg superheroes exhibit "control of his weapon system to a greater degree than ever before," including one popular superhero "who exercises control over his system at a cellular level."[22] This precise control is inherent in the "extraordinary nature" of the cyborg hero; yet, Mitchell Hundred clearly does not possess this control. His commands are often taken too literally, as when Hundred accidentally shuts down the entire power grid while trying to turn off a radio. A more troubling lack of control is seen in the "Off the Grid" storyline, when a shotgun "lies" to Hundred, falsely telling him that it is unloaded.[23] It has become clear that Hundred's relationship with technology is more complex than that of any of the typical superhero archetypes. After a complete loss of worldview and identity, The Great Machine does not attempt to alleviate cultural anxiety through raw force and physical power; instead, the post-9/11 hero is stuck within the disaster itself, working within the limitations of the system to rebuild and repair it.

The Great Machine on 9/11

The most crucial parallel between *Ex Machina*'s post-9/11 superhero and pre-9/11 superhero narratives is the failure of the superhero and his powerlessness in the face of cultural tragedy. As mentioned earlier, some superheroes, such as Superman, admitted their fictional limitations; others, such as Spider-Man, emphasized post-disaster cleanup. *Ex Machina* is unique in that it explicitly depicts the main character's actions during the terrorist attacks on the World Trade Center. The first page of the entire series shows The Great Machine in flight before a passenger jet that is later revealed as one of the planes used in the attack. At first glance, the image may be read as a conflict between the hero and the airliner, as The Great Machine's pose (mirroring the classic flight pose of Superman) places his closed fist across the turned nose of the plane. It is only at the end of the first book that we understand the true meaning of the initial image. In a second flashback depicting the afternoon of September 11, Hundred faces criticism from Jackson Georges, his NSA handler, who blames the hero for not attempting to help at the Pentagon. When Hundred counters that he is doing everything within his power, Agent Georges replies:

> We're all useless, "Great Machine." Maybe you can talk to airplanes, but you can't talk to monsters. They'll find a way to kill us all soon, and there's nothing you can do to stop them.[24]

Later in the series, we see a flashback in which The Great Machine is seen flying toward a jumper, her limp body just out of reach. He is using his "command voice," shouting "Please!" It is not until his later explanation that Hundred describes his actions:

> I made it back to Ground Zero about ninety minutes after I diverted the second plane, forced it to make an emergency landing. There wasn't a civil engineer alive who thought that tower would go down, but still, I . . . I tried to help everyone who was trapped by the fire. I tried to convince the jumpers to hold on, but . . . but people don't listen to the goddamn "Great Machine" the way . . . Whatever, I tried to catch them, but there were so many. I'm not that fast, not that strong.[25]

While Mitchell Hundred was able to parley his fame and celebrity status from that day into his successful election attempt, it is clear that on 9/11, The Great Machine was still a failure. The final page of the first issue in the series encapsulates the sense of powerlessness: a single, full-page panel of the Manhattan skyline, with the remaining WTC tower standing next to a memorial column of light. Hundred's words are the only other objects on the page: "If I were a real hero, I would have been there in time to stop the first plane."[26] After the events of September 11th, it seems irresponsible to expect superheroes to save the day. However, the superhero is just as important to post-9/11 America as he was before the terrorist attacks. The superhero represents the American ideal, its core cultural understanding.

A later story arc shows the death of Hundred's father as a reversal of the iconic murder of the Waynes in the Batman mythos. While Bruce Wayne's virtuous parents were killed by a mugger while the young Bruce watched, Mitchell Hundred's mother accidentally kills her alcoholic husband (the Hundreds, like the Waynes, are named Thomas and Martha) in self-defense, then lies to young Mitchell about his father's death. As Bruce Wayne continually defined his role as the Batman through his memory of his parent's death, Hundred also chooses his career as an engineer to honor his father's blue-collar career. However, when Hundred later finds out the truth of his father's death, he chooses to ignore the truth rather than allow the violent past to define his present. Hundred defines himself by his father's supposed ideals, allowing rebuilding and progress to emerge from the traumatic event.

On the first page of the first issue of the series, the protagonist of *Ex Machina*, Mitchell Hundred, tells us that his story "might look like a comic, but it's really a tragedy."[27] Fundamentally, the series examines the parallel systems of power where the costumed superhero and the politician each function. For both, it is not enough to simply have good intentions or ideals—well-meaning gestures and decisions have catastrophic consequences. *Ex Machina* reminds us that, in many cases, public statements from a political figure can be just as damaging as out-of-control super-strength or heat vision.

Worse, *Ex Machina* suggests that both politics and superheroics also share a common, if often unnoticed victim—the political or heroic agent is often destroyed by his or her own attempts to preserve order. Mitchell Hundred's presumed victories in both facets of his life are shown to be truly tragically hollow. While the Great Machine sealed the dimensional portal in the final issue of the series, the "immigrants" who had been trying to invade the Earth remind Hundred that not only is their return inevitable, but that the true invasion force is actually led by a multitude of alternate Great Machines and corrupt alternate Mitchell Hundreds.[28] Similarly, even though Hundred's last act as mayor of New York City is to use his appointment as ambassador to the United Nations to gain the support and funding to rebuild the lost World Trade Center tower, his political success has come at the cost of the ideals he holds most dear. The final pages reveal that Hundred has managed to get elected to the White House in 2008—but as the Vice Presidential running mate of John McCain. By presenting this new political Mitchell Hundred as analogous to a partisan figurehead like Sarah Palin, Vaughan speaks volumes to the loss of Hundred's fundamental belief that he can affect real change from within the system. Instead of working within the "great machine" of government, Hundred is simply a smiling, ineffectual public celebrity.

At its core, the post-9/11 superhero presented by Vaughan presents a model for coping with a cultural disaster. Like the classic superheroes, the post-disaster hero is essentially impotent: he is unable to prevent the disaster, nor can he actually correct it. The first issue of *Ex Machina* ends with a starling image—a solitary, iconic building standing in the night sky next to a beam of light—as we find that the Great Machine was able to only save one of the Twin Towers. While the hero cannot stop the destruction of the worldview, he can nevertheless participate in the construction of a new dwelling-place. The true power of the post-9/11 hero is what Kenny calls "mastery"—the determined effort of the individual to persevere in his or her existence even after the disaster has destroyed everything. In *Y: The Last Man*, Yorick Brown deliberately chooses to continue his Sisyphean struggle to find his fiancée in Australia, despite the prevailing logic that she cannot be waiting for him. Similarly, Mitchell Hundred is determined to continue his heroics in a new form; the Great Machine may be powerless, but Hundred's real achievements are seen in his accomplishments as mayor.

After the cultural trauma of 9/11, it becomes clear that the traditional superheroic figure cannot repair or rebuild the traumatized culture. As Matthew Wolf-Meyer notes, superpowered attempts at utopia fail not due to a weakness of the superhero, but because the superhero is fundamentally a representation of conservative social order. Traditional superheroes can only attempt to simulate what has been lost in the trauma, rather than to create a new "Master Narrative" that serves a post-trauma society.[29] Smelser suggests that the response to cultural trauma is "often a prolonged process of collective groping, negotiation, and contestation."[30] When Hundred retires as a costumed hero, he recognizes the need for a different kind of solution:

> At best, I've been maintaining the status quo. At worst, I've been jeopardizing lives. I realize that now. That's why I've decided to retire as the great machine . . . and run for mayor of New York City.[31]

The post-9/11 superhero is one who works within the system, not as an all-powerful tyrant, but as a representative of the culture itself. Hundred embraces the ideals of the American ideology, as he truly becomes the "Great Machine," a leader originally described by Thomas Jefferson:

> He is no more than the chief officer of the people, appointed by the laws, and circumscribed with definite powers, to assist in working the great machine of government erected for their use, and consequently subject to their superintendence.[32]

American culture can successfully cope with the massive cultural trauma of September 11th, but the traditional superhero will not sweep out of the clouds to restore that which was lost. In his place, a new hero emerges from within the traumatized culture, reconstructing it from within.

Notes

1 Bill Ellis, "A Model for Collecting and Interpreting World Trade Center Jokes," *NewFolk: New Directions in Folklore*, 5 (2001), http://www.temple.edu/isllc/newfolk/wtchumor.html (accessed May 23, 2010).
2 Bradford W. Wright, *Comic Book Nation: The Transformation of Youth Culture in America* (Baltimore: Johns Hopkins UP, 2003), 287.
3 Robert Wade Kenny, "The Phenomenology of Disaster: Toward a Rhetoric of Tragedy," *Philosophy and Rhetoric* 39, no. 2 (2006): 99–100.
4 Ibid., 120.
5 Neil. J. Smelser, "Psychological and Cultural Trauma," in J. C. Alexander, R. Eyerman, B. Giesen, N. J. Smelser, and P. Sztompka, eds, *Cultural Trauma and Collective Identity* (Berkely: University of California Press, 2004), 32.
6 Ibid., 38.
7 J. Michael Straczynski (w), John Romita Jr. (p), and Scott Hanna (i). Untitled. *Amazing Spider-Man* v2 #38 (December 2001), Marvel Comics. Captain America was also working to clear wreckage at Ground Zero in the first issue of the Marvel Knights "Captain America" series. John Ney Rieber (w) and John Cassaday (a). "Enemy: Chapter One—Dust." *Captain America* #1 (June 2002), Marvel Comics.
8 Steven, T. Seagle (w), Duncan Rouleau (p), and Aaron Sowd (i). "Unreal." *9-11: September 11, 2001: The World's Finest Comics Book Writers and Artists Tell Stories to Remember*, volume 2 (New York: DC Comics, 2002), 15–16.
9 Gary Engle, "What Makes Superman So Darned American?" in Jack Nachbar and Kevin Louse, ed., *Popular Culture* (Bowling Green, OH: Bowling Green State University Popular Press, 1992), 334.
10 Brian K. Vaughan (w), Tony Harris (p), and Tom Feister (i). "The Pilot." *Ex Machina* #1 (August 2004), Wildstorm/DC Comics, 8–9.
11 Brian K. Vaughan (w), Tony Harris (p), and Tom Feister (i). "Fact v. Fiction: Conclusion." *Ex Machina* #14 (November 2005), Wildstorm/DC Comics, 6.
12 Brian K. Vaughan (w), Tony Harris (p), and Tom Feister (i). "Tag: Conclusion." *Ex Machina* #10 (June 2005), Wildstorm/DC Comics, 4.
13 Brian K. Vaughan (w), Chris Sprouse (p), and Karl Story (i). "Life and Death: Part 2 of 2." *Ex Machina Special* #2 (August 2006), Wildstorm/DC Comics, 14.
14 Brian K. Vaughan (w), Tony Harris (p), and Tom Feister (i). "Tag: Chapter 1." *Ex Machina* #6 (January 2005), Wildstorm/DC Comics, 1.
15 Daniel Robert Epstein, "Brian K. Vaughan, Writer of Pride of Baghdad," Suicide Girls, October 31, 2006, http://www.suicidegirls.com/interviews/Brian+K.+Vaughan+writer+of+Pride+of+Baghdad/ (accessed November 21, 2011).
16 Richard Reynolds, *Super Heroes: A Modern Mythology* (Jackson: UP of Mississippi, 1992), 16.
17 Vaughan, et al. "The Pilot." 13.
18 Vaughan, et al. "Fact v. Fiction: Conclusion." 6.
19 Brian K. Vaughan (w), Tony Harris (p), and Tom Feister (i). "State of Emergency: Part 4." *Ex Machina* #5 (December 2004), Wildstorm/DC Comics, 6.
20 Brian K. Vaughan (w), Tony Harris (p), and Tom Feister (i). "March to War: Chapter 1." *Ex Machina* #17 (March 2006), Wildstorm/DC Comics, 19.

21 Mark Oehlert, "From Captain America to Wolverine: Cyborgs in Comic
    Books: Alternative Images of Cybernetic Heroes and Villains," in David
    Bell and Barbara M. Kennedy, eds, *The Cybercultures Reader* (New York:
    Routledge, 2000), 118.
22 Ibid., 118.
23 Brian K. Vaughan (w), Tony Harris (p), and Tom Feister (i). "Off the Grid: Part
    Two of Two." *Ex Machina* #16 (January 2006), Wildstorm/DC Comics, 17.
24 Brian K. Vaughan (w), Tony Harris (p), and Tom Feister (i). "Tag: Chapter
    Four." *Ex Machina* #9 (May 2005), Wildstorm/DC Comics, 3.
25 Brian K. Vaughan (w), Tony Harris (p), Tom Feister (i), and Karl Story (i).
    "Fortune Favors." *Ex Machina* #11 (July 2005), Wildstorm/DC Comics, 18.
26 Vaughan, et al. "The Pilot." 29–30.
27 Ibid., 3.
28 Brian K. Vaughan (w) and Tony Harris (a). "Vice." *Ex Machina* #50
    (September 2010), Wildstorm/DC Comics, 20–25.
29 Matthew Wolf-Meyer, "The World Ozymandias Made: Utopias in the
    Superhero Comic, Subculture, and the Conversation of Difference," *Journal of
    Popular Culture* 36, no. 3 (2003): 49.
30 Smelser, "Psychological and Cultural Trauma," 38.
31 Vaughan, et al. "The Pilot." 26.
32 Thomas Jefferson. "A Summary View of the Rights of British America," in
    John P. Foley, ed., *The Jefferson Cyclopedia* (New York: Funk and Wagnalls,
    1900), 963.

INDEX